Praise for
Well
of
Souls

NAMED ONE OF THE MOST MEMORABLE MUSIC BOOKS OF THE YEAR BY
NO DEPRESSION: THE JOURNAL OF ROOTS MUSIC

"So vividly does [Kristina R. Gaddy] write, and so enthusiastically does she convey her meaning, that many of the songs play unbidden in your mind, through the rhythm of her sentences, the lyric of her vocabulary. As much as *Well Of Souls* is a gripping, fascinating, story, it is also a beautifully written one . . . a novel in documentary's clothing."

—Dave Thompson, *Goldmine*

"For many years, the banjo's early Afro-Caribbean history has been shrouded in mystery. Part of this is because the information has been locked away in deep archives accessible only to curious specialists interested in the deeper roots of the banjo. I have spent a great portion of my career advocating for much of this history to be placed in the forefront. For the very first time, a reader's version of a few of the earliest written observations of the instrument are on full display. With thoughtful and masterful writing [Gaddy] opens a new window into seventeenth-, eighteenth-, and nineteenth-century world history by those who lived it and saw the strange new cultural connections brought by a brutal plantation system. Her observations lead the reader back into the twenty-first century to contend with and reanalyze the crooked road of America's musical past."

—Dom Flemons, American songster, Grammy Award–winning musician, and cofounder of the Carolina Chocolate Drops

"[Kristina R. Gaddy] has written exactly the book the banjo world needs right now. . . . [C]onnect[s] today's musical strains to their deep roots that are just beginning to be rediscovered and acknowledged."

—Chris Wathen, *Bluegrass Unlimited*

"Superb. . . . Gaddy's lively storytelling re-creates scenes from 17th-century Jamaica to 19th-century Washington, D.C., and beyond, illustrating not only the birth and development of the banjo but also its co-optation by white people."
—*BookPage*

"Kristina R. Gaddy has provided a great service to lovers of the banjo. In this heartfelt, absorbing telling, you see the story unfold through the eyes of the historical contemporaries, thus bringing a welcome human dimension to the tale of an instrument often stereotyped, but as Gaddy points out, one with a history that imbues it with 'sacred' qualities."
—Tony Trischka

"This is a glorious and invaluable chronicle for music lovers and everyone interested in American culture."
—*Booklist*, starred review

"Kristina R. Gaddy's deep and rich history of the banjo reveals that the instrument was for centuries the portal to a social and spiritual life through which African Americans tasted freedom, however fleeting. I'll never hear, see, or enjoy the banjo again without reflecting on how the horrors of Black slavery gave reason and form to 'America's Instrument.'"
—Dale Cockrell, author of *Everybody's Doin' It: Sex, Music, and Dance in New York, 1840–1917*

"Profound and invigorating, exhaustively researched and brilliantly conceived, Kristina R. Gaddy's *Well of Souls* carries the reader across the globe and through centuries to restore our understanding of the banjo's central place in the spiritual and ritual life of the African diaspora. The meaning and significance of the insights to be found here, and the worlds summoned, will change you. It is a stunning, and major, achievement."
—Tom Piazza, author of *A Free State*

"Kristina R. Gaddy recenters the banjo as a Black instrument and as an icon of the African diaspora, before and beyond its perversion in the hands of Blackface Minstrels. Like a skillful archeologist, with empathy and respect, Gaddy excavates the sites, sightings, and citations of Black banjo as a central part of dances and rituals of celebration, remembrance, and resistance throughout the Americas. The erasure of this soulful history is an injustice that Gaddy corrects."

—Marc Fields, director of PBS's *Give Me the Banjo* and creator of The Banjo Project digital museum

"Kristina R. Gaddy has crafted a sensitive, insightful narrative of the 'hidden histories' of the banjo as an emblem of African endurance in exile. Centering the courage and the human costs of the African diaspora, *Well of Souls* provides historiographic insight and human connection that, while unblinkingly cataloging the horrors of the slave trade, also celebrates the creativity and cultural resiliency of those who resisted erasure. Through the lens of the banjo's history and recovered meanings, Gaddy honors the traditions and the humans who carried them."

—Christopher J. Smith, author of
The Creolization of American Culture:
William Sidney Mount and the Roots of Blackface Minstrelsy

WELL

of

SOULS

Uncovering the Banjo's Hidden History

KRISTINA R. GADDY

W. W. NORTON & COMPANY
Independent Publishers Since 1923

For information about permission to reproduce selections from this book, write to
Permissions, W. W. Norton & Company, Inc., 500 Fifth Avenue, New York, NY 10110

For information about special discounts for bulk purchases, please contact
W. W. Norton Special Sales at specialsales@wwnorton.com or 800-233-4830

Manufacturing by Lakeside Book Company
Book design by Chris Welch
Production manager: Lauren Abbate

Library of Congress Cataloging-in-Publication Data

Names: Gaddy, K. R., author. | Giddens, Rhiannon, 1977– writer of foreword.
Title: Well of souls : uncovering the banjo's hidden history / Kristina R. Gaddy ;
[foreword by Rhiannon Giddens].
Description: First edition. | New York : W. W. Norton & Company, Inc., 2022. |
Includes bibliographical references and index.
Identifiers: LCCN 2022027189 | ISBN 9780393866803 (cloth) | ISBN 9780393866810 (epub)
Subjects: LCSH: Banjo—History. | Slaves—America—Social life and customs. |
Slaves—America—Social conditions.
Classification: LCC ML1015.B3 G24 2022 | DDC 787.8/809—dc23/eng/20220614
LC record available at https://lccn.loc.gov/2022027189

ISBN 978-1-324-07448-9 pbk.

W. W. Norton & Company, Inc., 500 Fifth Avenue, New York, N.Y. 10110
www.wwnorton.com

W. W. Norton & Company Ltd., 15 Carlisle Street, London W1D 3BS

1 2 3 4 5 6 7 8 9 0

To

MR. BAPTISTE

WILLIAM

TOBY

PRINCE

JOB

GEORGE

BLACK BILL

AND ALL OF THE KNOWN AND UNKNOWN BLACK MUSICIANS
THROUGH WHOSE HANDS BANJOS PASSED.

Contents

2nd Movement

3rd Movement

Foreword

Rhiannon Giddens

The banjo is a tricky instrument. It is a physical object with skin, wood, gut, metal; it is a means to make music, rhythmic, melodic, drones, arpeggios; it is an emblem of culture, of nationalism, of ephemeral yet deeply rooted heartstrings and of made-up histories used as weapons. It's got a lot going on. Anybody who studies the banjo knows they are walking into a swamp of unknown players, scraps of primary sources, dead ends, flashes of brilliant understanding and also of utter despair. How is something so integral to American culture so badly understood and so widely misrepresented? It has taken a small army of dedicated researchers to correct the record—to do good work in the world of the banjo is to have insatiable curiosity, exacting patience, and an awareness of where you are as the observer. All of these things, plus an excellent writing style, sense of humor, and keen brain; yes, it's demanding! And Kristina Gaddy has it all in spades. And boy are we banjoists lucky to have her.

When I first started my banjo journey I had no idea where it would take me; I just knew I loved the sound. But as I played more, and learned the history, and as I picked up older styles of banjo and began to take in the warm sound of older-styled wooden-rimmed and gourd instruments, more akin to the instruments that Kristina begins with in her book than the ones you hear in modern banjo music today, I became aware also of an extra-musical feeling when I played. An urge to make little musical offerings when I picked up the instrument. An eventually unshakeable belief that when I played my banjo, I was connecting with my ancestors in a way I can only describe as spiritual. But I never really talked about it too much because of the image the banjo holds in popular consciousness; even if you can get past the "pickin' and grinnin'" sometime goofball image of the banjo, it's touted mainly as a great dance instrument; and sometimes it gains a soulful aura when a singer-songwriter uses it to sing a plaintive air, or a traditionalist croons a lonesome ballad. But nowhere is it talked about as a ceremonial instrument, a spiritual instrument—until Kristina's painstaking yearslong work to document this unbelievably important aspect. Reading Kristina's book was like being told, "Yes, Virginia, there is a Santa Claus—you knew it all along." That yes, this precious artifact was more than a dance instrument for our people—those feelings could be footnoted! It was incredible. It was unexpected. It was so needed, especially now, in these contentious times—connections to the past that are joyous and beautiful and deep should be treasured. Such as this book. Treasure the knowledge about to unfold before you—I know I do.

Prelude

Centered between two small houses somewhere in swampy lowlands next to a creek, three people begin to dance. A woman in a green dress bends over slightly. She lifts her heels, stirring the sandy ground beneath her feet. Suspended between her hands, she holds a white-and-blue-striped cloth, pinched by her index fingers and thumbs. She raises and lowers her hands, shaking the cloth in front of her. She wears an apron, a scarf around her shoulders, and a scarf around her head tied at the back. Next to her, another woman dances, a cloth outstretched between her hands. They dance on their toes. They look like they are floating. The women face a man. He's bent over too, with a dark wooden dowel in his hands. He raises and lowers the staff as he moves his feet, his blue jacket rising as he lifts his arms, his bare feet and red pants gliding across the makeshift stage.

Two instruments drive the music of this dance. To the left of the dancers sits a man with a drum pressed between his knees. He holds a slender stick in each hand, beating out a rhythm. To his right, a man in a hat sits with the round body of a stringed instrument squarely in his lap. The tan, dried gourd amplifies the sounds that burst from the strings.

To modern eyes this instrument may not look like a banjo. It has no circular wooden body, no metal parts. Instead, a flat piece of wood bisects a round gourd, forming the neck and sound chamber. A piece of animal skin sits taut across a circular hole cut into the side of the gourd, a skin that creates the top of the instrument and the soundboard. Around this white circle, the maker has cut intersecting lines into the gourd. Strings extend from the bottom of the gourd, across the soundboard, over a bridge that holds them up, and along the board-like neck to where it comes to a triangular point. Here, at the headstock, three cylindrical shapes stick out from the piece of wood. The strings attach to these tuning pegs; turning the pegs allows the musician to tighten and loosen the strings to the pitch he wants. Halfway down the neck is another peg, for a shorter string. The short string, flat fingerboard, skin soundboard, and tuning pegs are some of the banjo's defining characteristics.

When the white slaveowner John Rose saw this scene of enslaved Black people before 1790, he felt it was interesting enough to commit to paper. He dipped his paintbrush in a rich red for one man's coat and a warm tan for the stringed instrument, the drum, and a ceramic vessel by the banjo player's feet. Rose was an amateur, but he painted details like the patterns on the cloths the women tied around their hair and the pegs and sound holes of the banjo. There is care in this work: in his brushstrokes and with the people's movements. Looking at it, you feel almost instinctively that something significant is happening.[1]

Nearly 150 years later, in 1935, art curator Holger Cahill had the gut feeling that the watercolor was important and bought it on behalf of Abby Aldrich Rockefeller, who was collecting American folk art for an exhibit in Williamsburg, Virginia. The watercolor was unlike anything Cahill had seen, and its depiction of uncaricatured Blacks in the early United States still makes it unique. In the years since it was first displayed, the image has gained the title *The Old Plantation* and has been reprinted in books, on museum walls, and on CD and record covers. This rare piece of art is one of the most significant images of early African American music and dance in North America, and one of the earliest images of the banjo. It was not until the early 2000s that decorative arts librarian Susan P. Shames discovered that Rose was the artist. She considered that the "painting demonstrates one of the closest links between the cultural life and practices of African Americans and the cultural life and practices of their heritage in western Africa," although she had no definitive evidence that the dance was of West African origin.[2]

Most scholars and historians have assumed that what Rose painted was a social dance or a secular celebration. Some have suggested that two of the dancers are jumping the broom, a marriage ceremony among enslaved Blacks in the United States. This reading seems wrong. The painting has no broom. Moreover, the broom ceremony was not a tradition in Africa, hasn't been documented during the period of the painting, and is a folk custom likely introduced to the Americas by Europeans. Other scholars have simply accepted that the painting depicts an African dance, even though searches for an analogous dance in Africa have yielded no results.

In 2017, my partner Pete Ross and I wandered through the Rijksmuseum in Amsterdam, which explores eight hundred years of Dutch history through the visual and decorative arts. After hours spent looking at old masters and other paintings from the Northern Renaissance, we heard an announcement that the museum would close in half an hour. We looked over the map, trying to decide which of the myriad rooms to visit before we had to leave. Tucked away in a corner on the first floor was a room with art from former Dutch colonies.

Pete and I play a game in art museums, a kind of treasure hunt that we had always lost. A trained artist and luthier, Pete has spent decades staring at images of early banjos, researching early banjo accounts, and making gourd banjo recreations and reproductions for museums and musicians. Each time we visit a museum, we joke, "Today we are going to find an image of a banjo that no one has ever noticed before." We come across works we've seen in print or online. At the New-York Historical Society in Manhattan, we found ourselves in front of *Negro Life at the South*, a well-known 1859 oil painting of a scene in Washington, DC, with a Black man playing a banjo. The idea of finding a lost banjo image always feels both ludicrous and hopeful.

On one hand, how would we discover something new in a painting that has been hanging on a museum wall and been seen by thousands of people every day? Surely we would have known of it already, or we could find it on the internet with a simple search. On the other hand, we know that the banjo's early history, its African American history, has been willfully hidden and distorted. Only three early gourd-bodied, African American-made banjos exist today, and Pete and I are the only people to have examined all three. It wasn't until the 1970s that the white librarian Dena Epstein published a book outlining pre-Civil War sources that mention Black banjo playing, and she admitted that even after looking through tens of thousands of pages of documents, she still hadn't mined every source. Known images of the banjo before 1820 number less than fifteen.[3]

This all makes it feel like we could find a treasure in our game. We chose the room of Dutch colonial art because two of these three earliest banjos are from the South American nation of Suriname, formerly Dutch Guiana. We thought the art would expand the landscape of Suriname for us and might help us understand those banjos better.

Entering the room, we saw a wall of dioramas, each about as wide as a dining-room table. As I moved from one intricate papier-mâché scene of Suriname in the early 1800s to the next, I felt like I had been transported. Blue, white, and green buildings line a waterfront as sailors hoist the canvas that will take them away from this South American jungle. Black men in white uniforms and top hats row a green boat. Mules drag wagons past women in light-colored dresses with umbrellas over their shoulders. A cow munches on grass.

Then I saw it.

"There it is," I said, astonished.

He's no bigger than my thumb: a Black man leaning against a tree. He wears white pants, a blue shirt, and a headdress of feathers. He tucks an instrument into his right shoulder. It can't be bigger than my fingernail, but there it is: a gourd banjo. The back of the instrument rounds where it meets the player's body. The neck, though, might be shorter than that of a banjo.

I read the information card: *Waterkant van Paramaribo*, 1820, by Gerrit Schouten.

I coaxed Pete over. He looked less excited than I thought he should. His disposition is calmer than mine, but he also wasn't convinced that the instrument was interesting. The way the man holds it up on his shoulder makes it look like a fiddle. Pete has seen many indistinct images of banjos, images that he didn't think were accurate enough to learn something from. Feeling that this was probably just another inexact or caricatured version of the banjo, he moved on.

I started snapping photos with my phone anyway, trying to get the largest version of the man I could. Pete wandered over to the next diorama. I don't remember his exact words, but "holy shit" is a favorite expletive.

"That's it. That's *The Old Plantation*," he said.

The scarves. The man and women facing each other as they dance. He'd been staring at that watercolor for decades, never satisfied with the cursory explanations that it just showed a dance. He thought John Rose had painted something unique, something significant, which had never been successfully deciphered. And here was something almost identical. It was almost as if the diorama had been created from the painting. We knew that would have been impossible. Rose had never framed the watercolor, and after his death, it stayed in the family until a woman named Mary Lyles bought it from one of Rose's descendants and sold it to Cahill. It wasn't publicly displayed until the 1930s.

The fact that there was no banjo in the diorama didn't matter to Pete, nor did it matter that the scene was in South America rather than South Carolina. His gut told him that this dance was related to the one in Rose's watercolor. I looked again at the information card next to the diorama. Once again, Gerrit Schouten. I snapped a few more photos, and in the gift shop I bought a book on Schouten and the dioramas. We didn't open it until we got home to Baltimore. But when I dived into it, the next "holy shit" moment occurred. The book led me to sources and information about the cultural context of the banjo that had been forgotten. When I looked at Rose's watercolor with this new information, I saw cultural practices and belief systems. It showed me the early banjo in the hands of enslaved Africans and people of African descent, and demonstrated that the banjo was part of a culture extending from Suriname to South

Carolina to New York. It changed what we knew about the instrument's origins, which I feel also changes our understanding of something that is both symbolic of and important to American culture.

The banjo is the quintessential American instrument and an object in our material culture that can tell us the story of the United States. The banjo did not exist before it was created by the hands of enslaved people in the New World.

Banjo history is also symbolic of African American history: it has been ignored and distorted. All three early banjos are housed in European museums and were only rediscovered in the last forty-five years. Many more that were collected and taken to Europe have disappeared from museums and private collections. "The banjo is African" is often repeated on National Public Radio and in *Smithsonian* magazine and the *New Yorker*. But it is not true: the banjo is a uniquely American instrument, crafted by people of African descent. It is structurally different from any African instrument. The rabbit hole I went down made me realize that, like a creolized language or foodway, the banjo can help us explore the way in which African cultures transformed in the Americas and transformed the Americas.[4]

I compulsively researched early accounts of the banjo, which are scarce because those playing the instrument often didn't have the opportunity to record their own history and white people in proximity to the instrument often didn't care to document banjos. As the scholar Saidiya Hartman writes, "Every historian of the multitude, the dispossessed, the subaltern, and the enslaved is forced to grapple with the power and authority of the archive and the limits it sets on what can be known, whose perspective matters, and who is endowed with the gravity and authority of historical actor." I read and reread every available source for descriptions that might be valuable and rediscovered lost sources—ones researchers, historians, and librarians had used in pursuit of other topics, but not to analyze early American music. Along the way, I became frustrated that white supremacy has distorted this history and that better sources don't exist. I used these sources to understand the context in which the banjo was played and tried to interrogate the bias of writers and observers by learning more about them and the world they lived in. I also looked at my own bias as a Swedish American white woman trying to understand a culture that isn't my own but is integral to American culture.[5]

During my research, I saw the same cultural elements appear in images of the banjo, descriptions of the banjo, and the three existing early instruments. As archeological evidence of the banjo's beginnings is scant, these elements became stand-in artifacts: evidence of behavior, movement, and relationships. The banjo appears in Suriname and New York and everywhere in between. What does that geographic spread say about the culture and lived experience of the people of African descent who created, played, and listened to the banjo? Is it really an American instrument, as we commonly think of it today?

Our biases have limited the banjo to being a secular instrument: it is in the hands of a lone white man on a porch, a backup instrument in a bluegrass band, or a driver of melodies for a square dance or clogging routine. The stereotypes of the instrument from the last 180 years create these images in our minds. The assumption is that the banjo must have always been a secular instrument—from the Latin word *saeculum*, meaning of the present world. This is putting a Eurocentric worldview on an instrument born of African beliefs and traditions.

From my research, I realized that the banjo once served a higher purpose. The instrument was sacred—a word derived from the Hittite *šaklāi*, meaning custom or rites, something of an otherworldly realm, of spirits, ancestors, and worship. The banjo was not just a musical instrument but a spiritual device, and it fit into a cultural complex of music, dance, and spirituality. In the 1970s, when scholars of the African diaspora still had to argue that the enslaved who arrived in the Americas had not been denuded of their culture, poet and scholar Edward Kamau Brathwaite wrote, "There is no separation between religion and philosophy, religion and society, religion and art. Religion is the form or kernel or core of the [African] culture." He warned that when religion is mentioned, a full cultural complex should be considered. In this book, I hope to reveal that cultural complex and to have the banjo take us on a journey to remember the hidden, the willfully ignored, the forgotten, and the lost.[6]

1st Movement

•

"Whenever there's an injunction on something as integral to the livability of this world as joy, there is an underground activity, a fugitive cooperative of feeling, a commune of love that isn't to be perceived by the dominant eye."

—Billy-Ray Belcourt, *A History of My Brief Body*

I

The Atlantic Ocean, 1687

They sit in this ship, this wooden prison, 375 men, women, boys, and girls, not knowing what awaits them. Rumors circulated that they would be eaten by the white cannibals, their bodies crushed to make oil or ground into gunpowder, or their skin would be made into sails and their blood used to color the flags of the ships offshore.[1]

Ships that came and went from this part of the Central African coast had flags of different colors, patterns of red, white, blue, and orange. The ship these people were on was named the *Benjamin*, and the red cross, white stripes, and blue triangles on its flag represented England and the people who had come for them—not the people who had taken them from their homes, but the white people who would take them from this shore and across an ocean. The Europeans arrived on the coast in their wooden ships with tall masts and billowing white sails, perhaps firing cannons to signal their arrival. The Dutch, British, and French flew flags of different colors, but they all wanted the same thing from this place: people. On other parts of the continent, the Spanish, Portuguese, and Danish landed their ships for the same purpose. From Brazil to the Caribbean, the few hundred plantations growing sugar were expanding to thousands, and slaveowners wanted tens of thousands more Africans each year to work in cultivating and processing the ever-more-valuable crop. The demand was almost insatiable. The people forced onto the *Benjamin* in the late months of 1687 would not literally be eaten by the white people waiting for them across the Atlantic. But they would be forced to sacrifice their bodies to produce the sugar that Europeans devoured in everything from salmon to spirits. On the ship, they did not know that yet.[2]

Caravans in Central Africa had taken captives from inland towns and cities as far east as Lake Nkunda and the Kongo River basin to the coast, a journey that could last months. These trade routes had formed in response to the European demand for copper and ivory found in the interior. Now human beings, taken against their will, became part of the trade. When the caravans arrived at the coast, those bound for the *Benjamin* and other ships were held in a port somewhere south of the Sette River and north of the Zaire River, along what the white men called the Loango Coast. The next part of their forced journey would take them onto the waiting ships.[3]

A *mafouk*, a trader designated by the leader of the region, took a canoe or sent a messenger to the ship to discuss the transaction with the captain. The ships brought guns, gunpowder, cloth, and alcohol to barter for the people they wanted. The local merchants on the Loango Coast wanted control over trade, and so Europeans were not allowed to own permanent buildings to operate from, unlike on the Gold Coast to the northwest, where trading companies built massive structures they called castles. Instead, on the periphery of the port, the captain would rent a building called a factory where he could store his goods. He and his crew never knew how long it would take to get what they wanted; they might be on the coast for four months or eight months, waiting for their cargo: the people kidnapped in the interior.[4]

The captains came ashore, looking at the Africans available for purchase and gathering news of the region. From the inland caravans, the *Benjamin's* captain, Edward Daniel, bought men, women, and children, maybe in small groupings, a few at a time. These people were then taken to the factory's makeshift prison, where they spent the night before being transported to the ship.

Although it had been months since they were taken from their homes, what the captives experienced next might have been the most terrifying. They were told to get in a canoe while the water around them roiled, bubbling and foaming white as the waves crashed against the shore. The never-ending waves don't make noise so much as mute it, creating a damper that sucks up the sound of voices, perhaps yelling and screaming. The captives could hear nothing over the roar. This part of the ocean is perilous, notorious for large swells of surf and underwater earthquakes. The canoe rose and sank with the waves until it reached the side of the ship, where six cannons faced outward. The *Benjamin* was not large; four men could lie head-to-toe and reach from one side of the ship to the other, and someone could easily throw a rock from the stern to the bow. Even anchored, the ship would have swayed and bobbed, making a voyage across the ocean seem treacherous at best, impossible at worst.[5]

The captives might have sat there for days, weeks, or months while canoes arrived with new people, until the ship could hold no more or no more people could be bought. On this voyage, Captain Daniel was ready to leave when 375 captives, including about 60 children, were aboard his ship, below deck in the cargo holds retro-fitted to transport people, the smell of sweat, excrement, and fear choking the air.[6]

The people who had been forced aboard spoke Bantu languages, but assuming they could speak with one another was like assuming that the Englishman Captain Daniel could understand a Dutch captain. While some Bantu languages are mutually intelligible, more like dialects, familiar-sounding but not quite the same, others would have sounded as foreign as the tongues of the white captors.

In the communities and societies they had lived in, these people had beliefs about how the world worked, music that they used to invoke their god or gods, and instruments that made those songs and dances come alive. These things would live in their memories as they rocked in the hold of the ship.

This voyage, like any other in a supply chain, required hard calculations to succeed. Captain Daniel and the Royal African Company which hired him took into account weather patterns, shipping routes, supply and demand. It seems that Daniel had lost money on his last two voyages and needed to make it up on this trip. Some things he couldn't control, such as smallpox outbreaks on board. Others he could. The hold was overcrowded and the captives were given a meager diet of dried beans and grains, as the slavers considered physical and mental health only in the light of maximizing their profits. Daniel also would have considered that his cargo was capable of destroying itself. Captains sailing for the Dutch West India Company, which was founded in 1612 and had complete control over the sale of the enslaved in Dutch colonies until 1738, had specific instructions to purchase drums. They thought dancing and exercise on deck would keep the slaves healthier, and might possibly decrease the discontent that would grow on board.[7]

Rumors flourished on board these slave ships. The fear of being eaten drove some people to jump into the sea. For others, revolt seemed possible. On the *Benjamin*, the Africans outnumbered the crew fifteen to one. If they could just get their hands on a knife, a scrap of metal, a stone even, they could break the shackles holding them and turn them into weapons. Some captains didn't shackle the women and lodged them closer to the crew, which exposed them to rape and violence but also gave them better opportunities to attack. The first and most important abolitionists have always been the enslaved themselves.[8]

As an experienced captain, Daniel knew these risks. The people his ship was carrying could sell for almost 7,400 pounds sterling, at a time when unskilled male laborers earned less than two pounds a year. He might have also been carrying gold, ivory, or pepper purchased along the African coast for sale in Europe. The Royal African Company was acutely aware of protecting its investment. Captain Daniel may have bought men the Royal African Company called guardians—enslaved men given a cat o' nine tails and the authority to police the others. Dutch captains employed spies who reported on planned escapes and revolts. Crews kept loaded guns in a chest on the quarterdeck, ready to fire at someone trying to secure their freedom. Or, they might simply fire guns in the air, making thunder ricochet across the ship's deck in a show of power.[9]

During the *Benjamin's* trans-Atlantic voyage, no major mutiny occurred. The ship arrived in Jamaica on December 31, 1687, to no fanfare beyond the clamor of plantation owners and managers eager for new workers to labor in the fields of sugar cane. Six of the people the Royal African Company had bought on the Loango Coast died during the voyage. Those who disembarked, now designated as slaves for their rest of the lives, would experience weeks of shock and sickness, mental and physical exhaustion, as a result of their possibly yearlong journey to the Americas. They must have felt lost, terrified, and alone. And yet, they were not alone. The year was 1687, but Portuguese ships had begun forcibly transporting people from Africa to the Americas in 1526. Ships originating in Europe and the Americas would make over 36,100 voyages through 1866. The people aboard the *Benjamin* were among an estimated 12.5 million people taken from at least 180 ports across the African continent, from Gambia to Ouidah to Madagascar. Millions died before they arrived in the Americas, and millions more would be born enslaved, descendants of those who had been taken.[10]

Like most ships that trafficked people, the *Benjamin* did not record the names of the men, women, and children on board. But this does not mean they were invisible. They had names, families, religions, likes and dislikes, good traits and bad traits. They affected culture, economics, and politics. In the face of enslavement, brutality, denigration, and generations of oppression, enslaved Africans and their descendants would create new languages, new foodways, new religions, new dances, new music, and new instruments: cultures that would become foundational to every colony and country they lived in.

II

Jamaica, 1687

Twelve days before the *Benjamin* arrived in Jamaica, Hans Sloane looked out into the harbor of Port Royal, the activity onshore matching the anticipation he felt. After more than three months at sea and the headaches, nausea, and vomiting that seasickness had brought him, land would feel good. Jamaica was going to provide him an opportunity that he knew few men like him would have.[1]

His journey to Jamaica, like those of other white Europeans, began very differently from that of the people aboard the *Benjamin*. In September 1687, Sloane had willingly boarded the *Assistance* in England, excited for what awaited him across the Atlantic. The ship was part of a fleet accompanying the new governor of Jamaica. Carrying forty-four guns and two hundred soldiers on behalf of the King of England, the ship was both much larger than the *Benjamin* and less crowded. As he took over the duties of governor, Christopher Monck, the 2nd Duke of Albemarle, had invited the twenty-seven-year-old doctor to be his personal physician. Sloane understood this as more than a chance to ingratiate himself with England's royalty. His work as a doctor was closely tied to his interest in the natural world and the medicinal properties of plants and minerals. He and his colleagues yearned for new discoveries, but they rarely made trips like this themselves. Sloane knew that seeing and collecting specimens from Jamaica and anywhere else the ship stopped could elevate his career and his stature among his fellow naturalists.[2]

As the *Assistance* entered the harbor, all the ships raised their flags and prepared their cannons to fire a salute to the new governor. The town was growing, the colony on the edge of transformation, and Port Royal's waters were always crowded. The *Margarett*, a ship from New York that had arrived earlier in December, was probably still in the waters, selling enslaved people taken from Madagascar, while the *Mary*, another British ship, had transported enslaved people from Barbados to Jamaica. Ships bound for Europe loaded sugar, indigo, cotton, and lumber—products of the labor of the enslaved. Ships from the North American colonies arrived with salt cod, wheat flour, and apples.[3]

In town, two hundred men of the militia manned the guns at each fort, while near Fort Rupert, on the eastern end of town, another 1,300 gathered on the Parade to welcome the governor and his entourage. The beating of drums and the blare of trumpets joined a chorus of explosions from the cannons of the ships and forts. Soon, the ministers of state would board the *Assistance* to greet the Duke, and then they would go to St. Paul's Church for the ceremony where he would be inaugurated as governor of Jamaica. Into the night, the residents of Port Royal found reason to celebrate and beat drums, sound trumpets, play music, and light bonfires. Hans Sloane was fascinated.[4]

Both the *Benjamin* and the *Assistance* were in Port Royal because of Jamaica's economic expansion. England had taken the island from the Spanish and made it a royal colony in 1660. The Spanish had tried to enslave the native Taino, but when they resisted, the Spanish began bringing enslaved West African laborers to Jamaica. England's capture of the island coincided with King Charles II's return to the throne after Oliver Cromwell's death and the end of the English Commonwealth. Between 1660 and 1687, England had been building more ships, engaging in more manufacturing, and trading those manufactured goods for commodities like lumber, agricultural products, minerals, textiles, and spices. Port Royal had become the commercial center of the British Caribbean colonies, while Jamaica's growth was fueled by larger and larger sugar plantations. Dutch planters in Barbados had introduced the English to sugar cultivation in 1640, and the increasing consumption of sugar in Europe had expanded cane fields into the fertile soil of Jamaica, the Caribbean's third largest island. If Sloane had arrived in Jamaica just ten years earlier, before the sugar boom began, the number of enslaved Africans would have been only about 1,000 more than the white inhabitants. Between 1676 and 1685, Dutch, British, and North American ships forcibly brought almost 34,000 people from Africa—twice the number of the previous ten years combined. By 1690, there would be three to four times as many enslaved people in Jamaica as white residents.[5]

The air in Port Royal felt thick and wet, and Hans Sloane found the heat and humidity extraordinary. It probably didn't help that he wore stockings, a jacket, and his white wig whenever he left the house. Port Royal would have felt familiar, yet different. The multistoried houses built of brick, with glass windows, that belonged to the politicians, merchants, and representatives of the Royal African Company looked like houses in London. Yet here, their design made them look out of place, too dark and heavy for the bright sun and sea breezes of the island. Just as he might in London, Sloane could buy fish at a market on Thames Street and fruits, herbs, and plants at another market. At the High Street meat market, he could find the usual chicken and beef, and turtle meat, too. Like most towns and cities, Port Royal's sanitation left much to be desired, and the tropical sun cooking the decay made that stench worse.[6]

Sloane could walk past taverns, brothels, and music houses, all of which he might have seen in London. But Port Royal was known as a wild place, and visitors thought these establishments were not only less respectable than those in London, but "more rude and antique than 'ere was Sodom, fill'd with all manner of debauchery." Sloane limited his alcohol intake and thought others should do the same. He knew it was bad for one's health. But the taverns and music houses offered more than alcohol, and sailors, plantation managers, merchants, politicians, and visitors went to these establishments, where the prostitutes, servers, and musicians may have been enslaved men and women.[7]

On Saturday afternoons and Sundays, when those who were enslaved were given time for themselves, they gathered outside to eat, dance, and sing. On holidays that aligned with the Christian calendar, these events would turn into festivals. Sloane attended a festival in 1688 that was unlike anything he'd seen and anything he'd ever experience again after he left Jamaica in the early months of 1689. As a man of science, he strove to observe, collect, and analyze the experience.

Sloane watches and listens as movements and music flow into one another. He notes that on their legs and wrists the dancers wear rattles made of nuts, pieces of wood, or even animal-skin pouches with pebbles sewn inside and intricately tied together with string—a type of percussion instrument worn by Kongo, Igbo, and Fon dancers. While the *Benjamin*, having come from the Loango Coast, brought captives that may have been Kongo, by 1687 more than twice as many people had been taken from ports northwest along the Bight of Benin and the Bight of Biafra, where the Igbo and Fon communities live. The dancers in Jamaica have also adorned their bodies with cow tails and other things Sloane can't describe other than to write that the outfits give "them a very extraordinary appearance."[8]

The dance is outside his realm of experience, too. In London's ballrooms, men and women approached each other and retreated with the simple walking steps of an English country dance. The dances Sloane sees in Jamaica "consist in great activity and strength of Body, and keeping time," he notes, although he doesn't describe any steps specifically. Being unfamiliar with these movements, other white observers couldn't adequately describe the dances, either. John Taylor, a white English mathematician who visited Jamaica in early 1687, wrote that on Sabbath days and holidays, the enslaved dance in an "antique" and "confused manner, seeming all mixth men and women together."[9]

The musicians are easier for Sloane to describe. A woman holds a rattle in her hand and shakes it, the rhythm in time with the beat of the musician tapping his hand on an opening cut into a gourd. Sloane knows that musicians at these festivals were once allowed to have drums, made of a "hollow Tree" covered on one end with a skin, "But making use of these in their Wars at home in Africa, it was thought too much inciting them to Rebellion, and so they were prohibited by the Customs of the Island." Trumpets were outlawed for the same reason. A fairly large dried gourd isn't as loud as a drum, but can provide the beat needed for the music.[10]

Musicians also play stringed instruments, instruments that feel both foreign and familiar to Sloane. One seems to be functionally the same as a sanku or seperewa, a box lute played by the Akan people of the Gold Coast. Other stringed instruments, he writes, are "in imitation of Lutes." The lutes that Sloane knows have a teardrop-shaped wooden body that is rounded on the back and flat on the front, with many strings, and a flat fingerboard with raised ridges called frets. An instrument with frets allows only the notes of the European scale, rather than the microtones, or in-between notes, characteristic of African music. The term lute can also be used to describe a class of instruments, and, using the most generic definition, it refers to any instrument where strings run parallel to the soundboard and up a neck. Lutes can be played either by plucking the strings or by drawing a bow across them.[11]

At the festival, Sloane sees one musician playing a lute made of a round gourd that is larger than a grapefruit but smaller than a cantaloupe. A broad, flat neck enters the gourd through the tube-like extension where the fruit was once attached to the vine, continues through the body, and exits where the fruit's flower once grew. Into the flat neck, the maker carved intersecting lines on the fingerboard: crosses and diamonds. Instead of attaching a wooden soundboard, as on a European lute or violin, the maker cut a hole in the side of the gourd and pinned an animal skin over it. Across the skin soundboard run strings made of "Horse hairs, or the peeled stalks of climbing Plants or Withs," which connect to tuning pegs at the top of the neck.[12]

The mathematician John Taylor also described lutes in Jamaica, but called them "a kitt (made of a gourd or calabash with one twine string)." A kit was another name for a pochette—a small, narrow violin that dance teachers played during lessons in the seventeenth and eighteenth centuries, a fiddle so small it could be slipped into a pocket. Taylor's description is brief and he doesn't say whether he calls the instrument a kit because of its size or because it is bowed like a violin. The instrument Sloane sees is small, too, about three-quarters the length of the musician's arm, and has two visible strings, with one or two holes where a short string tuner may have been. Another musician plays a lute with a slightly more oblong gourd body and more ornamentation. On the fingerboard, carved lines swirl like smoke rising from a fire, while others move in sharp angles and straight lines, forming triangles, diamonds, and rectangles. The gourd, too, is decorated with triangles and rectangles.[13]

Like the rattles the dancers wear on their ankles, these lutes evoke instruments from many different ethnic groups across the African continent. In addition to the people taken from the Bight of Benin, the Bight of Biafra, and the Loango Coast, primarily British ships brought just under 7,000 people from southeast Africa and the Indian Ocean islands and less than 2,000 people from Senegambia and Sierra Leone. While the Royal African Company brought people from West and Central Africa for enslavement, the English East India Company and independent ships from British North American colonies brought enslaved Malagasys in the last ten years of rapid plantation expansion. While we know the generalized locations of departure, who exactly was taken and from which ethnic groups and communities they came is less clear. People from the westernmost and easternmost regions of Africa might have had the greatest impact on the lutes that Sloane saw. In Senegambia and Sierra Leone, the Jola play the akonting, while the gewel praise singers of the Wolof play the geseré and xalam geseré, all lutes with a long neck that sits in a notch on the rim of a gourd body. North of the Bight of Biafra, professional Kotoko musicians play the gulum, while the Hausa play the gurmi and gurumi, all two- and three-string instruments with a neck extending through the gourd or calabash body. Unlike the instruments Sloane saw, all these have rounded dowel necks with the strings tied to rawhide rings that slide up and down the neck, called tuning rings. The lutes of East Africa, Zanzibar, and Madagascar—the bengala, gabbus, kabosa or kabosy, and kenanda—all have flat fingerboards and tuning pegs like the instruments Sloane saw; however, they most often have carved wooden

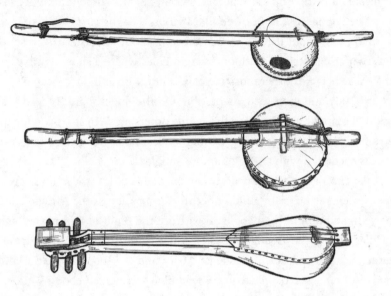

African stringed instruments, not to scale. The gurmi (top) is a two-string gourd lute played by the Hausa in eastern West Africa. The neck enters and exits the side of the gourd. The akonting (also spelled ekonting; middle) is a three-string lute played by the Jola in far West Africa. The neck sits in a notch on the rim of the gourd and is held down by the skin soundboard. The kibangala or gabusi (bottom) is part of a family of East African wooden-body lutes related to the Yemeni qanbūs. © *Grace van't Hof*

bodies rather than gourd or calabash resonators, and the bodies are teardrop-shaped, like Moorish and European lutes. The instruments that Sloane sees are not a copy of any of these African instruments entirely: they have both a gourd body and flat fingerboards and tuning pegs.[14]

Sloane's description of the instruments in Latin translates to "1.1.2.2. Strum Strumps, lutes of the Indians & Blacks, made of different hollowed-out gourds covered with animal hides." Even with this and the engraving later published in his book, he's not providing all the information he could have gathered about the instruments. He doesn't give the lutes' names, even though they look very different, calling two of them Strum Strumps, which perhaps speaks more to the manner in which they are

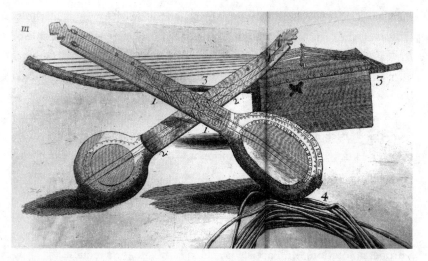

The three instruments in Hans Sloane's book *Voyage to the Islands*. The Strum
Strumps in this c. 1707 engraving are considered the earliest image of a banjo. *University
of Minnesota Libraries, James Ford Bell Library*

played than what the musicians call them. The musicians playing the
Strum Strumps press their fingers onto the strings to change the pitch of
the note, creating patterns of sound as they pick or pluck the strings with
the other hand.[15]

Sloane does not explain what he means when he says the instruments
are played by "Indians and Blacks," which can be ambiguous terms.
Elsewhere, he notes that "The Inhabitants of Jamaica are for the most
part Europeans, some Creolians, born and bred in the island Barbados,
the Windward Islands, or Suriname who are the masters, and Indians,
Negroes, Mullatos, Alcatrazes, Mesities, Quarterons, &c. who are the
Slaves." By "Indians," he could mean East African or Malagasy people who
were taken from the Indian Ocean region, those who could have played
the kabosa. He could also mean Native Americans—not the Taino people
native to Jamaica, but indigenous people taken to Jamaica from Central
America or Florida. By "Blacks," he likely means people born in Africa,
who were not a homogenous group, as Sloane noted himself when he
wrote that they were from "several places of Guinea"—which could mean

the Gold Coast specifically, West Africa generally, or Africa as a whole. However, the term Black wouldn't necessarily exclude enslaved people of African descent born in the Americas. For Sloane, European descendants born in the Caribbean are Creolians or Creoles, and so too are enslaved people who were "born in the Island or taken from the Spaniards."[16]

As with a botanical specimen, Sloane wants to capture what he hears from the musicians and singers at this festival. Notes, music, melody: these things he knows from the music rooms and concert halls of the European elite. But, whether or not he can read or write musical notation, the music he hears is too complex for him to record. Instead, he asks Mr. Baptiste, "the best Musician there to take the Words they sung and set them to Musick." Having both familiarity with the music and the ability to write European notation, Mr. Baptiste is able to fulfill Sloane's request.[17]

Sloane likely named Mr. Baptiste as the best musician there because he was of African descent but was also a professional. In French, Spanish, and Portuguese colonies, the Catholic Church trained free and enslaved boys and young men of African descent in religious music. They could continue working within the church or become teachers and performers throughout the Caribbean. Mr. Baptiste's name, which may have also been spelled Baptisto or Baptista, suggests a French, Spanish, or Portuguese background—colonies where Blacks were baptized into the Catholic Church. Baptiste could have also been born in the kingdom of Kongo, where King Alfonso I introduced Catholicism after his own baptism in 1491 and African and European music styles blended within the church tradition. Sloane may already know Mr. Baptiste as a man who plays for the governor's parties, balls around town, or at one of the taverns in Port Royal.[18]

Mr. Baptiste listens to the music at the festival. Perhaps he's heard it before at another festival, or perhaps he has a virtuosic ability to notate music he hears only once. Using his blended knowledge of African and European music, he is able to record music that was blended, too—music not from one community or ethnic group or kingdom in Africa, but the result of the forced mixing of cultures that resulted from enslavement. As notes float through the air, he places them into European notation: quarter notes, dotted quarter notes, eighth notes, sixteenth notes, and triplets. He transliterates the songs in creolized languages into words that Sloane can read and then hear again, but gives each piece a name that evokes a community in Africa: Angola, Papa, and Koromanti. African societies name musical types after the people who perform them. "Angola" might reference people from Central Africa, like the captives on the *Benjamin*; "Papa," the Papah or Popo from the kingdom of Dahomey on the Bight of Benin; and "Koromanti," the Akan from the Gold Coast. Music types can also be named after the main instrument of the performance or the dance which the music accompanies.[19]

In "Angola," the singer's voice starts high and drops as she sings, "Ho-baognion." One of the lutes responds with a melodic run. The melodies from the voice and the instrument combine as the chant continues. This could be the induction of the festival, calling out to a specific god or spirit to allow those gathered to call in different ancestors and spirits.

Nineteen notes, hopping through what a European musician might think of as arpeggios, make up "Papa." Where a musician who has had exposure only to European music might not understand the intricacies of this song, Mr. Baptiste notates it with syncopation. "Papa" does not sit on the steady beats of a one-two-three-four pattern, with an emphasis on what would be notated as the first part of a measure or phrase. Instead, the notes fall just after where a European musician might expect, creating movement, a dancing of the melody. Mr. Baptiste transcribes this using a brief rest, then a brief note, then a note, then a brief rest, then a brief note. The notation ends abruptly, but it's unlikely that the music did. As in many compositions in traditional music, those nineteen notes form a circle that doesn't repeat so much as continue on endlessly, dancers moving and musicians improvising, perhaps the repetition putting dancers, musicians, and spectators alike in a trance.

Under the title "Koromanti," Mr. Baptiste records three sections that seem like individual pieces. The first section is in twelve-eight time, a beat that puts four groups of three notes together, as in a jig. While some notes roll up and down, more or less in order, in one section they jump from a high note to a low note and back again—a structure perfect for the Strum

Strumps, with their higher-pitched short strings and lower-pitched long strings. The musician might have transitioned seamlessly to the next section, playing fast scales that make his fingers run across the neck like a spider, lower note following lower note with breaths of syncopated notes in between. Then, in the last section, the notes flow more freely, rising and falling as someone sings "Meri Bonbo mich langa meri wá langa," words whose translation Sloane does not share, even if Mr. Baptiste told him.[20]

Sloane believed that the "Indians and the Negros have no manner of Religion." For Sloane, these ceremonies, dances, and "plays" were far from "Acts of Adoration of a God," because they were bawdy and lewd. This dance was too heathen, too un-Christian, too different, to be religion. But part of him must have seen the connection between the festivals and religion, since he mentioned the two in the same sentence. For him, adoration of God can only be seen through a European–Christian lens, which makes little room for the type of practice that people of African descent were developing in Jamaica.[21]

※

The new governor would die less than a year after the arrival of the *Assistance*, and even though Sloane was the governor's personal physician, this didn't tarnish his reputation. Jamaica was just the beginning for him. His time there had allowed him to observe and collect, and when he returned home, he put his findings, together with engraver Everhardus Kickius's illustrations, into *Voyage to the Islands of Madera, Barbados, Nieves, S. Christophers and Jamaica*, two volumes which are each the size of a small briefcase. Here Sloane presented the images of the Strum Strumps and Mr. Baptiste's transcription.[22]

Mr. Baptiste's notation of the music he heard jumps out at the reader, with larger text and notes that boldly run up and down the pages. Any musician's first instinct would be to hum the melody, and perhaps in the early 1700s, after it was published, wealthy Londoners would want to try to play along on their harpsichords, viols, and lutes. They may have even clapped their hands and sung "Alla, alla," as the text suggests. Mr. Baptiste's transcriptions capture these early moments of exchange between African music in the Americas and Europeans, of notes from those lutes being forced into even beats on a treble clef.

The engraving of the three instruments spans two pages, and while Sloane called the lutes Strum Strumps, today we call them banjos. This engraving is the oldest known image of the instrument. Sloane was so fascinated by the Strum Strumps and the harp that he brought them back to England. We don't know how he got the instruments, who he got them from, or who made them. An enslaved person had no property rights, and so Sloane could have just taken them or had someone take them for him. He may have traded for them. Maybe someone made the instruments for him, or maybe he obtained old instruments, often-played and worn.[23]

Sloane couldn't stop collecting. During the course of his life, he brought over 71,000 objects into his home, creating a cabinet of curiosities. After marrying the widow of a Jamaican planter in 1695, Sloane received income from the forced labor of those enslaved on the plantation, which allowed him to invest in the slave-trading South Sea Company and collect objects of natural history and material culture from around the world. Predominantly white European men used these collections, which could range in size from a drawer to a cabinet to a room to a house (like Sloane's), to showcase natural and man-made wonders from around the world. Sloane said the cabinets of curiosities he viewed in his youth had increased his fascination with the unknown; that was what had led him to Jamaica and to collect the Strum Strumps in the first place. Cabinets of curiosities were not necessarily laid out by subject, with instruments or all of the items from Jamaica together in a single area, for example. Those who put together the collections were not always curators. They were creators, who by placing objects intentionally next to one another made something new. These collections could reflect on the beauty or strangeness of the world and all that was in it.[24]

To add to his collection of Jamaican instruments, Sloane obtained a "Strum Strump made of a round large gourd" from Virginia, catalogued as item number 1369 in his collection. He received it from a Mr. Clerk, who around 1730 also sent Sloane a drum. Catalogued right before the Virginia

Strum Strump, as number 1368, it is described as "An Indian drum made of a hollowed tree carved, the top being brac'd with peggs & thongs, wt the bottom hollow, from Virginia." If all we had was that description, we would never have known how significant this drum is. It survived in the collection and even in 1906 an anthropologist wrote, "Although this drum is described in the old catalogue as being of Indian [Native American] origin, it was probably made by negroes, and may even have been taken to Virginia from Africa." A later scientific analysis showed that it is made of *Cordia africana* and other species of tree native to the African continent. That this drum was not made in Virginia, but brought to the Americas from Africa, may show Sloane's and other white collectors' inability to fully understand what they were seeing and taking. However, as *Cordia africana* grows in East Africa and Madagascar, there is a possibility that by "Indian" Sloane meant from the Indian Ocean region. The drum was also amended in the Americas. The head is deerskin, probably replacing an earlier goat or cow hide.[25]

Upon his death at age ninety-two in 1753, Sloane donated his collection to the British nation and it became the foundation of the British Museum. If his banjos were still in the British Museum, we could examine them and be able to make better guesses about the musicians and makers. But at some point, the Strum Strumps from Jamaica and Virginia and the harp were lost. We'll never know what type of wood the luthiers chose for the neck, whether the designs were carved or burned, and whether the designs extended around the body of the gourd. We don't know how similar the instruments from Jamaica and Virginia were to each other. We can't see the fine craftsmanship and care it took to make the instruments. They are gone.

III

Martinique, 1694

Outside Father Jean-Baptiste Labat's chapel, thin strips of green shimmied in the warm breeze, and the stiff and pointed leaves of sugar cane crinkled against each other like pieces of parchment being shuffled as frogs and crickets added a chorus of chirps. These winds brought the dry season. The view of the cerulean sea may have been beautiful, but brutality was built into the sugar behind him. Soon, enslaved people across Martinique would be tasked with shearing the tall, ripe canes as close to the root as possible, then stripping off the wispy leaves and chopping the inch-thick stalks into smaller pieces to begin the process of making sugar. It wasn't quite that time yet; the harvest would begin in the new year. The shift in the seasons offered a brief moment of respite before the harvest and processing season, so, for the enslaved and free alike, December and Christmas meant celebration. For Father Labat, it meant Mass.

The Christmas before, in December 1693, Labat had been aboard *La Loire* on his way to Martinique from France. On the ship, he'd regularly held Mass and marked the end of the Christmas season with a symbolic baptism representing the Feast of the Baptism of the Lord. He'd arrived in the French Antilles a few weeks later, in January 1694, as a missionary in the Dominican Order, a job which involved both religious duties and the practical administration of a parish. He traveled from Fort Saint Pierre to Fond Saint-Jacques, where the order owned a sugar plantation. As he crossed the small island, each monastery Father Labat came to was smaller and worse-kept than the one previous, and at Fond Saint-Jacques he found just three wooden buildings with a badly laid-out sugar works. Of the sixty or so enslaved people owned by the order and kept on the property, fifteen were malnourished children and ten were too old or sick to work. It wasn't surprising that the mission wasn't making money, and instead had a debt of about seven thousand pounds of sugar, which was more than twice as much as the whole island of nearby Montserrat would export in 1700.[1]

Labat had continued to the parish of Macouba, where he arrived at the well-kept but small church where he would be responsible for Mass and services, and, this December, the celebrations honoring Jesus's birth. Inside the chapel, he stood at the altar and looked out at the congregation. Within these walls, everyone, free and enslaved, white and Black, were his parishioners. He moved at the front of the chapel as he repeated liturgy in Latin. The black cloak he wore over his white habit distinguished him as a Dominican. Capuchins and Jesuits also had Catholic missions in the Antilles, missions that, like Labat's, included plantations and enslaved laborers as part of their property. People in Martinique could see Father Labat's cloak and understand who he was, and Labat could easily see where people fell in the island's hierarchy by what they wore. Free men dressed in silk stockings, waistcoats, suits, and plumed hats, if they hadn't shed European formal wear in exchange for something that suited the heat better. Enslaved men and women wore knee-length pants or petticoats and loose shirts, and Christmas might be the time of year when they were given a new set of clothing. If any of them were allowed to earn extra money, as was sometimes the case, they might spend it on clothing they'd wear for a special occasion.

Father Labat and his fellow French Catholic missionaries had both a religious and political duty to bring Christianity to people of African descent. In 1685, the French king Louis XIV instituted the Code Noir, a series of laws that regulated the treatment and behavior of the enslaved in

French colonies, and specified how white people—free or indentured—were supposed to interact with them. The second article of the code stipulated that all enslaved people should be baptized and instructed in the Catholic faith and that all other forms of religious worship be banned. Both white Europeans and Americans debated the question of whether a slave should or could be baptized. Godefridus Udemans of the Dutch Reformed Church argued in 1638 that the "lovely yoke of our Lord Jesus Christ" and the "yoke of human slavery" were mutually exclusive, and eleven men in New Netherland used their baptism as a reason why they and their families should be free in a 1644 petition to the Dutch West India Company. In 1655 in Virginia, Elizabeth Key sued for her freedom using her baptism in the Church of England as one of her arguments, the idea being that a Christian could not enslave another Christian, only a heathen. To forestall this type of manumission, baptism and enslavement were no longer considered mutually exclusive in Virginia by 1668. Catholic French missionaries, who incorporated the Spanish and Portuguese racist myths of African inferiority and European supremacy, believed that baptizing and converting enslaved Africans would not only save their souls but make them better workers and more beautiful by European standards. So, Father Labat and his fellow Dominicans baptized the enslaved and educated them in Catholic teachings, believing that a person could be both Christian and enslaved.[2]

As Father Labat traveled around Martinique and the French Antilles, he observed what he believed to be a lack of religion among most of the Africans. "Nearly all the slaves are idolaters," he wrote, save for some who were Muslims. Similarly, almost "all the adult slaves who leave their land are sorcerers, or at least they have some acquaintance with magic, sorcery and poison." However, many were eager to be baptized. One man who had been baptized came to Father Labat to ask for a bag that another priest had taken from him. This man's owner had told Labat that the man was a sorcerer who could find lost objects and see events that hadn't yet happened. Father Labat spoke with the man and realized that, yes, he was clairvoyant. Labat was still willing to accept him into the church, as long as the man stopped believing in his pagan practices. The man agreed, but soon he asked Father Labat for the bag again. Why? What is so important in this bag? Labat asked. The man replied that since losing the bag, he'd become "poor and miserable." Father Labat didn't care how bad his life was without his bag, and "threatened to hand him over to the judge, who would certainly have had him burnt." Then Labat destroyed the bag and its contents, including a terra cotta figure and a ball of thread. Labat's destruction of the spiritual objects was his own choice, but it also followed the Code Noir.[3]

Sugar and the wealth it brought impelled the debate about whether enslaved people could be baptized and remain enslaved. On Martinique, Jamaica, and throughout the Caribbean, sugar was causing the expansion of plantations and slave labor. It seemed that every piece of well-drained, fertile soil would soon be covered in *Saccarum officinarum*, the species of sugar cane that had originated in the Pacific islands and now drove economic expansion on the Caribbean islands. Europeans couldn't get enough sugar. Father Labat himself, a well-fed Frenchman with a round face and thick neck, jotted down the extravagant food he consumed in the West Indies, much of it dense with sugar, from shipboard meals of stewed fruits with added sugar to cacao confit, which, he wrote, "requires great care [to make], and uses a great quantity of sugar." Sweeteners had once been a luxury, but now sugar was used to turn gooseberries into a sweet wine, sweeten tea, and make luxurious desserts. In the ten years between 1690 and 1700, the importation of sugar to England would almost double.[4]

Sugar cultivation and manufacturing required a complex process that had to be followed exactly. Sugar cane needs attention, and needs it in very specific ways, from the moment it begins to grow to the moment, after it is harvested and processed, when the last drops of moisture evaporate, leaving behind only the coveted crystals. The Europeans understood that this type of attention meant labor, and when they wanted to expand their sugar production and profits they wanted slave labor instead of having to worry about wages and fluctuations in the availability of laborers.

Having been in Martinique for a whole year, Father Labat had seen the process. On Fond Saint-Jacques in May or June, when the clouds grew large and heavy with water and thunder, the Dominican overseers forced enslaved people to dig trenches for new plants. The workers took cuttings and placed them in the soil, forming mounds where new roots would grow and give rise to new stalks of sugar cane. From June to December, they would weed, thin, hoe, and fill in the gaps where plants had died with new cuttings. After a few years, when the canes became less productive, they would be torn out of the soil. The slaveowners saw the workers, like the stalks, as expendable. Planters in the Caribbean often found it easier to bring in new captives than to keep the people they already owned alive. One out of five newly arrived Africans would not survive three years in the forced labor camps of the West Indies. If a worker died on Father Labat's plantation, he could rent an enslaved person from a nearby plantation or buy one of the thousands of people who arrived each year on ships from Ouidah, Senegambia, or Benin.[5]

Late December and early January, the time between the wet and the dry season, between the growing and the harvest season, offered a brief moment when work might slow or cease. The parishioners at Father Labat's chapel in Macouba may have gathered at a midnight Mass on Christmas Eve, a tradition that had been popular since at least the twelfth century and combined the celebration of the birth of Jesus with the darkest days of the year. Later, he would hold another Mass to recognize the arrival of the Wise Men and Jesus's baptism. Enslaved parishioners who had been in Martinique for a while would have been familiar with these services by now, as would people who had been taken from the kingdom of Kongo—although Central Africans made up only a small portion of the 21,000 people taken to Martinique between 1646 and 1695. While Catholics from Kongo observed these holy days, they celebrated them differently than Labat did. Christmas became a time when all those in slavery could have their own holy days. And so, after any church service they attended, or when they were done with work, they would celebrate with *le calenda*.

"Their passion for this dance is beyond imagining; it animates the old and the young right down to children who can barely stand up; it is as if they had danced it in their mother's belly," Labat wrote. The calenda was the favorite and most common dance of the Africans, he added, and when "their master does not allow them to dance on the plantation they will travel three or four leagues," which could be up to twenty miles, "to be somewhere where they know there is a dance."[6]

So, sometime during the Christmas season, close to the chapel or somewhere else on the north side of the island, a deep, resonant sound rises. A drummer strikes a large drum with four fingers of his hand, the goatskin head as wide as his forearm and the drum's body half as long as his own. A higher-pitched note that moves more freely comes from a smaller drum called a baboula. This drummer shifts his rhythms with the movements of the dancers and the songs of the chorus.

Labat can only hear two sounds coming from these drums. He thinks the large drum has an even and sedate rhythm, while the baboula is fast and sharp. His experience of rhythm is likely to have come from hearing military bands, which may influence how he hears these drummers. In the military, the beat of a snare drum regulated a troop's steps and could signal a call to battle. Labat thinks that the larger drum must be regulating the dancers' steps because the rhythm is so even. The other drum, he thinks, "only serves to make noise, rather than marking the cadence of the dance or the movement of the dancers." What he may not be able to understand, and therefore hear, are the nuances of the drumming. Just as on any instrument, the musician can choose notes, tonalities, and styles. A drummer has only one drum and two hands, and yet can create a multitude of sounds based on where, how hard, and with which part of the hand they hit the goatskin. Hitting closer to the middle of the goatskin head produces a lower, lasting, and resonant note, while pressing down on the skin with the other hand at the same time changes its pitch. Hitting closer to the rim of the drum clips the sound. The drummers use their skill to create specific melodies of percussion, patterns that might signal and respond to what the dancers are doing. A change can signal forward movement in the ceremony or a switch to a new dance. These rhythms may also have a deeper meaning, a meaning Father Labat would never have been told of. In the Zar ceremonies of Sudan and Ethiopia, every spirit has its own beat, its own rhythm, and the drummers invoke these spirits with their drumming. Women jump up to dance to the drumming when the spirits take possession of them, dancing in a particular style for each spirit. In Ewe dances of the Gold Coast, a lead drummer guides the ceremony, pushing dancers to spirit possession, using his beats to win the favor of ancestors and deities visiting the dance and letting people rest when they need it.[7]

As the drummers play on Martinique, men and women join the calenda, in which there is no real differentiation between spectator and participant. Those who want to dance do so, while those who are too tired to dance or don't feel the music moving them to dance form a circle around the dancers and drummers. The dancers form two lines, the women facing the men. They hold their arms out to the side almost parallel to the ground, and the only comparison Labat can think of is to people playing castanets. As they dance, they jump and twirl, the men and women stepping toward each other but leaving a distance between the lines, then stepping backward, away from each other. This isn't unlike English and French country dances, where sex-segregated lines move forward and back.

Then, Labat hears the rhythm change. The shift signals a change in the dancers' movements, and now the distance between the men and women disappears. Father Labat thinks at first glance that the torsos of the men and the women are hitting against each other, then he realizes that the dancers are striking their own thighs, and sometimes they strike the thigh of a dancer of the opposite sex. The dancers pirouette, spinning around and retreating on a signal from the drum, only to approach and bring their bodies together again. Sometimes, in between these steps, a man and a woman approach each other, interlace their arms and spin around two or three times, slapping their thighs and giving each other a kiss. This is not a dance Father Labat can imagine taking place in Europe and he considers these movements "most indecent."

As the men and women dance and the drummers play, everyone participates. Children dance off to the side, learning the movements. One man sings out a line of song, while those standing in the circle around the dancers sing back in a chorus. They clap their hands, adding another dimension of sound to the rhythms of the drums.

Another musician might join the music, playing an instrument that

Labat cannot name but refers to as a "sort of guitar." He must have seen it
often, since he says that "they almost all play" the instrument; his "they"
refers to people of African descent. To play it, the musician pinches and
beats on the strings. Labat must have observed it up close, since he gives
a fairly detailed description of it. He writes that the body is made of a half
calebasse—literally, calabash, but could also translate to gourd. (Although
both calabashes and gourds leave similar-looking hard, hollow shells after
they've been dried, a calabash is the fruit of a tree and a gourd is the fruit
of a vine.) Attached to the body is a "fairly long neck." According to Father
Labat, where the fruit has been cut in half, the hollowed body is covered
with a piece of animal skin that has been "scraped down to the thickness
of parchment," on top of which sits a bridge that holds up four strings
about an inch or so above the skin. Like those on the Strum Strumps, the
strings are made of plant filaments, but Labat adds that they can also be
made of silk or bird intestines prepared with castor oil.[8]

Like Sloane, Labat has seen an early banjo.

In all of these rituals, the dancers move to the sound of the drums,
the chorus sings in unison, and the drummers and instrumentalists create melodies. The union of music, dance, and song can create an ecstatic
experience. Singing in a chorus has the potential to strengthen bonds
between people, to make us feel more secure and trusting of others. In
a place where families could be torn apart at any moment, where communities had to adjust to new arrivals and unexpected departures in the
form of sale and premature death from illness, overwork, and murder,
these ritualized dances helped create a sense of family and community.
The pulse of drums can change the body's own rhythms. After about
ten minutes of listening to drums, our state of consciousness can shift.
Music that feels energetic, fiery, and triumphant can make us feel more
self-confident, reduce feelings of helplessness, reduce negative ideas,
and produce constructive and motivating thoughts. More than creative
expression, the music and dancing of the calenda provided an opportunity to build family, community, and resistance.[9]

And resistance is why people on Martinique were not supposed to be
dancing the calenda. As early as 1654, the council of Martinique made

"the dances and assemblies of Negroes" forbidden under penalty of death. In 1678, they again gave notice that dances were banned, specifically the calenda, and in 1685, the Code Noir again prohibited enslaved people from gathering at any time, at any place, outside of their forced labor. Labat understood why: large groups dancing happily "under the influence of brandy, could stage a revolt, an uprising, or thieving raids." He was inclined to let the people the order owned "dance all sorts of [African] dances, except the calenda" and had tried to teach them French dances, including the minuet, courante, and pass-pied. He had even paid a violinist and "given several jars of brandy to entertain each other all together," in hopes of preventing the calenda. But, he laments, "I firmly believe that in spite [of] all my precautions they dance the calenda as hard as they can when they are not afraid of being discovered."[10]

Although Labat puts the blame for these dangerous ideas on the festive nature of the gathering and the alcohol that is being passed around, what he doesn't see is that through these rituals, the strengthened bonds and synchronized spirits create a cohesion among the people where they are more than separate individuals, where they might plan to gain their freedom by killing the master or running away.[11]

Labat believes that the calenda came from the Coast of Guinea— a good assumption, since two-thirds of the people who were forcibly brought to Martinique had begun their trans-Atlantic voyages there. But his language indicates that he knows there is something different about it. While the calenda is the most popular dance, he sees other dances that he designates as belonging to particular African ethnic groups. The enslaved whom he thinks are from Kongo have a dance very unlike the calenda, where the dancers stand in a circle, their bodies bent over slightly but not moving, and lift their feet in the air and hit the ground "with a kind of cadence." Here too, one person leads a story in song, while the others respond in refrain. Those who don't dance clap their hands. People from the Akan region, Gambia, and the Cape Verde Islands have their own dances, too, he observes.

The calenda does not originate with a specific group of people, he says. Instead, it is danced by all the enslaved, and even some Europeans.

Despite how "opposed to decency" the calenda is, Father Labat says the dance is also a favorite of "the Creole Spaniards of America," which likely means those of Spanish descent born in the Americas. They dance the calenda for entertainment, and it even "enters their devotions" in churches and during processions. Labat complains that even the nuns can hardly keep from dancing it on Christmas Eve, an idea that must horrify him.[12]

He sees the influence moving from African to European culture. But could it go the other way, too? Both the name and the dance steps could have been influenced by European traditions. *Las calendas* was the name given to festivities in Spain that represented the time between the Virgin Mary's search for a place to give birth and the appearance of the Magi. Calenda could have become the name for dances done during this time of year by enslaved and free people in the Caribbean. However, the meaning must have broadened from dances held at just that time of year, since during the wedding of an enslaved couple in August 1678, a planter allowed a "kalenda" that lasted a whole day.[13]

In Paris, a craze of the late 1600s was the contredanse, a French adaptation of English country dances. As in the calenda, rows of women and men face each other, with music dictating the movement of feet and arms as the dancers twirl by themselves and spin, linking arms and reaching hands from one partner to another. The calendas could have been influenced by French dances, or Europeans might have seen the similarity in some steps and assumed they were European-influenced. They would have had no real experience with African dance traditions. For all of the similarities between the calenda and European dances, Father Labat believed that this was a purely African dance, and not an African dance influenced by European set dances nor a European dance influenced by African dances.[14]

African dance traditions were at the calenda's core, and it may have been influenced by the contredanse, the Spanish *calendas*, or other European dances. But it was a dance for all of the people of African descent, and perhaps this was where its power lay. It had been created in the Americas and could bring enslaved people together in a new way, a necessary way.

Just like the calenda, the guitar-like instrument Father Labat saw many people playing had origins in Africa but was created in the Americas. Labat never assigned the banjo he saw to a particular ethnic group. Like the dances he described, if he had known its origin he would have classified it as an instrument of the Kongo, the Akan, the Gambians, or the Cape Verdians. While Sloane gave a similar instrument the name Strum Strump and John Taylor called it a kitt, Labat had no name for it. He remained in the West Indies for twenty-one years and traveled from Martinique to Guadeloupe, Grenada, St. Kitts, Saint-Domingue, and St. Thomas, and when he wrote his reminiscences, starting in 1716, he had still not learned what this instrument was called. This is not strange, though. Before Labat's book was published in 1722, written records of banjos were scant; we know only of those by Sloane, Taylor, and the historian John Oldmixon. In his 1708 history *The British Empire in America*, Oldmixon writes that during their "Diversions on Sundays" the Blacks on Barbados "dance, or wrestle all day, the Men and Women together" to the sound of drums and "a Bangil, not much unlike our Lute in any thing." This is the first time the instrument has a name that seems like a progenitor of the word banjo. Oldmixon calls it a lute, which offers a generalized view of an instrument with a body, neck, and strings. But he had never been to Barbados and hadn't seen the instrument for himself, so he may have been recounting correspondence from one of his acquaintances in the Caribbean.[15]

Just as Sloane didn't believe the festivals in Jamaica could be worship, Labat didn't think that a calenda, or any dance, could be religious, even though he had examples of when it became devotional. As a Catholic, he believed in select representatives of God and Christ on earth. But other religions have a more egalitarian view of the human relationship with the divine, where any practitioner can receive divine inspiration. In many religions, ecstatic experiences and music cannot be separated from each other. For the Hausa in Africa who practice Bori, possession poses no threat and a trance induced through the music of two-string plucked lutes called garayas, one-string fiddles called goges, calabash rattles, and drums is central to their religious practice. Women are called the mares of the gods, and spirits "mount" them. Beliefs like these and religions like these came to the Americas, and had to be adapted and amended to fit in not only with the European religions of the slaveowners but with the religions of other Africans, including Islam and Catholicism, as well as polytheistic religions. At the same time that music and dance bring communities together, they can allow spirits to inhabit the body and worshippers to speak with ancestors and gods.[16]

The calenda lasted but a moment in the scope of work and life. When wet days gave way to dry, the harvest of the sugar cane began. These months, from January to May or June, required even more work than the planting and growing months. The sweetness of sugar cane disappears quickly; the juice dries and the stalks ferment. The enslaved workers had to process the cane as soon as they cut it, carrying it to the sugar mill where men fed the stalks into rollers that squeezed out the juice. This was a dangerous job. Limbs could get drawn into the rollers and crushed like the canes.

Fond Saint-Jacques, like all sugar plantations, had a man referred to as the boiler, one of the most valuable enslaved men on the estate, who oversaw the boiling and clarification of the cane juice. His knowledge and skill had developed over years, and in the complex process of boiling, skimming, and straining, his decisions could determine the quality of the sugar, which in turn could determine a plantation's ultimate profit or loss. Although jobs in the boiling house may have come with preferential treatment or other benefits, anyone working there was at risk of severe burns from the sugar cooking or the fires that kept the sugar boiling. Slave labor, accidents, and death made *Saccarum officinarum*. And all who enjoyed this sweet substance, from Father Labat on Martinique to the lower-class woman in London who could now afford it for her tea, were beneficiaries of the institution of slavery.[17]

IV

New York, 1736

Outside, the clouds gathered with rain, typical wet weather for a New York shifting from winter to spring. Inside his home on the tip of the island of Manhattan in March 1736, James Alexander leafed through the latest edition of the *New-York Weekly Journal*. It looked more like a pamphlet than a periodical, just a single sheet of paper folded in half to make four pages of text, but claimed to offer "The freshest Advices, Foreign and Domestick," like many other papers. Alexander believed in that tagline and, for him, this single sheet of paper held power. In the early 1730s, Alexander had joined New York's anti-government Popular Party. The party had a lot to say about the governor and the British Crown but no way to get its message across, so the *Journal* became the answer. Alexander became the editor and wrote much of the copy. Since none of it was signed, he and his colleagues had no fear of calling the governor an idiot and revealing his improprieties, while also writing more proper essays about the value of free speech and freedom of the press. Regardless of what they thought they should be allowed to say and write, these critiques of the government led to a charge of seditious libel against the printer John Peter Zenger, just two years after the 1735 founding of the paper.[1]

In the spring of 1736, that lawsuit was still a year in the future. Although the primary purpose of the *Journal* was political, Alexander added advertisements for revenue, essays for intellectual discourse, and, sometimes, opinion editorials that blurred the lines between fact and fiction to make a point, like the one Alexander would have read on that rainy morning.

"Mr. Zenger: By an odd Chance I got a Copy of the following Letter, which I desire you to insert in your Journal, and oblige one of your constant Readers," it began.[2]

Did Alexander chuckle to himself when reading this line? He, the most faithful of all readers of the paper as the editor, may have written not only this introduction but also, probably, the letter itself. In a work some might call speculative nonfiction, Alexander filtered what he knew to be true through the eyes of an outsider, someone unfamiliar with the customs of New York. This wouldn't have been hard for him to do. He had not always been a prominent New Yorker and newspaper editor. He was born in Scotland and had studied science and mathematics in Edinburgh. There, too, he'd had a problem with the government and joined the Jacobites in an uprising to bring the Stuarts back to the British throne. He came to the North American British colonies and became a politician first in New Jersey and then in New York. For this letter, he adopted the persona of an outsider, perhaps the newly arrived Scotsman trying to understand the nature of this colony. He called himself "The SPY."[3]

In the letter, Alexander invites the reader to Utopia, a reference to Thomas More's idealized place of good government and social conditions. At this, too, Alexander may have chuckled. His newspaper regularly pointed out how New York was definitely not Utopia, and the scene he describes in the letter would make that clear. He goes back in time to an Easter Monday in the near past.

Notes drift out from the kitchen, not a melody yet, but someone preparing a song. Alexander turns his ear toward it, and the notes come together into tunes. He knows the player is his "Landlord's Black fellow," that is to say, an enslaved man whose name he doesn't give. If Alexander passes six people on the streets of New York in 1736, one will be Black. This isn't nearly the ratio of white to Black in England's Caribbean colonies, but it's a higher proportion than anywhere else in the British colonies north of Maryland. In New York, many enslaved laborers lived in the house of a family, forced to labor there or in the industry in which the family was engaged. Others were hired out, with some or all of their earnings taken by their owner. Women worked as domestics, washerwomen, and street vendors; men as farmhands, shipbuilders, dockworkers, brewers, bakers, tanners, and millers. An economic system based on slave labor may not have been something Alexander was familiar with when he arrived in New Jersey in 1715, but by 1729, he owned six people.[4]

In the kitchen, the sound of this man practicing on his instrument is familiar. The musician, Alexander writes, "[is] very busy at the tuning of his Banger, as he call'd it, and playing some of his Tunes . . ." For Alexander or anyone reading his account, a banger is an instrument familiar enough that he doesn't need to explain what it looks like or how it is played. While neither Hans Sloane in Jamaica nor Father Labat in Martinique gave the lute they described a proper name, historian John Oldmixon called the lute on Barbados a bangil. Oldmixon writes bangil as if the reader should know how to pronounce it, but, as anyone who has learned to read English knows, the sound that a letter makes is not always clear. Is it ban-gil with a hard *g*? Or ban-jil, like the soft *g* in the name Nigel? The *g* in Alexander's banger seems to contradict the latter pronunciation, but only if the word is bang-er, as if describing an instrument that is banged on. The word could have had a soft *g*, sounding like ban-jer. In 1736 New York, many people still spoke Dutch, including people enslaved by Dutch families. The Dutch *g* is notoriously hard for English speakers to pronounce, an open fricative produced at the very back of the mouth that has no equivalent in English but sounds more like an *h*, and so banger might have sounded more like ban-her. Perhaps the variations in spelling indicate that Europeans were imitating a name in a language they were not familiar with, adapting their letters and pronunciation to a word they heard used by people of African descent. The similarity between bangil and banger, the fact that they are both plucked lutes, and the context in which they were played make it likely that they are the same instrument: the banjo.[5]

Alexander says he is "always delighted by music," even if he finds the music of the banjo rustic. He pretends to need to wash up and enters the kitchen to hear more. Notes fill the small space, usually reserved for the enslaved men and women who live here and labor to make the landlord's life more comfortable. They may have made this space their own as much as they could, placing beads, shells, spoons, or pieces of metal by doorways to protect them from harm. Alexander devalues the music, thinking it unsophisticated and rudimentary, but he can't hold back his enjoyment.[6]

"What is the meaning of your being so merry?" he asks the musician.

Alexander then recounts for the reader what he believes to be an accurate representation of what the musician tells him.

"Massa, today Holiday; Backerah no work; Ningar no work." On the holiday, neither the white man nor the Black man works. "Me no savy play Banger; go yonder, you see Ningar play Banger for true, dance too; you see Sport today for true." I don't know how to play banger well, but if you go to the edge of town, you'll see someone play banger well, and dance, too. Today, you'll see a real celebration.

In the field at the edge of town, where there are no houses, there's room for a dance. Alexander knows the place, sometimes called the Common. For white residents, this was a place to graze cows or collect firewood. For Black residents, this had become sacred space, as it was the only place where they were allowed to be buried. Trinity Church, where Alexander was a member, had banned burials of people of African descent in their graveyard in 1697.[7]

Before 1722, Black residents would have arrived at the Common at night for a funeral. They would have prepared their loved one for burial; maybe it was a man wearing a shirt and a prized pair of cufflinks, or a woman with a copper ring slipped on her finger. Then they wrapped the body in a shroud and placed it in a coffin. They might have placed a conch shell or oyster and scallop shells next to the body, or put a crystal in the coffin, or coins on the eyes. They might have decorated the simple wooden coffin with a pattern of iron tacks or writing. They buried newborn babies and small children, women with devastating injuries, young men with worn-out bones and joints, and older adults whose lives may have started on the African continent before they were taken to the Caribbean and then New York. They lowered their loved ones into the ground with their heads toward the west. The many ethnic groups that made up the Black population of New York would have had different burial traditions based on their own religions and belief systems, from Senegambian Muslims, to the Ewe and Fon Vodun practitioners, to Catholics from Kongo, to those who had arrived from the West Indies, where these different religions had already developed new traditions as they came into contact with one another and with various Christian and Jewish traditions. One belief that seemed to be common to all was the power of the ancestors, both those long gone and those recently departed, to be able to harm or help a person's current condition. A burial had to be done with care, with proper funerary rites to honor the new ancestor.[8]

At one of these funerals, the musician may have picked up his banjo and played as others drummed, danced, and sang. To outsiders, this looked like a celebration rather than a solemn occasion. When Reverend John Sharpe was proposing the advancement of religion in New York around 1712, he commented that the rituals at the Burial Ground were "heathenish rites . . . performed at the grave by their countrymen." While un-Christian behavior may have been the concern of a religious man, it was the threat of rebellion that worried politicians and slaveowners like Alexander. In 1712, six enslaved men fighting for their freedom had set a fire and killed nine white people. As a militia went after them, they took their own lives, dying free rather than be captured. They were buried in the African Burial Ground. The politicians believed that nighttime burials and gatherings on the Common could be used to plot uprisings like this one, so the city banned funerals at night in 1722 and limited them to twelve attendees in 1731.[9]

Alexander and other white New Yorkers saw the celebration the Black musician mentions as sport, a diversion, a fun time. While there may have been an element of enjoyment or rest on a holiday, the dance could have also provided the musician and other African-descended people in New York the opportunity to do something that had been banned: pay respects to their ancestors. In 1736, the banjo player in Alexander's letter could not bury a family member in the way that religion and tradition dictated, in the way that the deceased needed to be buried in order to cross over into the world of the ancestors. Perhaps Easter Monday and other days off became a stand-in for the funeral or simply another occasion to honor the ancestors, when Blacks could go to the public space of the Common and the Burial Ground and perform the necessary rites.

Like the calenda dances in the French Antilles, this gathering—with or without a burial—on the Common wasn't legal. In 1682, an order banned "Negros and Indian Slaves" from assembling, especially for the purpose of anything that might look like a celebration. The government felt that "exerciseing Severall Rude and Unlawful sports and pasetimes" on Sundays was a "Dishonour of God Profanation of his holy Day." Perhaps even worse, it disturbed the "Peace and Quiett of His Magesties Subjects many whereof are Likewise Drawed aside and Mislead to be spectators of such their Evill Practices." The enslaved gathered on Sundays and holidays because some were not forced to work on those days. They may also have been celebrating God in a way that was meaningful to them.[10]

Apparently, by 1736, not much had changed despite the 1682 decree. White, Christian New Yorkers who were supposed to be honoring the resurrection of Christ on Easter Monday were still being drawn as spectators to the celebrations of Black residents. At the edge of the city, Alexander saw the Common covered with little stalls, crowded with white residents and "Negroes divided into Companies, I supposed according to their different Nations." Alexander doesn't explain what he means by "Nations," but perhaps, like Labat, he was designating the people he saw by perceived African ethnic groups. The concept of origin, ethnicity, or nation was complex in the Americas. Europeans had created designations for African people that didn't always reflect what they called themselves. Many people, Alexander included, had no firsthand experience of Africa and were basing their knowledge on things they had been told or read. Alexander had lived only in Scotland, New Jersey, and New York, although as a trader he corresponded with people across the world, buying goods like cocoa from Curaçao and lace from England, and selling flour to South Carolina.[11]

Furthermore, enslaved people, whether African-born or American-born, created new identities in the Americas, perhaps based on cultural ideas and perceived African ethnic groups. Slave ships coming directly from Africa didn't arrive in New York often. In fact, when Alexander published the letter, the last slave ship traveling from Africa to New York had arrived five years earlier. Ships arrived more frequently from Charleston and Jamaica with just a few people to sell. Someone who had arrived on a ship from Madagascar and been in New York for decades, and someone else recently arrived from Jamaica who also identified as of Malagasy origin, might have felt they were a part of the same nation though their experiences in the Americas had been totally different. A person from Madagascar, with its Arab influence, might also have felt more community with a Senegambian, a Hausa, or other Muslims or Arabic speakers.[12]

This scene of nations on the Common described in the *New-York Weekly Journal* seems as if it could have been written by Father Labat in Martinique or Hans Sloane in Jamaica. In a clearing, Black dancers move to the sounds of drums, "made of the Trunck of a hollow tree," while others dance to the "rattling Noise of Pebles or Shells in a small basket," and some, like the man in the kitchen, play the banjo, and some even "knew how to joyn the voice [to] it," singing an accompaniment. Some of the "Companies of the Blacks" were not dancing but "exercising the Cudgel, and some of them small Sticks in imitation of the short Pike." Perhaps, like men in Kongo, they were engaging in a mock battle set to music, dodging and leaping while trying to strike one another, a performance that showed off their skills or presented a ritualized display of power.[13]

Although Alexander enjoyed the banjo music, the scene as he paints it in the letter is off-putting to him. He writes, "I leave it to you to judge whether all these confused Noises so near to one another didn't make a—cord"; perhaps a wordplay on chord and discord, the unharmonious sounds he perceives from this celebration. He leaves, wondering if "their Rudeness" isn't innate but rather because the people celebrating need a better education.[14]

This letter, like other pieces in the *New-York Weekly Journal*, appeared not as an actual recounting of events but as a reminder of the type of

Captioned "Blacks playing stick,"
from Moreau de Saint-Méry's 1791
voyage to Saint Domingue. While
Jean-Baptiste Labat described a
dance as *le calenda,* kalinda has also
been described as mock stick-fights,
like the ones described in the *New-
York Weekly Journal* in 1736. *University of
Minnesota Libraries, James Ford Bell Library*

debauchery that was occurring on what should be considered a holy day.
This letter and two other letters penned by the Spy appeared in the middle of Lent 1736, and provide fictitious yet representative accounts of the
un-Christian behavior of many white New Yorkers. After seeing the Black
music and dance, Alexander sees white visitors buy beer at a tent that's no
better than a brothel and get so drunk that the only noise they can make
is cursing, while fights break out and others gamble. The reader sees the
irony in calling this place "Utopia." At the end of the letter, Alexander
concludes, "In short, we have been used to Holidays in our Country, but
such as Observation of them in my Opinion, would hardly go down with
our civilized Heathens."[15]

Just as the New York Council observed with their ordinance in 1682,
white New Yorkers were drawn to the festivities the day provided,
although Alexander didn't place as much blame on the Blacks celebrating
as the government did. But the derogatory comments about the discord,
rudeness, and uncivilized behavior of the enslaved and free Blacks on the
Common illustrate the way in which white people increasingly began to
see the banjo: as an uncouth Black-originated instrument of little worth.

V

Maryland, 1758

The sprawling land around the stately brick mansion dissolved into a small marsh before becoming the Chester River, fresh water that led to the brackish water of the Chesapeake Bay. The house was quiet as James Hollyday settled into his study, a compact room full of books and natural light. He opened a letter and began to read. Hollyday had recently returned from London, where his half-sister Rebecca Lloyd Anderson and her family lived, and, as he had no wife or children, it pleased him to hear from them. Some of his favorite letters came from his niece Sarah, whom everyone called Sally. Her script was that of the studious young woman she was, unlike the weary scrawl of her uncle's replies. His family thought Hollyday serious and solemn, but he enjoyed these frivolous correspondences with his niece. Sally loved writing to her uncle, too. When he was in London studying law, he and Sally would play music together, she on the harpsichord and he on the flute. After Hollyday returned to Maryland, Sally sent along notes on music, plays, and gossip from London. In this December 1758 letter, she thanked him for a gift he'd sent: "We are much pleas'd and thankfull to you for the bangeau for altho' we can't make musick on it yet it is a great curiosity and makes a good figure as it lays on the Harpsicord."[1]

The image of the instrument he sent lying on the harpsichord in a townhouse in the upscale Tower Hill neighborhood of London amused him. Sally and friends of the family, Lady Browne and her daughter Mary Folkes, had wanted to see a bangeau, and Hollyday obliged by sending them one. Although Sally's mother, Rebecca, and father, William, were both born in Maryland, Sally's whole life had been in London. Not long after Rebecca and William married, they had moved to London so that William could sell Chesapeake tobacco and buy European goods for export. By the late 1600s, tobacco already dominated the Maryland and Virginia economy, and exports from these two colonies made up 30 percent of the world's supply. Like sugar, tobacco was a product in high demand in Europe, and, also like sugar, it demands intensive, year-round labor. At first, planters were willing to use white indentured laborers, but by the 1690s, Maryland and Virginia landowners were buying people of African descent to work the tobacco fields, as it cost twelve pounds for four years of a white man's service but only twenty-two pounds for the lifetime service of an enslaved Black man. The Hollydays and Lloyds were wealthy landowning families, and Sally's father saw that they needed an agent in London to sell their tobacco. More than fifteen years after moving to England, William Anderson was doing well in his merchant business. He'd also gone into a shipping business with Rebecca's brothers Edward and Richard Lloyd; their ships carried hogsheads of tobacco, iron, grain, pork, and lumber from the Chesapeake Bay to England, and household goods back to Annapolis and Oxford, Maryland. Their ships also sailed to and from the Caribbean, where they bought enslaved people in Curaçao, the French Antilles, and St. Kitts for their own use and for sale to other landowners in Maryland.[2]

Sally hadn't seen the tobacco and livestock farms that created her family's wealth and she hadn't seen the hundreds of people forced to labor on those farms. Hollyday must have told her about life at his home, Readbourne, on the Chester River, and, with her interest in music, maybe he told her about the enslaved people and their musical instrument, the banjo, or, as Sally writes it with a French transliteration, "bangeau."

Sally wrote to her uncle that Lady Browne and Mrs. Folkes had come to the house after the bangeau's arrival and "Mrs. Folks [sic] longs sadly to know how to play on it." Sally thought guitar lessons might help. In her next letter, Sally told him that Mrs. Folkes had found a teacher, and with the "scale of Music" from Hollyday, she will try "to make very pretty Musick on the Bangeau." Sally predicts that Hollyday will soon "hear of a new Fashion'd Instrument, much in Vogue invented by the Affricans." The name of the instrument, the idea that learning the guitar might help Mrs. Folkes learn to play the bangeau, and the knowledge that it was invented by Africans demonstrate that the instrument and its origins were becoming more widely recognized.[3]

What is remarkable is Sally's vision for the future of the banjo: it will become an instrument that entices white audiences. Still a young woman, she doesn't seem to have the bias that her uncle brought to seeing and hearing the instrument. Although she acknowledged that there was "great curiosity" to the banjo, in the sense that she'd never seen anything like it before, she also wrote, "'tis neatly made." She appreciated it as an object. Hollyday, on the other hand, was dismissive. In 1759, he wrote to Lady Browne's husband, Sir William, admitting, "I did not imagine the bangeau could have given them any entertainment but as a novelty, and should not have thought of sending so rude an instrument of music if it may be called, if Lady Browne had not desired it."[4]

Although the Londoners found it an intriguing novelty, Hollyday found the banjo quotidian. It was common, both in the sense that he saw it often and that it was not worthy of note. While he was in his study reading letters from his family in London, the house might have been quiet, but activity surrounded him. Some sixty enslaved people performed the labor that made his comfort and wealth possible, from dressing him, to cooking his food, to cultivating his tobacco, to playing music when he held parties and entertained guests at Readbourne. But his description of a gourd-bodied banjo—as crude, rude, primitive, or any number of words that suggest it is unsophisticated and something not of value, while giving no real details of the instrument—makes it lucky that any record of the banjo was made at all.

The banjo was easy for Hollyday to obtain: he sent it to Sally just months after returning to Maryland, although he gave no indication of where he obtained the instrument. By the mid-1700s, the banjo was known and even somewhat common in Maryland. A striking, yet disturbing example of this is in the advertisements placed when a person liberated themselves. These ads often begin "Run away, from the subscriber" or the slaveowner's name, and give descriptions of the person, including name, visual appearance, demeanor, languages spoken, and any distinguishing talents, including whether they were a musician. These ads provide more information on certain individuals than exists about most other people living in the mid-eighteenth century, and show how slaveowners like Hollyday paid close attention to the people they owned.[5]

In the years 1748 and 1749, advertisements were put out for the return of three different banjo players who escaped slavery in Maryland. Two of the men had been living near Hollyday's home on the eastern side of the bay. Sometime before June 1748, Toby escaped from William Harris, who lived across the Chester River in Fairlee, Maryland. The advertisement urging Toby's recapture notes that Toby was dressed finely, or at least had fine-quality clothes with him: a broadcloth coat and waistcoat, both lined with red fabric, a pair of wool breeches, a new pair of stockings, a hat, and "a pair of old Pumps"—attire that suggests Toby didn't do manual or field labor. It's also possible that these were not his regular clothes, but items he took because they would make him look like a free man. Toby probably planned his escape well, since he left in a canoe and took with him "a new Fiddle, [and] a Bonja, on both which he at times plays." Playing music was likely part of Toby's expected labor, and the fine clothes came from his owner's desire that he look good at parties.[6]

Like many musicians who escaped, Toby was a carpenter and sawyer. Skilled craftsmen, and especially carpenters, were among the most valuable enslaved people, as were musicians. As a carpenter, Toby would have had the skills to make his own banjo. He could also have made his own fiddle, although constructing a fiddle or violin requires more time and precise work than a banjo. If Toby was expected to play music, Harris could have also bought the new fiddle Toby took with him. He also took a howel, a woodworking tool used in barrel-making, with which he made bowls. Woodworking could have been a way to earn money once he escaped. Harris suspected that Toby might have gone to his former owner, Reverend James Williamson, who was Harris's relative.[7]

The next year in mid-August, a man named Prince sought his liberty, leaving the home of John Woolford in Cambridge, a town on the Choptank River forty miles south of Hollyday's plantation. Like Toby, Prince took with him nice clothing, including a new blue coat, a wool jacket, two linen shirts, a pair of leather and a pair of black cloth breeches, and a felt hat. The description of Prince as "yellow" suggests that he was light-skinned, perhaps of mixed African and European ancestry. He took "an old fiddle" with him when he left, and Woolford comments that he "plays very well on the Banger"—using the same word for the instrument as newspaper editor James Alexander. The advertisements use different but similar words for the instrument—banjo, bonja, bangeo, banjoe, banger—which suggests that there was starting to be some standardization of the name, and the lack of description suggests that readers knew what the instrument was, what it looked like, and that the ability to play it was distinguishing enough to be included in a description. And while some musicians listed in these advertisements, like Prince and Toby, played both the fiddle and the banjo, many more played just the fiddle.[8]

Perhaps at the very moment that Hollyday was reading Sally's letter, outside his window William, a man he owned, was practicing the fiddle. William worked in the house and may have played the fiddle at Hollyday's parties. He may also have been one of the musicians who Hollyday said played fiddle and banjo under the trees. Hollyday wrote that sometimes William led others in song, which may indicate his prominence among the Black people at Readbourne and even the surrounding area.[9]

Like so much of this history, what happened to William and the banjo Hollyday sent Sally isn't known. If William outlived Hollyday, he could have been listed as property in Hollyday's will, but Hollyday didn't itemize the enslaved people he called property and left his entire estate to his brother Henry. It is not clear in the letters between Hollyday and Sally whether the banjo stayed at the Andersons or was kept at the home of Lady Browne or Mrs. Folkes. Perhaps it found its way into one of the cabinets of curiosities that were popping up across London, or perhaps someone threw it out when the novelty wore off.[10]

VI

Jamaica, 1750

Thomas Thistlewood walked from his small house down to the even smaller ones. He passed pens of cattle, sheep, goats, horses, and mules, fields of corn and the corn mill, and the plots of land where the enslaved people of Vineyard Pen were allowed to grow their own food. It was Christmas day, 1750, and the time of year seemed, as Father Labat had written around fifty years earlier, to allow for something other than work. However, at Vineyard Pen they grew no sugar, and the work taking care of livestock and growing food for people on the sugar plantations was constant. Although Thistlewood wasn't a particularly religious man, he permitted a slight pause in work to acknowledge the holiday.

This was Thistlewood's first Christmas in Jamaica and he was still learning about his new life, including how to run the farm, earn money, and interact with the enslaved people he managed. Even if he gave the enslaved small freedoms, he more often used cruelty to control them. On his first day at Vineyard Pen, he was ordered to give three hundred lashes to a man named Dick who was responsible for taking cattle to surrounding plantations. Dick survived this brutal beating, and if Thistlewood had any qualms about striking another person, they soon abated. "Whipped and flogged," followed by an enslaved person's name, appears again and

again in his diaries, sometimes with a reason for the punishment, sometimes without.

He had emigrated from England to Jamaica earlier that year in hopes
of raising his station in life. As a second son, Thistlewood had no hope
of inheriting land or much money. Still, he had managed to pay his own
way to the Caribbean where, like other free white men, he could quickly
get work as an overseer or plantation manager. With fears of insurrection
rampant, Jamaica's Deficiency Law required that for the first ten enslaved
Blacks on any estate, two whites were needed as overseers, and for every
ten Blacks thereafter, one more white man had to be employed. This
meant that plantation owners, whether they lived in Jamaica or managed their estates from Europe, desperately needed white men to work
in administrative and managerial positions. If Thistlewood survived the
diseases that plagued new arrivals and managed to stay sober, he could
make good money. A white man in Jamaica was paid in cash in a country
that mostly worked on credit, and was on average more than thirty-six
times as wealthy as a white man in Maryland or New York and more than
fifty-two times as wealthy as a white man in England or Wales. Those
who came had ambition and often avarice and could easily live luxuri-
ously—but only if they were willing to fully embrace the brutal slavery
of the sugar plantations that were making Jamaica the wealthiest British
colony. Thistlewood did embrace it.[1]

Whether or not any of the forty-two enslaved people at Vineyard Pen
told Thistlewood what was happening on Christmas night in 1750, he
would have heard the music drifting across the landscape. He kept an
almost daily diary while at Vineyard Pen. He was well-read and regularly
bought books to add to his extensive library, but the short, neatly written
notes of his days are for himself and not the beginnings of an autobiogra-
phy or memoir. In that way, his records are different from those of someone like Hans Sloane, who expected that his time in Jamaica would be
temporary and hoped to publish a book about his travels. In his diaries,
Thistlewood seems frank about his actions and life.[2]

On Christmas, the men and women enslaved at Vineyard Pen gather to
have "Criolian, Congo, and Coromantee &c. Music & dancing." Like most

people getting ready for a celebration, they wear their finest clothes. One of the women dances slowly and fluidly, while a man moves with faster, more energetic steps. The woman sways her hips without moving her torso, while the man turns his body and lets his limbs move freely, both in time to the music. The musicians can choose to pause, slow the pace, and lower the volume of the instruments, giving the dancers a moment to catch their breath, before picking up again at a faster pace. The next night, December 26, Thistlewood saw dancing again. He wrote, "Tonight our Coromantee Negroes had a trick, which they call Tabrabrah, a rope 7 or 8 yards long, one end tied to a post close to the ground a person swung the other, whilst one danced in the middle above and beneath it."[3]

Thistlewood gives the names of the enslaved people who lived and worked at Vineyard Pen, but doesn't say who is dancing or playing music on either night. Sixteen men and seven women at Vineyard Pen were born in the Americas, described by Thistlewood as Creole or Criole. The other seven men and twelve women were African-born, including Charles, Marina, and Betty, and perhaps he learned that they were from the Gold Coast region, which he called Coromantee, or from Central Africa, which he called Congo. Like James Alexander in New York, Thistlewood may be making an observation that each community, or each "nation," has its own dance and music, or, like Mr. Baptiste's transcriptions in Sloane's book, that pieces of music and dances have their own ethnic designation. In Kingston, Thistlewood observed this division of people during song and dance "to the westward of the Town . . . odd Music, Motions &c. the Negroes of each Nation by themselves." The designations Thistlewood give may not discount that people danced something other than a dance of their own culture. Already by 1750, more than 450,000 people had been taken from Africa. While the first generations of enslaved Africans may have had an important impact on the development of Black Jamaican culture, the constant arrival of ships from ports across the African continent meant that traditions changed. While sugar plantations had hundreds of enslaved people, it may have been harder for the relatively few people at Vineyard Pen to create communities based on their African ethnic heritage.[4]

During his first years in Jamaica, Thistlewood recorded what he was learning about African and Creole culture. In his diary, he jotted down new terms he learned, and on February 2, 1751, he defined a musical instrument: "Merry wang, Banjor, Strum Strum, or Creolian Negroe fiddle." He doesn't mention where he learned these words, although he was familiar with Sloane's book on Jamaica and may have seen the term Strum Strump there. He called these instruments Creolian, meaning that Blacks born in the Americas—and not in Africa—made them, much like the "type of guitar" Father Labat saw. His definition of this instrument as a fiddle is also curious. Thistlewood wasn't a musician and maybe he didn't know the difference between a fiddle and a lute, or that a fiddle is bowed and a lute plucked. The word fiddle may have simply popped into his head, or perhaps the terms "merry wang" and "banjor" were still fluid enough to encompass both plucked and bowed instruments.[5]

Edward Long arrived in Jamaica not long after Thistlewood. Unlike Thistlewood, Long already had connections to the island, as his father owned a plantation, and quickly established himself in Jamaican society by marrying a plantation-owning widow. His writings on Jamaica are also the opposite of Thistlewood's. Where Thistlewood wrote private notes in his own shorthand, Long published three volumes under the title *History of Jamaica or, General Survey of the Ancient and Modern State of that Island*, in 1774. Here, he made note of the "favourite instrument" of the enslaved, the merry-wang. This "rustic guitar, of four strings . . . is made with a calabash; a slice of which taken off, a dried bladder, or skin, is spread across the largest section; and this is fastened to a handle, which they take great pains in ornamenting with a sort of rude carved work, and ribbands." Neither Thistlewood nor Long explains the name merry-wang, but it appears similar to the lyrics "meri wá langa" which Mr. Baptiste wrote down for "Koromanti." The word wang could be related to wanga, sometimes spelled *ounga*: a charm or talisman.[6]

Long observed different Christmas festivities from Thistlewood. He wrote that men in town would dress up in "grotesque" outfits, meaning a combination of human and animal forms, with "a pair of oxhorns on their head, sprouting from the top of a horrid sort of vizor or mask,

An illustration in Isaac Mendes
Belisario's *Sketches of Character* (1837),
featuring three percussionists and
the caption "Band of the Jaw-Bone
John-Canoe." *Rare Books and Manuscripts, Folio
A 2011 24, Yale Center for British Art.
Paul Mellon Collection*

which about the mouth is rendered very terrific with large boar tusks."
The man in the costume carried a wooden sword and danced at every
door, "bellowing out John Connu!" Women followed behind him, offering him alcoholic aniseed water. Long thought that the "dance is probably an horrible memorial of John Conny, a celebrated cabocero . . . on the
Guiney coast." John Conny was a chief and trader on the Gold Coast who
fought against the Dutch for the right to trade around 1720. He added the
title King to his name, a variant of the Dutch Konick. Sometimes this celebration was called Junkanoo.[7]

✍

More than twenty years later, in November 1773, Thistlewood heard
something after he'd gone to bed. It was ten o'clock on a Saturday night.
He left his house and went down to the area where the enslaved lived.
He had left his job at Vineyard Pen to manage a sugar plantation, then
bought his own land and now owned people who raised his crops and
livestock. The longer he stayed in Jamaica, the more sadistic and brutal he
had become. He raped women and invented forms of torture to threaten,
humiliate, and scare enslaved people into compliance. He believed slaves
to be human and yet also believed that he could treat them as he wanted,
that the rules of behavior he had learned in Europe did not apply because

his livelihood depended on the total subjugation of the enslaved. His diaries reveal no distress about slavery or his position as an overseer or owner of slaves. In fact, he seems to have understood that all of his actions, including his brutality, were part of the control that makes enslavement work.[8]

On this Saturday night, he "found Mrs. North's George playing upon the Banjar to Lincoln." Thistlewood had bought Lincoln in 1756, and in a strange way Thistlewood trusted him. Lincoln was Ibo, probably taken from the Bight of Biafra or the Bight of Benin. Thistlewood let him go hunting and fishing, and, using his favored position and earned trust, Lincoln would push the boundaries of his allowances. Sometimes Thistlewood commented that Lincoln was "lazy" or "headstrong." Lincoln might have acted so for the purpose of frustrating Thistlewood, as a not-so-subtle form of resistance, or Thistlewood might have been criticizing Lincoln to degrade him. Although enslaved, Lincoln worked within the system to gain a certain amount of freedom. In addition to being allowed to carry a gun on occasion, two years earlier Thistlewood had let Lincoln go to "a play, at the burial of a Negro at the Retrieve all Sunday night."[9]

Thistlewood allowed dances and allowed Lincoln to attend the funeral, but he didn't want anyone practicing "African superstitions," which was becoming known generally as obeah. As early as 1710, an English army officer in Barbados mentioned obeah in his letters to London, while the 1764 poem "The Sugar Cane" introduced obia as magic spells and conjuring. The word was used not just for the practices of the obiamen or conjurers who had abilities that transcended the physical world, but for any practice that could be seen as ancestor worship, calling on supernatural powers for aid, or superstition. Father Labat decried superstition and what he considered magical powers because he believed they interfered with being a Christian. Thistlewood wasn't religious, and most Jamaican slaveowners didn't care about Christianizing the enslaved. Instead, considering people of African descent idolaters fed the idea of African cultural inferiority, which supported white supremacy and enslavement.[10]

Even though Thistlewood wasn't a practicing Christian, he still had a problem with obeah. Punishing those who practiced it or believed in it was a way of maintaining control, and there was an implicit fear that if Blacks could use obeah against other Blacks, they would use it against whites. During one dance, Thistlewood saw a man who ate fire and struck his own arm with a blade "very hard, yet received no harm." Could the man who didn't suffer from hitting his own arm attack Thistlewood, knowing that he himself wouldn't be harmed?[11]

In 1760, this fear came into sharp focus. Before, the whites who instituted and upheld slavery could dismiss obeah as harmless superstition, but the uprising that became known as Tacky's Revolt proved to them that the practice could be dangerous. Men led by the Koromanti man Tacky attacked a fort, stole gunpowder and weapons, and began burning plantations after liberating the enslaved people on them. Those who participated in the revolt were said to have been bound by obeah oaths and protected against the violence of white men. While the island was in a panic, Thistlewood trusted Lincoln enough to give him a gun and keep watch. Afterward, the colonial government criminalized the practice of obeah.[12]

Where before Thistlewood would have observed music and dancing, he didn't tolerate it four years after Tacky's Revolt, and may have considered banjo playing and drumming a part of obeah practice. On a night in 1764 when he found a man named Job playing the banjo, he "broke Job's Banjar to pieces in the Mill house."[13] And when he found "Mrs. North's George" playing the banjo for Lincoln in 1773, it was not just that they were playing the banjo; worse, Lincoln, whom he trusted, was doing something illicit. Thistlewood grabbed the instrument and "chop't it all in pieces with my cutlass, & reprimanded them." Like many other whites, Thistlewood settled on the name "banjar." Unlike Sloane, Thistlewood decided it was an instrument that shouldn't be saved.[14]

VII

Suriname, 1773

The short dry season was ending as John Gabriel Stedman sat down for breakfast at the home of Mr. Demelley, a colonial official. He'd only arrived in Suriname a few months earlier, in January 1773, but had already gotten used to the splendor that the Dutch colony provided white Europeans like him. Stedman had boarded a ship in Texel, Holland, responding to a call from the Dutch States General for soldiers willing to sail to South America's northern coast. Having served in the Scots Brigade since he was sixteen, Stedman thought it would be a new adventure. The homes in Paramaribo, the colony's only city, had a distinctly European flavor, with their wealth on display. Crystal chandeliers hung shimmering from ceilings, while stiff portraits of people with soft, plump, pale skin sat in frames of gold. But nothing showed true wealth like the number of enslaved people who attended to a household. At the Demelleys' home, these included the fifteen-year-old Joanna. Stedman thought she was the most beautiful woman he'd ever seen and wanted to know more about her.[1]

Stedman was not in Suriname to eat fancy breakfasts and admire women, but to protect the colony. Founded in 1651 by the English, ceded to the Dutch in 1667 in exchange for the North American colony that would become New York, and belonging to the city of Amsterdam and the Dutch West India Company, the colony was home to wealthy planters who flaunted their riches while some 75,000 enslaved men, women, and children produced that wealth. As in other parts of the Caribbean, the forced labor camps stretching up the Suriname and Commewijna rivers mostly produced sugar. These plantations were seventeen times as large as plantations in Maryland and Virginia, with a ratio of sixty-five enslaved people to every free white person. The enslaved used this ratio to their advantage. Beginning in the 1600s, they escaped into the jungle to form new communities. In the 1760s, these Maroon communities started attacking plantations in hopes of freeing more people. In Berbice, a colony next to Suriname owned by the Dutch West India company, enslaved people had revolted in 1763 and almost took over the colony. The landowners and colonial authorities in Suriname knew that the Maroons could do something similar. Stedman was one of 1,600 soldiers, or Marines, shipped in to protect the plantations and fight these insurrections.[2]

At the waterfront in Paramaribo, Stedman saw a mix of Carib Indians, who came to town to trade and do business, and whites of European descent—soldiers, sailors, planters, and landowners. Those Europeans included Jews, who had the freedom to practice their religion, staff their own militias, and own land and buy Black people to work that land. But most of the people on the streets of Paramaribo were of African descent, coming from communities Stedman heard called Abo, Bonia, Blitay, Coromantyn, Congo, Gango, Konare, Kiemba, Loango, N'Zoko, Nago, Papa, and Pombo. Although the vast majority were enslaved, some Black people—a term in Suriname that meant someone who had only African ancestry—had gained their freedom, as had some people of color, who had mixed African and European ancestry. Joanna, Stedman learned, was not Black, but neither was she free. He found her elegant, like a goddess, and full of sweetness. He wrote about her expressive eyes, glowing cheeks, teeth "as white as mountain snow," and perfect ringlets in her dark brown hair.[3]

Before going into the jungle to fight the Maroons, Stedman partied almost constantly, like a sailor on shore leave. He attended a ball the colonel threw for the Prince of Orange's birthday and danced to the music of two fiddlers. Another night, he danced on the deck of a ship until seven in the morning and then rode around town in a carriage. He went to a ball hosted by free people of color and got drunk at the tavern. And he took full advantage of his position of power over the women in Suriname. Shortly after his arrival in Paramaribo, he wrote in his diary that, after getting drunk, he went to sleep at the home of his friend Mr. Lolkens and "I f—k one of his negro maids." Had she resisted him, this enslaved woman could have been physically abused or killed.[4]

To say enslaved women didn't have agency would be to underestimate their resistance. One of brutal plantation manager Thomas Thistlewood's frequent sexual partners was Phibbah. She could not deny his advances, but she used the money and gifts he gave her to increase her own wealth to the point where she could own property and better support her family. The inherent power structures of American colonies allowed men to have sexual encounters with any enslaved woman they wanted, no matter how the women felt. Stedman continued to take advantage of his position and had sex with multiple women.[5]

But Joanna was more captivating than any of these women, and Stedman asked Mrs. Demelley to tell him more about her. Her father was a Mr. Kruytoff, white and "respectable"; her mother was Cery, a Black woman owned by a man named Mr. De Borde. Mrs. Demelley told Stedman that Kruytoff had tried to buy Cery, Joanna, and his other children, but De Borde refused to sell them. Kruytoff died, depressed about his inability to free his family, and the situation for Cery and Joanna deteriorated. The best carpenters ran away from De Borde's estate, causing the plantation to collapse. Unable to pay his debts he fled the colony, leaving his wife in debtors' prison and Joanna enslaved to some future, unknown buyer.[6]

Less than two months later, Stedman declared he was in love with Joanna and that she made him "perfectly happy." What they had wasn't an unusual arrangement, although it wasn't technically legal. Because of the imbalance between white men and women in the colony, the men entered into "Suriname marriages," which Stedman called "as common as it is almost necessary." The man had "a female slave" who didn't necessarily belong to him but might have been hired to clean, wash, knit, sew, and attend to him when he was sick. Sexual relations would have been a part of the relationship, even though sexual contact between people of European descent and people of African or Indigenous descent was outlawed. The man usually paid money to the woman's family, and this economic exchange put further pressure on the woman to accept the transaction.[7]

Even if Stedman loved Joanna, they could not be lawfully married because enslaved women could not be granted that "Christian privilege and Ceremony." Decorum and law didn't really matter to Stedman. One day he declared to Mrs. Demelley that he wanted to purchase Joanna's freedom, take her to Europe, and marry her. Even though this went against the general principle of the Suriname marriage, he felt no shame in announcing his feelings.[8]

Mrs. Demelley gazed back at him in "wild astonishment." This wasn't how men usually behaved, and Stedman may not have known how difficult what he was proposing was. He may not have cared. Stedman was the type of man who grabbed an electric eel just to feel the shock, and he had decided that because he loved Joanna, the common practice and opinion of others could be damned.[9]

But Stedman soon began to feel the complexity of the relationship. By June 1773, he resolved "to ly no more [with her] for certain good reason," perhaps because she was enslaved or because he was leaving for the jungle. Yet while in the jungle, poorly equipped and battling Maroon troops who knew the land better, Stedman received letters from Joanna. Then, in October, he learned that Theodore Passalege and his son Issac had bought De Borde's plantation and everyone enslaved there, including Joanna. When Stedman returned from the jungle in January 1774, he recommitted himself to Joanna and was determined to purchase her.[10]

Stedman had gotten used to traveling by boat. Enslaved men rowed hollowed-out trees shaded with tents to protect the passengers from the equatorial sun. Every piece of river- and creekfront for miles around Paramaribo was the edge of a plantation, a mini-port where people and goods were loaded and unloaded, the waterway the only means of transport. Having been in the city and the jungle, Stedman now found himself on the way to L'Esperance, a plantation and military outpost, where he was supposed to keep watch for Maroon attacks.

On March 5, Stedman spotted a white handkerchief waving from a tent boat and was overcome with joy. It was Joanna, traveling with her aunt back to the old De Borde plantation, Faukenberg, four miles up the river from L'Esperance. Stedman joined them for the last part of the journey and at Faukenberg he met Joanna's grandfather, "a venerable old slave" who said he had been born on the Coast of Guinea in Africa. For all of Joanna's beauty and light skin, Stedman couldn't deny the "misfortune of her birth and conditions," as he put it. Then he received wonderful news: Mr. Lolkens, the manager of the Faukenberg estate, wanted Stedman to take Joanna to L'Esperance. Stedman could write to the Passaleges and ask to buy her.[11]

Stedman had the enslaved people at L'Esperance build a house for him and Joanna, who joined him in April. He considered their life together idyllic: he painted, played music, swam in the river, and practiced shooting, with Joanna always by his side. She also became central to his ability to understand Suriname and Surinamese culture. To communicate with her, he learned Sranan, the English-based Creole spoken in the colony. He learned remedies used by the enslaved to cure illnesses and recorded the cultural practices of the Afro-Surinamese. He saw people wearing obias, protective amulets. The word obia is the same as obeah, the religion considered dangerous by Jamaican colonists; in Suriname, it refers to spiritual objects. Stedman may have learned things like this from others who lived on the plantation besides Joanna.[12]

Stedman had felt he was settling into a life with Joanna, but in May it was disrupted. The senior Passalege died, and Joanna would be sold again. And it was no longer only Joanna's freedom he had to consider. She was pregnant.

"Heavens, not only my friend, but my offspring to be a slave, and a slave under such government," Stedman wrote. What should have been an impending joy was clouded by the realization that his child would be owned by another man. Like Adam, Stedman thought, he had tasted the forbidden fruit, and now his situation was just as wretched. Would he have felt differently if he owned Joanna? Would he have cared whether his actions had created another enslaved person?[13]

Stedman wrote to a lawyer asking whether he could buy his child's freedom. He could, with the "proprietor's consent." But Stedman didn't even know who that proprietor would be. Stedman believed he was exceptional and that his relationship with Joanna was exceptional. She was not just a Suriname wife, but a woman he planned to bring to Europe and marry. And yet, his ancestry and status as a European man did nothing for his child. All he could do was wait. "This news perfectly completed my misery."[14]

As Joanna neared the end of her pregnancy, in November 1774, Mrs. Lolkens took her to Paramaribo, where they all thought it would be better for her to give birth. Stedman stayed at L'Esperance and regularly visited Faukenberg and other nearby plantations. One day, Gideon de Graav invited him to Knoppemonbo, his plantation on the Cassewinica Creek. De Graav had recently bought new men and women to work on it and was giving everyone a holiday where there would be music and dancing.[15]

Although a soldier, Stedman had received an education in art and music, played the fiddle, and made note of the music in Suriname. In his diary, he writes of small bands of Black musicians in Paramaribo, the singing of women who scrubbed floors, and even includes the musical notation of a bird call in the forest and a transcription of a vocal melody, a song he supposed an enslaved soldier might sing before going into battle.[16]

At Knoppemonbo, Stedman wrote about the Loango dancing he saw. Like Thomas Thistlewood in Jamaica and James Alexander in New York, Stedman believed that he was seeing people from a particular African ethnic group doing their own dance. He could have been grouping the dancers based on a shared language, like KiKongo, or the same place of origin, like the Loango coast of western Central Africa.

The participants gather around a makeshift stage where a man and woman begin the dance. A drummer sounds out a rhythm. He sits astride the drum. The drum looks like a log, a wooden tube with animal skin covering both ends, fastened with strings or gut. He beats out the time, and Stedman thinks it sounds like a bass. Another drummer might join in sporadically on a smaller version of the instrument, which is similar to the baboula drums Father Labat saw in the French Antilles.[17]

Stedman thinks the dance, which lasts for hours, is "like a play, divided into many acts." Instead of losing energy and moving more slowly as the dance continues, the dancers become "more and more active and animated." Stedman admits that the dance might turn "an Englishwoman's face from white to scarlet," but, unlike Father Labat, he doesn't go into details of why. These dancers "think what they are doing is perfectly right," Stedman writes, guessing that they would find European set dances boring.[18]

During this dance, or a similar dance on the same plantation or another one nearby, Stedman hears singing. He calls it "melodious but without time," and notes the call-and-response format. Later, Stedman learns of another kind of dance. Whether he actually sees it for himself or hears the description from others he doesn't make clear. What he does know is that this other dance is more secretive, and more dangerous.[19]

Joanna gave birth to a boy on November 27, 1774. Stedman didn't meet his son until the end of December, when he presented Joanna with a gold medal that his father had given his mother on the day of his own birth. Stedman and Joanna named their son Johnny.

Joanna now had a new owner, Dirk Luden, who selected Stedman's friend de Graav to manage Faukenberg and its operations. De Graav promised to help Stedman free Joanna, but her freedom had not yet come.[20]

Paramaribo was a small town, and Elizabeth Godefroy had heard of Stedman's predicament. Godefroy, one of the few white women in the colony, understood life in the Caribbean colonies. She was born in Suriname to a family that had lived in the Americas for nearly one hundred years, was twice a widow, had a home in Paramaribo, and managed her plantation on the Commewijne River. She invited Stedman to dinner and told him she wanted to help. A month earlier, in July 1775, Stedman had learned from de Graav that he could purchase Joanna and Johnny for 200 pounds, an amount of money he didn't have. But, as many people who bought slaves did so on credit, Stedman asked de Graav if that would be possible, telling himself he'd survive on bread and salt in order to pay off the debt. Godefroy offered another solution.[21]

"Permit me, then, to participate in your happiness and in the prosperous prospects of the virtuous Joanna and her little boy," she said to Stedman, offering to lend him the money to buy Joanna and Johnny's freedom. Stedman hardly knew what to say. When he told Joanna, she cried, "Gado sa blessa de woma"—May God bless the woman.[22]

In Stedman's telling, Joanna insisted she should be mortgaged to Godefroy until the debt was paid off, although Johnny should immediately be freed. Stedman wrote, "Without here endeavoring to paint the struggle that I felt between love and honor, I shall bluntly say that I yielded to the last . . ." Why did Joanna not accept her freedom? Was she afraid that if she didn't negotiate for her son's immediate emancipation, Stedman might default on his debt and they would both return to slavery? Was deep motherly love keeping her enslaved, at least temporarily?[23]

Godefroy accepted the arrangement and told Stedman that Joanna would be more companion than servant. Stedman paid de Graav for his family, and the next day, "praises [were] sung through the town of Paramaribo" for what he had accomplished.[24]

Although Stedman wanted Joanna and Johnny's freedom, he was no abolitionist, and his thoughts, words, and actions are riddled with contradictions. He felt that the "African Negro" was his brother and though treated "by some stupid Europeans as Brutes, are made of no inferior clay." He saw how many people were being forced to labor on "the whole American settlements" and concluded that "in twenty years, two millions of people are murdered to provide us with coffee and sugar." However, he also felt that under "a mild government, no Negro's work is more than a healthy exercise, which ends with the setting sun, when the rest of his time is his own . . ." And when it came to disciplining enslaved men, he wrote, "I flog 3 negroes" with no note of remorse. Stedman wasn't alone in this cognitive dissonance. It was what led George Washington to free the enslaved people he owned only after his death and Thomas Jefferson to have a relationship with Sally Hemings, free their children but none of the other people he owned, and never free her. Washington and Jefferson could change laws, but did not advocate for abolition and were not willing to give up their wealth and lifestyle.[25]

Stedman imagined a place where people of African descent were truly content despite being enslaved. In this theoretical place, the enslaved men, women, and children were cared for, fed, housed, and treated with respect, even as they worked without pay and without freedom.

Writing about spirituality, religion, music, and dance, Stedman tried to show that enslaved people were happy—and thus could remain slaves. They had a God: "All Negroes believe firmly in a God whose goodness they trust more than many whining Christians." They had spiritual ceremony, in the form of a dance he calls the "winty play, or dance of the mermaid." The play centers on an older woman, someone Stedman would describe as a matron rather than a young woman. The women that take this role are "a kind of sibils . . . who deal in oracles" and dance "till absolutely they froth at the mouth and drop down." The woman could command anything—murder your master, desert into the woods, rebel, be free—and the others would do it. Stedman learns that "whatever She says to be done during this fit of madness is sacredly performed by the surrounding Multitude." He knows that others think this dance dangerous, but even when "this piece of fanaticism is forbidden" by colonial authorities, people cannot be kept from their spiritual practice. In the "winty play," Stedman sees both music and dance, and connects it to a religion simply by referring to the women as sibyls, a connection white Europeans could not often make when observing the music and dance of other cultures.[26]

During burial rituals and death celebrations, spirituality and music mixed again. Stedman thought that the enslaved had no fear of death, because they believed "they will see again some of their friends and relations in another world." A feast for a relative that has left this earth finished with "a joyful dance and songs of praise in memory of their dear relation."[27]

Once every few months an owner or manager like de Graav might give permission for a grand ball, where the enslaved would gather, play music, and dance. The women dress in their best cotton petticoats imported from Europe or North America, and men don their best Holland trousers. Instruments provide music, and during these dances, Stedman says the men and women always dance in couples. The men "figuring and footing," the women turning "round like a top" as their skirts begin to float upward and expand in a move they call *waey cotto*. The revelers cheer, shout, and clap. The dance music Stedman hears is always in 4/4 or 2/4 time sounding "Tuckety Tuck and Tuckety Tuck ad perpetuum," but "never triple time" like that of a waltz or jig.[28]

Women wipe the sweat from the brows of performers and musicians, while others stand and watch. The manager or owner might give them rum or kill-devil, another alcoholic byproduct of sugar manufacturing. Stedman has seen these dances many times and "known the drums to continue beating without intermission from sunset on Saturday night till that celestial orb again made its appearance on the Monday morning following." He believes these balls are purely social in function, but he may be unable to see the difference between spiritual music and social music.[29]

At one of these musical performances Stedman saw a banjo he called the Creole-bania. He wrote, "This is like a Mandolin or Guitar, being made of a Gourd covered with a Sheep-Skin, to which is Fixed a Very Long Neck or Handle. This instrument has but 4 strings, 3 long and one short, which is thick and serves for a Bace; it is play'd by the Fingers, and has a Very Agreeable sound, more so when Accompanied with a Song."[30]

The line "thick and serves for a Bace" was changed to "thick and serves for a bass" in Stedman's published memoir, a change that seems minor but is significant. "Bass" implies that this string would be tonally the lowest. Yet, to make lower tones, strings must be thicker and longer, whereas this one is short. If, instead, "Bace" is taken to mean base, that might suggest that the short string serves as a foundational element of the song, a source of rhythm. In down-stroke banjo playing, the thumb hits the short string each time the hand brushes down on the long strings. This creates a single note that repeats—either in quick

The Creole-bania collected by John Gabriel Stedman before his return to Europe in 1777. *Collection Nationaal Museum van Wereldculturen. Coll.no. RV-360-5696*

succession, making it sound almost like a fast, tight drum, or as a single repeated note that can set the pace of the music.[31]

Stedman did not record where he was when he heard this instrument, or if he did, that information hasn't survived. The name of the instrument reveals some of its origin, as Stedman frequently described an instrument using a designation for the group of people who played it: Kiemba, Ansokko, Loango, Papa, and Creole. Although he never explained where those designations came from, Creole might be the clearest. To Stedman, a Creole is a person of African descent born in the colony, someone considered more "American" than "African." So the Creole-bania was played by people of African descent born in Suriname.[32]

The suffix "bania" is more difficult to parse. The suffixes of other instruments he names are categories for drum, horn, or flute. He uses bania to name other instruments, including the Ansokko bania and the Loango bania. The Ansokko bania is like a xylophone or marimba and the Loango bania is similar to a thumb piano or kalimba. Like the Creole-bania, they could carry a melody, and perhaps melody is what bania means. But how could bania—so similar to words like bangil and bonja—mean anything but banjo, a stringed lute with a skin soundboard?

✍

By the middle of 1776, John Gabriel Stedman knew that his time in Suriname was coming to a close. Elizabeth Godefroy had allowed Joanna and Johnny to remain at Stedman's cabin on L'Esperance, where they cultivated a vegetable garden as if he were going to stay in Suriname forever. Sometimes Stedman went to town and visited his friend Mr. Schouten, taking rides in his chaise and examining his cabinet of curiosities. He also called on other prominent Surinamers like Graman Quacy, a locoman, or sorcerer, healer, and naturalist.[33]

During his visits with Godefroy and Graman Quacy, he had conversations about what would happen to Joanna and Johnny when he left. They were not free, and by law the government had to agree to their manumission. Stedman, Joanna's family, and Godefroy made an agreement that Joanna would be bound to Godefroy alone (or Stedman), meaning that she could not be sold again. If Stedman could not pay Godefroy back, Joanna would be enslaved until Godefroy's death, at which time Joanna would receive a house and some land. He also made a will naming Johnny the heir to his estate and wanted him to be christened, but the priest refused, saying that Stedman could not guarantee that Johnny would receive a Christian education. Stedman wrote to the governor of Suriname in August 1776 requesting Johnny's manumission, but by the fall, he still hadn't heard anything. At one point, he considered taking Johnny with him to Europe, as Graman Quacy had told him that this would result in automatic manumission after six months. However, Stedman also knew that taking Johnny from Joanna would be the equivalent of "plunging a dagger in his mother's bosom."[34]

Finally, he received word that Johnny's freedom would be granted on March 11, 1777. Joanna cried "tears for joy and gratitude." Neither had expected the request for manumission to come through, and the news came right when it was needed. At the end of March, Stedman was set to return to Europe. He still wanted Joanna and Johnny to go with him, but Joanna refused on the grounds that she was still bound to Godefroy.

Stedman believed that in fact she preferred to remain in Suriname. She would rather be "one of the first among her own class in America, rather than, as she was convinced to be, the last in Europe," he wrote.[35]

Monday, March 31, 1777. The boat was at the dock. At home, Joanna's mother took sixteen-month-old Johnny from Stedman's arms. Joanna's brothers and sisters gathered around him, "crying and invoking Heaven for my health and for my safety." Joanna took his hand but didn't speak. Stedman brought Joanna and Johnny to his chest, feeling their bodies, smelling their hair for what might be the last time ever. He looked into Joanna's face, her eyes shut with tears forming around her eyelashes, her lips devoid of color. She bowed her head and sank into a chair. Dragging out the goodbye would only cause them more anguish. Stedman walked to the Waterkant, boarded the boat, and sailed home.[36]

VIII

South Carolina, 1780s

Somewhere along the Coosaw River, people emerge from their small houses, laid out in rows at the edge of fields. This land is called the Sea Islands, and sometimes the border between its flat earth and the brackish water that seeps into the Atlantic Ocean is imperceptible. There, the land isn't land at all, but thick marshes where the water can swallow someone or hide someone who doesn't want to be found. During the 1780s and early 1790s, rice and indigo fields made up the firm portion of the land. When they were allowed to leave those fields, people walked barefoot across the soft sandy ground to these one-room wooden cabins. They tried to find time for themselves at the end of the day and at the end of the week. Like the enslaved people in Jamaica, Martinique, New York, Maryland, and Suriname, they were forced to labor for others, but they found ways to do something for themselves.

On Saturday evenings, Sundays, and holidays, when they might be given time off work—if their owner believed in the Sabbath or a day of rest—they, like the enslaved across the Americas, prepared for traditions and celebrations, often in the form of a dance that could bring them closer to one another and to the places from which they came. A white man named John Rose saw this dance once. He must have been fascinated by it, since at some point, he drew it in watercolors on a piece of paper.

Rose owned property in the town of Beaufort on Port Royal Island. In 1775, at the age of twenty-three, he became the Clerk of the Court of Common Pleas, the civil court, of the Beaufort district. He was educated, had studied Greek and Roman literature, "sang by note, painted in watercolors, and played upon the hand-organ." At some point after becoming clerk, Rose bought 813 acres of land about ten miles from town along the Coosaw River, probably on Ladys Island, cementing him as a man of means.[1]

While some planters in the Sea Islands may have worked in their fields, absentee ownership was more common, as it was in the Caribbean. One visitor to South Carolina in 1785 wrote, "There are many who call themselves planters who know little about the process & art of planting—some ignorant of its most ordinary courses." With his job in the court, Rose was likely a planter of this type, and by 1790, he owned forty-nine people who worked either in his household in Beaufort or on his land on the river. Johann David Schöpf, a German physician who worked for the British during the Revolutionary War and then traveled in the United States and Caribbean afterward, commented that in South Carolina, "The headmen in this sort of [agricultural] work are commonly negroes, and if they thoroughly understand the management of the indigo, a great value is set upon them." Whether Rose grew indigo or rice, he likely had someone managing his property. Most plantation owners avoided living in the countryside during the summer months because of the heat and the fear of yellow fever, so perhaps it was around the Christmas holiday when Rose saw the dance.[2]

Outside the small houses along the Coosaw River, a woman in a green dress bends over slightly, shaking a white and blue cloth in front of her. Another woman, dressed in a thin white dress, dances next to her, also holding a cloth, a corner in each hand. They both wear pieces of fabric around their heads, tied at the back. They face a man, who is bent over and holds a wooden dowel in his hands.

Behind the male dancer stands a woman. She is the most finely dressed of the women and wears a blue-and-white checkered scarf on her head and a bright white dress trimmed in cream. Next to the woman in white stands a man in a red jacket. Behind the female dancers, three men and two women are sitting or standing, it's hard to tell, perhaps waiting for their turn to dance or perhaps forming a chorus of singers.

Two men provide musical accompaniment for the dance. They wear vests, knee-length breeches, and fine blue jackets, perhaps indicating that this is an indigo plantation. One sits with a drum pressed between his knees, beating out a rhythm with two sticks. The other plays a banjo made of a gourd, a board, and an animal skin. The round form of the banjo's body is echoed by a ceramic jug placed between the player's feet. The bottle Rose painted next to the musicians is a translucent green, with a stopper on top and a curve on the inside bottom visible.

While others left written records of what they saw or heard, Rose left an image with incredible detail. In the background is another plantation, with a main house, outbuildings, and slave cabins, perhaps an attempt by Rose to convey where the dance took place. In the foreground, the

John Rose's c. 1785 watercolor of enslaved people dancing and playing music in South Carolina. *Colonial Williamsburg Foundation, gift of Abby Aldrich Rockefeller.*

feet of the dancers don't just look as if they are moving, they look real; they have toenails and a half-circle where the fibula meets the foot. The men's jackets, vests, and pants have neat buttons, while their shirt cuffs tighten around their wrists in folds of fabric. The women's dresses seem to be shaped by stays, and the white dress of the woman dancing looks semi-translucent, her legs almost visible under the fabric. These are their best outfits, their special-occasion clothes. The faces of the people aren't well-rendered, but they are individualized, with different expressions and facial features, suggesting that Rose knew these people. The watercolor is small—a little over eleven by seventeen inches—and yet you can stare at it for an hour and keep seeing new details.

Rose doesn't give the name of the dance or the instruments. He doesn't say who the dancers, spectators, and musicians are, or whether he owned these people or if they were enslaved elsewhere. His records provide no clues to the narratives of their lives, except for the fact that those who were participating could have been Ansell, Cain, Dianna, Dick, Hagar, Hamon, Isaac, Maryann, Mingo, Peter, Phillis, Quilla, Sabina, Satyra, Soloman, Tom, Young Tom, or Tybee—all people Rose owned at the time of his death who were the right age to have been adults at the time he made the watercolor.[3]

Rose doesn't say what the music sounded like, what the dancers looked like when they moved. Could he have written precise descriptions if he had wanted to? Had he spoken to these people, asked them about their dance and their music? Was that worthy of his time? And even if he had, how clouded would his perceptions have been by his own worldview? Was the dance "lascivious," in the word of Father Labat? Was the banjo "rude," in the word of Maryland lawyer James Hollyday? Rose left only this one vibrant and detailed watercolor image: a relic that has to be decoded and understood not just in the context of South Carolina history but in the context of African-derived culture of the Caribbean and North America.

ℒ

The first generation of enslaved Africans brought to Carolina may have been predominantly from the Gold Coast, Akan and Ga speakers. The

Portuguese, Spanish, Danish, and Dutch called them Amina, Elmina, or Mina, while the English called them Coromantee or Koromantin. Within this region, there were multiple language dialects, ethnic groups, and political communities, and yet their similarities made them part of one nation in the Americas. They may have made up a large part of the first generation, since Barbadian planters, who settled the colony of Carolina in 1670, had designated them as being best-suited for sugar plantation work.[4]

These people of African descent now in Carolina, who had toiled in Barbados, were twice removed from their original homes and cultures. They were adapting their beliefs and practices to their new circumstances. In 1647, English traveler Richard Ligon indicated that the enslaved in Barbados came from an area spanning from the Gambia River in West Africa south to the coast of Central Africa, and because they spoke different languages, "one of them understands not another." Ligon didn't recognize that some of the languages he heard had already been created so that people could in fact understand one another. He wrote that a Black woman called her child "Pickaninny," which he didn't realize was a European-derived word; it comes from the Spanish *pequeño niño*, meaning small child, or the Portuguese *pequenino*, a diminutive form of the word for small, and appears as *pikin* in Surinamese Sranan and *pickney* in Jamaican Patois. Even those enslaved people who first arrived in Carolina probably already spoke a creolized language. In Barbados, the language would become known as Bajan, and on the Sea Islands it became Gullah. Using vocabulary and grammar from both European languages— including English, Spanish, French, Dutch, and Portuguese—and African languages—including Umbundu, BaKongo, Mbundu, and Mayombe— Gullah is a linguistic manifestation of the blending of cultures.[5]

Ligon had also witnessed the blending of musical cultures in Barbados, some forty years before Sloane arrived in Jamaica. He wrote that on Sunday afternoons, when the enslaved were not forced to work, they played music on "kettle drums" of several sizes, and "upon the smallest the best Musician playes." He saw people dance to this music, "men by themselves, and the women by themselves"—a very different description from that of Father Labat on Martinique.

Ligon wrote that Macow, an enslaved man, picked up Ligon's lute and began to figure out the scale. By placing his fingers on each fret and plucking the string, Macow noticed how, as he moved his fingers farther from the peghead toward the body of the instrument, the vibrating part of the strings became shorter and the sound higher in pitch. Later, Ligon saw Macow creating a melody instrument by placing pieces of wood of different lengths next to each other, cut precisely so that when Macow struck them, they would play the notes he wanted. This instrument is similar to the Ansokko bania that John Stedman saw in Suriname and instruments from Kongo and Angola called marimbas.[6]

Although small, Barbados was a place of convergence and dissemination of people and culture. In 1640, Dutch settlers had introduced knowledge and techniques from the Brazilian sugar plantation system to the island, which led to the importation of enslaved workers. Starting in the 1650s, Barbados became a stopping-off point for white people wishing to increase their wealth by settling areas in the Americas as yet unclaimed by Europeans. Some formed the colony of Suriname in 1651, which was suited for growing sugar, and in 1670, English settlers left Barbados to colonize the mid-Atlantic coast of North America, forming the colony of Carolina. Since the climate there wasn't good for sugar, enslaved laborers tended cattle and harvested trees, providing food and lumber to West Indian plantations.[7]

The Barbadian-now-Carolinian planters and slaveowners made slavery a part of their economic and social structure from the beginning. By contrast, in Virginia and New Amsterdam, comprehensive slave codes and laws of lifetime enslavement based on the race of a person's mother took time to develop. Carolina followed the models of Jamaica and Barbados, and imposed Jamaica's 1684 slave code. Among other provisions solidifying chattel slavery, it decreed that slaves who became Christians remained slaves and created monetary rewards for the recapture of runaways. Carolinians adopted the Barbadian practice of bringing enslaved people to trial to punish them for crimes.[8]

What Richard Ligon saw in Barbados might have been some of the cultural expressions of the first Africans in Carolina. But as time passed, culture shifted, adapted, and changed. Part of that shift was due to the new Africans brought to the colony. Southern Carolina's economy became increasingly focused on plantations near the coast and in 1712, North and South Carolina became two colonies. The South Carolina slaveowners had an interest in where people originated, making an assumption that this could indicate personality or the type of work a person would be suited for. In the early eighteenth century, slave owners shifted from providing the Caribbean with lumber and meat to providing the European market with rice and indigo. Although a majority of enslaved people arriving in South Carolina were from Central Africa, potential buyers could also find advertisements for people taken from Calabar on the Bight of Biafra or from the Gold Coast, and they began to value people from Senegambia and the Windward Coast, who had knowledge of rice cultivation.[9]

White slaveowners and white servants knew their lower numbers made them vulnerable, a fear which came to fruition on a Sunday in early September 1739 when a man named Jimmy and twenty other people thought to be from Angola freed themselves. They stole firearms and marched playing drums and carrying banners, burning buildings, killing almost every white person they came across and growing to a group of sixty. When they reached a field, they started dancing, singing, and playing drums, perhaps in order to signal others to join them or to prepare for war by dancing a sangamento, as was common in Kongo. More enslaved people joined in before a militia attacked, killing the rebels or causing them to flee. The uprising became known as the Stono Rebellion, and retaliation for it worsened the lives of enslaved people in South Carolina. Like the Code Noir of the French colonies, the 1740 Negro Act of South Carolina developed in the aftermath of the Stono Rebellion banned Blacks from certain behaviors, such as carrying weapons, unless they could show a pass from their owner. It also laid out regulations for whites in South Carolina, including a ban on teaching Blacks to read or leaving them on a plantation without a white supervisor; they did, however, have to give them "sufficient" clothing and food.[10]

The aftermath also included a moratorium on the international slave trade, which greatly reduced the number of new people arriving from

Africa and slowed any new infusion of African beliefs. Even fewer people arrived from Angola and Kongo, since the instigators of the rebellion
were thought to be from Angola, and therefore all Central Africans were
thought to be rebellious.[11]

The lawmakers took into account the idea that people in bondage
who were treated poorly would be more likely to cause problems such as
insurrection. Slaveholders did not take away opportunities to celebrate
during holidays. Instead, with the government's aid, they handled those
in bondage in a controlled manner. If enslaved people wanted to gather
somewhere other than where they lived, they would need passes saying
they had permission to be away. Still, gatherings were to be discouraged,
with the code noting that:

> all due care be taken to restrain the wanderings and meetings of
> Negroes and other slaves, at all times, and more especially on Sat-
> urday nights, Sundays, and other holidays, and their . . . using or
> keeping of drums, horns, or other loud instruments, which may
> call together or give sign or notice to one another of their wicked
> designs and purposes.[12]

The government was supposed to remain on the alert. Twenty-six
years after the Stono Rebellion, in 1766, South Carolina governor William
Bull heard that "some plots are forming & some attempts of insurrection
[are] to be made during these Holy days" and gave directions to the militia and patrols to be vigilant. While danger was in the eye of the beholder,
it could be hard to tell how much difference there was between a meeting
to dance and one to plan a revolt.[13]

Even with the laws of 1740 in place, enslaved people in the South
Carolina Lowcountry—like enslaved people in Martinique who disre-
garded the banning of the calenda—gathered anyway. In 1772, the *South-
Carolina Gazette* published an account written by the pseudonymous "The
Stranger," where he describes a large festival, which he calls "a Country-
Dance, Rout, or Cabal." As dusk falls, Black people begin to gather on
the outskirts of Charleston, carrying "heavy hickory sticks or clubs" and

baskets filled with food and alcohol. They also have "Music, Cards, Dice, &c.," although the Stranger doesn't say whether by music he means instruments. The evening's entertainment begins with a play of sorts. The men and women copy the manners of the whites, "relating some highly curious anecdotes," poking fun at them and engaging in subtle resistance. They follow this with dancing, games, and fights. He says these meetings are common, have as many as two hundred attendees, and happen within a mile of Charleston.[14]

These meetings caused anxiety among the whites since "their deliberations are never intended for the advantage of the white people." The Stranger hears people talking in low voices and suggests that runaways might be present, then demands to know why the "patrol-duty" hasn't stopped the meetings. He suggests that the fault lies with those who should be enforcing the laws "but yet permit them to be trampled upon."[15]

John Rose seems to have had no problem with enslaved Blacks gathering or playing drums—maybe because he thought this would keep them from revolting or sabotaging work, or because he didn't see a dance as dangerous. The drum in his watercolor could have been a qua-qua, which John Gabriel Stedman described as "a hard sounding-board elevated on one side like a boot jack, on which they beat or drum time with two pieces of iron, or two bones." In the watercolor, the musician presses the drum, which might be made from a gourd, between his legs and holds two slender sticks in his hands. J. F. D. Smyth, a traveler in the newly formed United States, speaking of "poor negroe slaves" generally without specifying a state or region, wrote that even if a man is tired after work, he "walks six or seven miles in the night . . . to a negroe dance." Here, the percussionist plays "a quaqua (somewhat resembling a drum)." The second instrument that accompanies the dance is "a banjor, (a large hollow instrument with three strings)." A better description comes from German physician Johann Schöpf, who wrote that "Another musical instrument of the genuine negro is the Banjah." He describes it in detail: "Over a hollow gourd (Cucurb lagenaria L.) is stretched a sheepskin, the instrument lengthened with a neck, strung with four strings, and tuned like a chord." The instrument is used to accompany dances, he writes, adding, "Their melodies are almost always the same, with little variation. The dancers, the musicians, and often even the spectators, sing alternately."[16]

Although Rose left no written description, his image provides almost a blueprint from which to make a banjo. The neck, extending from the gourd into the player's left hand, is flat and ends in a triangular point where three cylindrical shapes stick out: the tuning pegs. Halfway down the fingerboard is another peg for a shorter string. Rose has sketched in a bridge just below the player's hand, and at the bottom of the gourd is a tailpiece that holds the strings to the instrument on the opposite end from the tuning pegs. One of the things we can see, which is one of the most amazing things about this banjo, is that it is constructed in the same way as the Strum Strumps in Sloane's book about Jamaica from almost one hundred years earlier. Those instruments also have a flat neck with tuning pegs and long and short strings. On both instruments the neck enters the gourd where it attached to the vine, and the side of the gourd has been cut off for placement of the skin. The Strum Strumps have decorative crosses on the fingerboard, while in the Rose watercolor the sound holes form crosses. The engraving in Sloane's book does not offer a view of sound holes in the banjo, but the harp in the background has a cross-shaped sound hole. The lutes in these two images are more similar to each other than either is to any African instrument.[17]

Rose could have read Stedman, Sloane, or Smyth's books, all of which were published by the time he made this watercolor. But his banjo is unlike Sloane's or Stedman's, and clearly he portrayed an event he had witnessed on the South Carolina Sea Islands. Watercolors bleed easily into one another when the pigment is wet, so Rose would have had to let parts of the painting dry in order to make such a detailed work of art. He might have sketched the scene in pencil and worked on the painting after he saw the dance, or he might have seen it so often that he could paint it from memory. The level of detail and care suggests that he must have been intimately familiar with the dance and the people in it. And he was proud of the watercolor. He mentioned it specifically in his will, but he would never know its lasting significance.

IX

Cap François, Saint-Domingue, 1782

Sundays were more than the Lord's Day in Cap François, the city in northern Saint-Domingue that everyone called Le Cap. While the church bells rang from the cathedral, Médéric Louis Élie Moreau de Saint-Méry walked the city with his new wife. Moreau was born in Martinique and at age nineteen moved to Paris to study. He became a lawyer, then returned to the Caribbean and settled in Saint-Domingue, the French portion of the island of Hispaniola and the most profitable French colony. He married into a prominent family in 1781 and by 1782 was practicing law and serving in the government.[1]

One stop on a Sunday stroll could have been the *marché des blancs* (the white market), where Moreau liked to walk even if he didn't plan on buying anything; it was simply what one did on a Sunday. He wasn't a visitor or temporary sojourner like so many who would write about the Caribbean. He felt he knew this place and wanted to share what he considered its splendor with others.[2]

Compared to other ports around the Caribbean, Le Cap was a real metropolis, with hospitals and schools, theaters and plazas. The city was laid out on a grid, with house numbers and street names; some of the streets were even paved. It was modeled on European cities, but for the

French, this city of 18,000 people would always be inferior, a place with little to offer besides the large profits it generated. This was part of the problem, as Moreau saw it: the people who made the laws and decisions about the colonies didn't understand them. He could write about the colony with more knowledge than a visitor, and he believed that with the benefit of his insight the French government could make policies and laws that benefited it. Of course, Moreau's background deeply influenced his view of Saint-Domingue and what he would write.

Even though Moreau was of French descent, being born in the Caribbean made him of lower social status than someone born in France. He emphasized the distinction between white Creoles like himself and people of African descent. He advocated for the slaveowners and opposed the abolition of slavery and the granting of rights to anyone of African heritage, even if they were free people of color—that is, those not enslaved whose ancestors were born in both Europe and Africa. Free people of color were gaining wealth and the whites in the colony enacted laws controlling their behavior, making sure that distinctions based on ancestry were codified. These laws went so far as to ban free people of color from "affect[ing] the dress, hairstyles, style, or bearing of whites," a "bearing" which could include riding in a carriage or furnishing their homes in certain ways.[3]

Like the waterfront in Paramaribo, Le Cap's harbor bustled on Sundays. It wasn't just white strollers like Moreau and his wife who were out. The Code Noir—the code of law meant to control the behavior of the enslaved in Martinique, which also applied in Saint-Domingue—stipulated that enslaved people be given the day off from labor on Sundays. They could visit the markets, attend Mass in the cathedral, and, within certain parameters, do as they wished, including gathering to dance. Le Cap may have been different in some ways from other Caribbean towns like Paramaribo, but the allowance for dance, even when against the law, seems to have been essentially the same from Suriname to New York.

Moreau was working on a compilation of the laws and constitutions of the French American colonies, in what would end up being a six-volume work. As a historian and legal scholar, he had likely read Father Labat's descriptions of Martinique from almost a hundred years earlier, which were popular and well-received. Moreau might have also been compiling information for the history of Saint-Domingue he would publish fifteen years later, in 1797. Researching history, laws, and culture was all part of his effort to elevate the role white Creoles like himself played in the colonies. But he couldn't tell that story without also exploring the lives of the enslaved, including their dances.[4]

On a Sunday, men and women gather together at a flat area of ground and form a circle. Some people play rattles made of calabashes filled with pebbles or corn seeds, with a long handle. They shake, beat, and tap out rhythms, as did the percussionists Sloane saw in Jamaica one hundred years earlier. The women clap their hands and form a chorus, like the calenda singers in Martinique, and respond to one or two principals who "improvise songs."

Central to the dance are the drums, creating not just a beat but music to which the dancers respond. The description of the drums is familiar: a hollow piece of wood, one end open and the other covered by a piece of sheepskin or goatskin. While Father Labat referred to the smaller drum as a baboula, Moreau spells it "bamboula," and writes that this is the name "because it is sometimes made of a very large bamboo." The drummers sit astride their instruments, patting the drumhead with the heel of the hand and the fingers. One drummer plays a spare line with fewer beats, while the other plays a more complex rhythm. Moreau finds this "monotonous and dull," but the way the dancers move suggests they find it enlivening and inspiring.[5]

Couples enter the circle, and each male dancer faces his female partner. The man begins the dance by extending his foot and drawing it back, sometimes with his toe on the ground and sometimes his heel. Moreau thinks it looks like the steps of l'Anglaise, a contredanse or English country dance. Other steps may also remind him of the formal set dances that were popular in the ballrooms of Europe and the Americas. Here, the male dancer turns and then his partner turns too, waving a handkerchief she holds by the corners, just like the women in John Rose's watercolor. The dancers change places. The man lowers and raises his arms, his fists almost closed, his elbows close to his body. Moreau thinks the music makes the dance lively, animated, and graceful. The twirls and turns, the movements of arms and bodies forward and back, are akin to Father Labat's description. Was Moreau influenced by this or did he really see the same dance? He calls it *le Calenda*, using the same name that Father Labat used for the dance he observed in Martinique a century earlier.

Moreau notes another musician as well: "When they want to make the orchestra more complete, the Banza joins in, a kind of rough violin with four strings on which you pluck." Why did Moreau think the banza like a violin, when others described it as a "type of guitar"? It may be because he saw the banza player holding the instrument high on his chest or shoulder, or because violins have four strings while guitars have six. Or perhaps he thought the comparison to a violin would be more easily understood by his readers.[6]

A detail of an engraving in Moreau's *Atlas* where a banza player stands next to a drummer, holding the instrument high on his chest like the person in Schouten's *Waterkant van Paramaribo* diorama. University of Minnesota Libraries, James Ford Bell Library

Moreau published *Recueil de vues des lieux principaux de la colonie françoise de Saint-Domingue* in Paris in 1791, an illustrated atlas that was intended to complement the book he was working on. One engraving presents a dance at the port of Nippes, in the southern part of Saint-Domingue. The movement captured by the engraver, Nicolas Ponce, makes the scene come alive. One couple throws their hands out to the side with both feet leaving the ground, as they push their hips forward. The other couple looks as if they are running toward each other, hands outstretched but not touching, a back foot leaving the ground as they spring forward. Around the dancers stand men and women, some under parasols who might be free people of color or interlopers like Moreau himself.

As Moreau describes, there are two drummers. They sit astride drums as large as barrels, hands beating a rhythm. Next to one drummer is a musician playing a stringed instrument he holds up against his chest. This must be the banza that Moreau writes of, since the musician brings his hands up to the strings as if to pluck them, rather than placing a bow on the strings as he would if the instrument were a violin. This banjo doesn't look like the one in John Rose's South Carolina watercolor—it's smaller and held differently. Ponce may or may not have ever seen a banjo. He lived in France, but was well-read and wrote about classical art. Although there is no evidence of a banza in Paris when Ponce worked on these engravings as there is of a banjo in London, that doesn't exclude the possibility that he may have seen one.[7]

The scale of the banza in the Nippes scene is similar to that of the Strum Strumps in Sloane's book. Both instruments are a little longer than a fiddle, which means that holding them up against the chest to play wouldn't feel awkward. The body of the banza in Ponce's engraving is oblong, rather than the rounder gourd body on the one Strum Strump or the banjo in the South Carolina watercolor. While Ponce's image is detailed, the banza as it appears on the page is no larger than a thumbnail. Perhaps it is not an accurate representation of the instrument, but an engraver's shorthand—close enough so that those who see the image will recognize it from the words that Moreau has used to describe it in his text.

However, Moreau felt that the violin was the instrument preferred

by musicians of African descent on Saint-Domingue. Father Labat similarly noted the proficiency of Black violinists, and that the enslaved could
earn money from playing at marriages or other celebrations. The fact
that Moreau and Labat did not call this instrument a "gourd violin" or
"Negro violin" suggests that they are writing about the European violin,
not something like the one-string lutes played with bows in West Africa,
such as the ruudga of the Mossi and the goge of the Hausa. Perhaps, as
with Toby in Maryland, slaveowners in the French Antilles bought European instruments for these violinists. Moreau notes that the violinists he
observed played by ear rather than learning musical notation. They were
taught by another Black musician "who indicates to them the position of
the strings and that of the fingers."[8]

Moreau, like other white residents of Le Cap, could see calendas on
Sundays at the edge of the city or on local plantations—if he knew where
the dances were being held. But Moreau could have also seen a calenda
under completely different circumstances, in a way that would fore-
shadow the usurpation of Black culture by whites in the Americas. In
early January 1783, the play *Jeannot et Thérèse, a negro parody of Le Devin
du village, by Mr Clément*, was staged as part of an evening of theater. The
white actors performing "with blackened faces . . . [and] a calenda or slave
dance by several amateur dancers" promised to "render this parody most
agreeable and pleasing to the public."[9]

The musical play centers around Jeannot and Thérèse, who are
described as *nègres*, likely meaning that the characters were enslaved.
Although a parody of a French theatrical piece, the writer Clément made
it a thoroughly Saint-Domingue production. The play was in Kreyòl and
included specific references to the cultural and racial dynamics of the colony. Thérèse and Jeannot are in love, but Jeannot has left her for a wealthy
mulâtresse, a free woman of color. Angered, Thérèse says she could have
left him for both a wealthy free man of color and a white man. The performance has musical interludes of popular songs, and the calenda as a finale.
Here, on stage in Le Cap, whites and free people of color could experience
what Moreau says took place mostly clandestinely.[10]

One of the surviving manuscripts of the play suggests that the dance at the end is actually a contredanse. Like Moreau, the actors may have only seen the calenda as unwelcome spectators, and danced a European set dance which they thought they could make more "African" with their body movements. The play's directions give no indication of the instrumentation for the dance. Perhaps the musicians were, like Mr. Baptiste in Jamaica, enslaved or free men of color. If so, they may have been familiar enough with African-derived music to play something that felt authentic, but was toned down. Or, perhaps, they were more daring and played drums and a banza.[11]

The fact that the lead characters in *Jeannot et Thérèse* were of African descent (even if they were portrayed by whites in blackface) demonstrates that the audience of European descent had a curiosity about the life and culture of the enslaved, which they would have considered exotic and exciting. But just as most people at the time wanted to read travel books in their European drawing rooms rather than make the trip to the Caribbean, whites in Le Cap wanted to see this performance safely on stage on a Saturday night rather than watch a calenda on a Sunday outside the city being danced by people they owned.[12]

Furthermore, the Code Noir banned the calenda (a ban that was reiterated in 1772), which may have kept whites from wanting to be seen at the Saturday and Sunday rituals. Like the governments in Jamaica and South Carolina, Saint-Domingue authorities knew that gatherings for dances created the potential for people to plan acts of resistance or escapes. In the 1750s, the self-emancipated man François Makandal and his followers had poisoned slaveowners. The rumor was that Makandal had magical packets and invoked higher powers. Even within the safe bounds of the stage, *Jeannot et Thérèse* does not disarm these worries. An enslaved character named Papa Simon opens a wanga, an object imbued with spiritual significance, and begins to chant. The presence of magic and music suggests that perhaps the slaveowners do not have complete control over the people they own.[13]

There is no mention in the play's stage directions that the performers should mock the people of African descent they are portraying. But the play is a comedy, an example of the type of performance in which mockery, or at least caricature and stereotypes—including the oversexualized Black man and woman—prevail. Even Papa Simon is stereotyped, from his outfit—"the real costume of slaves," which may have meant worn-out pants, no shirt, and no shoes—to the lines he sings while grimacing: "oualili, quacoucou, Dahomé, coroco, calaliou." These are not Kreyòl words, the language spoken by most people in Saint-Domingue; they suggest that he is wild, uncivilized.[14]

The words that Papa Simon sings and the presence of the wanga refer to another illegal dance that is more dangerous than the calenda and would never have been performed onstage, as there is nothing comical or even vaguely European—as the calenda can seem—about it. Moreau calls it Vaudoux—the name of an all-seeing god who takes the form of a snake—and claims that the dance has been performed on the island "for a long time" and that the Aradas, people taken from Dahomey and the Bight of Benin, were its "true followers." And while Moreau believes it involved superstition and unusual rites, Vodou (as it is properly spelled) was a religion centered around the worship of gods and ancestral spirits, and daily healing and protection practices.[15]

Moreau describes "Vaudoux" rituals that occur secretly at night. Giving an account of one ritual, he notes that the initiates wear sandals and solid or predominantly red handkerchiefs. The male leader is the King and is distinguished by his beautiful, numerous handkerchiefs. He ties one solid red piece of fabric around his head, which "serves as his crown." The other leader is the Queen, who dresses in "simple luxury," with a red sash around her waist. They stand near an altar next to a crate where, just visible, is a snake that knows the "knowledge of the past, science of the present, and consciousness of the future." The King and Queen can communicate with the snake and are "entitled to the unlimited respect of those who make up the family" of Vodou practitioners. To disobey them is to resist God and to expose oneself to great misfortunes.

The followers ask the snake for favors and advice. This practice allows for spiritual forces to heal their pain and make their burdens easier to bear. It may also help them forget some of their troubles. The Queen serves as the medium through which answers are delivered. She stands on the snake's cage, convulsing when the god enters her and takes over her body. His words come out of her mouth. Sometimes the Queen speaks happily and calmly. At other times, she "thunders and bursts out in reproach."[16]

At this point, the dance begins. The King draws a circle on the ground and places a bundle in the hand of the person who wants to be initiated. The bundle, not unlike the wanga that Papa Simon uses in the play, is a packet consisting of herbs, horsehair, pieces of horn, and what Moreau terms "other equally disgusting objects."[17]

The King then taps the initiate on the head with a stick and begins his song:

Eh! Eh! Bomba, hen! Hen!
Canga bafio te
Canga moune de le
Canga do ki la
Canga li

The followers form a chorus, singing the lines back to him. Moreau doesn't know what the lyrics mean, and the performers may not have known either. Since he believes that the "Vaudoux" practitioners are Arada, they would speak Fon, and "Eh! Bomba" might be a bad transcription of *aboma*, the word for a large constricting snake in Fon and Sranan, the language spoken in Suriname. The lyrics following "Eh! Eh! Bomba, hen! Hen!" can also translate from Kongo as "Hold back the Black men / Hold back the white man / Hold back that witch, hold them," suggesting an invocation of Bomba, a Central African deity.[18]

The initiate begins to dance and tremble—"mounting Vaudoux"— in the circle until the King orders them to stop and hits their head. He moves the initiate to another spot, where the person swears to remain a member of the sect. Everyone begins to dance but all soon lose control. Spinning around, some "tear off their clothes or bite their flesh," while others collapse and fall down. Moreau claims they next engage in an orgy. He thinks they are deprived of reason, which is why the practice must be banned, without the allowance given the calenda.

Whether or not Moreau accurately recounted what is probably a sec-ondhand description of a Vodou ceremony, he is right that its ideas and practices were a threat to white control. The idea that God and his word spoken through the King and Queen cannot be disobeyed places the King and Queen at a level as high as—or above—the slaveowner. What if the King tells the followers to escape, or the Queen delivers a message that a white man needs to be poisoned? For the followers at the "winty play" in Suriname and the "Vaudoux" ceremony in Saint-Domingue, it is too dangerous to refuse.[19]

Moreau reports that Vodous ask the snake for the ability to control their masters—an incredibly dangerous idea. But perhaps even more dis-turbing for people of European descent on Saint-Domingue is the idea that they too are susceptible to the powers of the religion. Moreau has heard that if a white person is caught spying on the dance and is touched by a practitioner, that person will lose control of themselves and begin to dance, and only cease when they pay the Queen. When the enslaved dance, they lose complete control over themselves, and any control that a slaveowner or manager has over them is gone as well. Moreau under-stands the control and blind obedience that the religion and its priest and priestess have over the worshippers and determines that "[n]othing is more dangerous than this cult of Vaudoux."

He wrote this synopsis of the ceremony for his work *Description topo-graphique, physique, civile, politique et historique de la partie française de l'isle Saint-Domingue*, a history of the colony he began working on while living in Saint-Domingue and finished many years later. By the time the book was published in 1797, the danger this religion could bring was well known.

Moreau stayed in the Caribbean until 1784, when he left for France to work on *Description topographique*. After participating in the French Rev-olution and then falling out of favor with the new government, he fled to the United States in 1793. In Norfolk, Virginia, people told him first-hand what had transpired in Saint-Domingue two years before, begin-ning with an uprising of the enslaved led by a man named Boukman. The rumor was that Boukman drew on a religious power that allowed him to become a leader to whom others listened, and that he was able to use that power to defeat the whites. His followers made wangas, danced, and sang, likely asking for protection and power from their ancestors and the gods. Boukman had formed an army, leading others to freedom by killing managers and slaveowners and burning down plantations. The religion—what Moreau called Vaudoux—had brought about a revolution.[20]

The revolution continued even though Boukman was killed a few months after the rebellion started. Le Cap burned as whites and free people of color tried to protect their assets. More than 25,000 would arrive in the United States, at ports including Norfolk and New Orleans where they could keep their human property. Moreau could no longer safely return to Saint-Domingue, and decided to set up a bookstore and print shop in Philadelphia. He continued working on his book, but he was no longer fashioning a mere simulacrum of the colony. He was making an argument for slavery. He had long opposed giving free people of color the same rights as whites, and his book advocated for the status quo in Saint-Domingue by banishing the rebellion from it. But the Saint-Domingue he wrote about was already in the past. In 1804, Saint-Domingue became Haiti, the first nation in the world to permanently outlaw slavery and uphold the statement that all people are equal and should live free.[21]

X

England, 1787

"My Dear John, As the last good I can do for you in the world, I now join to the trifles I leave you these few lines, which bid you often to read for my sake, who always loved you so tenderly," John Gabriel Stedman began his letter to his son in January 1787. Stedman was no longer a soldier and Johnny, his son with Joanna, was no longer a child. Johnny was about to embark on life as a sailor, and although Stedman was not yet at the verge of death, he felt the need to write something his son could read after he did die. "Fear and love God, be honest," he wrote, and added, "To be Cruel is the portion of the coward while to be brave and humane goes hand in hand and pleases God."

Then one day, after Johnny has lived a good life, Stedman thinks, "We together—with your beloved mother my dear Joanna—have a chance once more to meet when in the presence of our heavenly benefactor our joy and happiness shall be eternal and complete."[1]

Stedman did not return to Suriname after he left in 1777, and Joanna never joined him in Europe. All these years later, he still missed her. He had said that she wanted to stay in Suriname, and that was probably true. But they wrote to each other. In July 1778, Stedman wrote that he received "a letter from lovely Joanna who sent me a case with confections &c.

which is not yet come from Amsterdam." He still imagined a time when Joanna and Johnny might come to live with him across the Atlantic.[2]

Since his return to Europe, the material that Stedman brought back—his notes and diaries, the objects in his house, the thoughts of his time in Suriname—had consumed him. His cold days in northern Europe were overwhelmed by memories from his past. The smell of tamarind and oranges in the morning, the warmth of the sun on L'Esperance, his days with Joanna and Johnny. He came home with instruments and items that had belonged to Indigenous people and enslaved Africans, drawings and watercolors he'd made, and notes, including a notebook he'd had to fish out of the water when he dropped it into the Suriname River. He had in his collection "an Indian bow," "a battle ax," "an Indian flute," and "cords of Silk grass," and likely many other items. An inventory of these objects from Suriname doesn't survive, if he even made one, and there is no record of where he obtained them. He could have taken them, traded for them, or bought them. Or, someone might have given them to him. He wrote that Mrs. Godefroy had "stocked me with presents for Europe too many to mention in this small journal." Quacoo, the boy that Stedman bought for 50 Dutch florins in 1775 and had brought to Europe, also may have helped him procure the items.[3]

Shortly after his return to England, Stedman formed the objects he brought back from Suriname into a collection. In February 1778, he wrote in his diary, "I finish me collection of indians, negroes && which leaves the admiration of all that see it." Like Hans Sloane, Stedman made a cabinet of curiosities that he could show off to his friends. Probably the objects also reminded him of his time in Suriname and provoked memories of Joanna and Johnny.[4]

One of the items in Stedman's cabinet of curiosities may have been the banjo he called the Creole-bania. As with the other items, Stedman's surviving notes don't mention where he got the Creole-bania or who made it. But the instrument itself leaves clues. It is skillfully crafted. The maker used a specialized tool to create a beaded edge along the box where the strings attach to the tuning pegs, which is usually called a pegbox and scroll on a violin. The maker carved a figure at the very top of the peghead, which at some point in time broke off. The body was made of a calabash cut lengthwise off-center from the top to the bottom of the fruit, with the resulting hole covered in a tacked-down skin—the exact same construction French botanist Richard Tussac described for banzas in the French Antilles, which he saw on his travels around the time Moreau de Saint-Méry was in Saint-Domingue. In 1810, Tussac published a detailed description of the banza, saying that to make the instrument, the enslaved Blacks take a calabash eight or more inches in diameter—specifying that it is the fruit of a tree—and cut it down the middle. They spread a goat-skin over the opening, pin it down with nails, and cut two holes in the skin. Although banjos aren't usually described as having holes in the skin soundboard, some African fiddles and lutes have such holes. A rough, flat piece of wood constitutes the neck, he wrote, and it is strung with three strings made of the fibers of the agave plant.[5]

The maker of Stedman's Creole-bania cut delicate S-shaped holes on the sides of the calabash. He found wood as dense as metal to make the tacks that hold down the skin soundboard. This is not a crude or primitive instrument. It took care and precision to make. The maker was likely a man: both lutes and drums were traditionally played by men in West Africa, and traditional gender roles placed men in positions to learn skills like woodworking. Inventories of property on a Suriname plantation show that *Timmerneger*, the Dutch word for enslaved woodworkers, were some of the most valuable men. The maker of the Creole-bania could have also been a free man of color. Stedman could have gotten the instrument from any number of people—Quacoo, Mrs. Godefroy, Graman Quacy, or one of Joanna's relatives—but it would be surprising if the owner willingly gave it away. This instrument contained power, a special significance.[6]

In 1782, Stedman's dream of a family reunion became impossible when he received word that Joanna had died. Some said she had been poisoned, "administered by the hand of jealousy and envy," while others said she died of a broken heart. Eight-year-old Johnny joined his father in England. Stedman was an attentive father: he put Johnny in school, took him to the theater, and taught him to play the violin. A few years later, Stedman married a European woman, who adopted Johnny. They lived as a family with George and Sophia, Stedman's children with his new wife.[7]

Stedman loved Johnny deeply, and perhaps this love and a desire to remember his "Dear Joanna" were what drove him to compile his diaries, drawings, and ideas into a book about his time in Suriname. In 1787, the year he wrote the letter to Johnny, he confided in his journal, "My only ambition remaining is to see my little writings made public. I wish to be an author but even that during my life [I] shall not attain."[8]

Three years later, he finished the manuscript. At the end, he wrote that Johnny had made "the Greatest progress in his education . . . [he] is at this moment on board the Southhampton frigate . . . ready to strike a blow at the Spaniards should they dare Quarrel with the Kingdom of Great Britain." European countries were already preparing for a power vacuum in the Caribbean if the French Revolution upset colonial power. Johnny was young, handsome, and wearing a uniform, and Stedman probably saw some of himself in his son. But why did Johnny become a sailor? Was he trying to please his father? Was he taking the best opportunity afforded to him? Or was he more comfortable as a sailor in the West Indies, as close to his childhood home as he could come, where more people looked like him? His father never related Johnny's motivations.[9]

Around the same time, Stedman received good news: London publisher Joseph Johnson had bought his manuscript. His writings on Suriname would be public; he'd be an author.

෯

"I should esteem myself very happy to have the honor of presenting a Painting to the Company that would be applicable to so noble, and useful an Institution," Samuel Jennings wrote from London in early January 1790 to his father in Philadelphia. Jennings was born to parents of white European descent and raised in Philadelphia, and, after attending the University of Pennsylvania, moved to London to continue studying art. He kept up with news from home and had heard that the Philadelphia Library was constructing a new building. As a budding artist, he felt that he could contribute a painting that would represent the knowledge and opportunity the library provided—perhaps of Clio, the Muse of history, or Calliope, the Muse of rhetoric and heroic poetry, or Minerva, the goddess of wisdom and the arts. But of course, he'd be happy to paint whatever subject the directors of the Library thought fitting.[10]

The directors welcomed the idea, although with some modifications. Instead of Clio, Calliope, or Minerva, they wanted "the figure of Liberty (with her Cap and proper Insignia) displaying the arts" and what freedom had to offer. They directed Jennings to paint a "Broken Chain under her feet, and in the distant back Ground a Groupe of Negroes sitting on the Earth, or in some attitude expressive of Ease & Joy." They wanted a painting that was patriotic, self-congratulatory, and reflected the goals of the abolitionists in the city. Benjamin Franklin, who was the founder of the Library Company, was also president of the Pennsylvania Society for Promoting the Abolition of Slavery, the Relief of Free Negroes Unlawfully Held in Bondage, and for Improving the Condition of the African Race. Liberty would not just break the chains of slavery; she would bring knowledge and joy.[11]

"I am happy to inform You, that I most readily coincide with You in Opinion, relative to the new Subject proposed," Jennings wrote back to the Library Company. He began formulating ideas of how to portray Liberty and the free Blacks. He painted at least one preliminary study, sketching a composition without high levels of detail. Then, he began work on the large version he would ship to Philadelphia.

In the painting, Liberty—the only white figure in the painting—sits in the foreground, clad in a white dress, handing the Catalogue of the Philadelphia Library to a Black man in a red coat, who bows in thanks. Next to the man are a well-dressed woman, child, and another man. Around Liberty are books, a lyre, sheet music, paints, and a globe. The painting bears the apt title *Liberty Displaying the Arts and Sciences*.

In the background, free Blacks celebrate in "an attitude expressive of Ease & Joy." A man in a red vest and headscarf dances with a person in yellow and a woman who wears a white headscarf and pearls, and holds a cloth in her hands. To their right, a banjo player provides music. The instrument is tiny on the canvas, but it clearly has a teardrop-shaped body, a rounded back, and a long neck that extends through the body.

The figures in the painting are not caricatured, suggesting that Jennings modeled them on people of African descent he had seen in Philadelphia or London. Had he also seen a banjo in real life? Or was he using an image or description he'd come across in a book? He painted the banjo three times: once in the painting, once in a smaller copy he made from which he hoped to make prints, and in the preliminary study. Each instrument is slightly different in shape, and although the three paintings are different in size and detail, this could mean that Jennings was generalizing the banjo's form rather than illustrating one he saw. However, in England in 1790, Jennings could have seen a banjo. Stedman probably still had the Creole-bania at his home in the countryside, Hans Sloane's Strum Strumps were probably at the British Museum (if they hadn't been lost yet), the bangeau sent by lawyer James Hollyday to his niece Sally Anderson could still have been in a London townhouse, and there might have been a banjo at the Leverian Museum in London, which was a cabinet of curiosities run by a Mr. Parkinson. On stage, Jennings could have seen the white musician Charles Dibdin performing "The Negro and His Banjer," a song in dialect about the instrument, although Dibdin didn't have a banjo with him on stage. Jennings's painting positions the banjo as quintessentially African American, yet also respectable enough to be played in a celebration of Black freedom.[12]

Jennings worked on the painting in 1790 and 1791, when talk of abolition seemed supremely relevant. The revolt led by Boukman, which began the Haitian Revolution, was international news. Slaveowners and governments were asking whether a violent overthrow might be possible in other colonies and wondering whether it wouldn't be better to abolish slavery in a controlled fashion, without destruction of property and life.

For years, petitions had been circulating in London asking the government to end the slave trade. In the late months of 1791, British abolitionists proposed a boycott on sugar and rum. "Thus it appears, that the legislature is not only unwilling, but perhaps unable to grant redress; and therefore it is more peculiarly incumbent upon us to abstain from the use

Samuel Jennings's study for *Liberty Displaying the Arts and Sciences*, where the banjo
has a slightly different shape and the neck almost seems to poke through the bottom
of the gourd body. *Metropolitan Museum of Art*

of sugar and rum . . . [until] we can obtain the produce of sugar cane in
some other mode UNCONNECTED WITH SLAVERY, AND UNPOL-
LUTED WITH BLOOD," the abolitionist William Fox declared in a leaf-
let in 1792.[13]

Stedman was unwilling to sign the petitions or boycott sugar, even
though his son's extended Suriname family was still in bondage and
Joanna had died enslaved. Ironically, one of the reasons that publisher

Joseph Johnson wanted to publish Stedman's manuscript was precisely because Stedman was so honest about the brutal conditions of slavery. Johnson was a radical and not afraid to publish books that advocated for political and social reform.[14]

Johnson liked Stedman's manuscript enough to buy it and publish it with the illustrations that Stedman believed would make the book better. But when Stedman delivered the completed manuscript in February 1791, Johnson was not satisfied with it. Beginning in 1794, Johnson hired an editor named William Thomson to work on it. What Thomson did, in fact, was rewrite the book, changing the tone and meaning in many places. The passage about "Suriname marriages" between African-descended women and white European men, for example, has a subtle undertone of sexism and racism in the final version, while Stedman, in his original draft, put the responsibility for this arrangement primarily on the men. Stedman wrote that the women "pride themselves" on taking care of the men; Thomson chose to replace this with the word "exult," as if the women could think of nothing better than to worshipfully serve a white man. Neither the printed book nor Stedman's manuscript acknowledges that for enslaved women, choice has an entirely different meaning and implication. Even though Johnson might have seen an abolitionist angle in the text, Stedman's original manuscript was not intended to be abolitionist, since he himself wasn't one. But Stedman did want to portray the enslaved people he had met with humanity and dignity. Despite Johnson's convictions, Thomson made Stedman's book more pro-slavery than the original text. Where Stedman wrote that people of African descent were not as ignorant or without religion as some Europeans imagined, Thomson went so far as to declare that they were "perfectly savage."[15]

Any pleasure in seeing his work published disappeared when Stedman saw the changes Thomson had made. This book he had spent thirteen years working on was "spoilt" and "mard" by Thomson and Johnson, he thought. The rewrite may have been especially hard for Stedman to stomach because, although his original manuscript presented an idealized version of his experiences in Suriname, it was all that remained of his life there. His Johnny and Joanna were not savage; they were his family. The book ends with a poem dedicated to Johnny, who drowned while serving as a sailor in the Caribbean in 1791.

To illustrate the volume, Johnson commissioned artists to make engravings from the watercolors and drawings Stedman had done in Suriname, and presumably from the items that were in Stedman's cabinet of curiosities. The first edition of Stedman's *Narrative* would include eighty-four hand-colored plates with maps, illustrations of plants and animals, and depictions of Stedman's time in the jungle, people he came across, and musical instruments. One of the artists Johnson approached was William Blake—a perfect person to capture the cruelties of slavery that Stedman had observed. Blake, a printmaker, poet, and painter, was also an abolitionist. Stedman's book would end up having an influence on Blake's work, providing evidence for the necessity of abolition. While Stedman wrote to Blake "to thank him twice for his excellent work," he was less pleased with the other artists and sent correction after correction to Johnson regarding their work.[16]

Stedman's specific objections don't survive, but he could well have

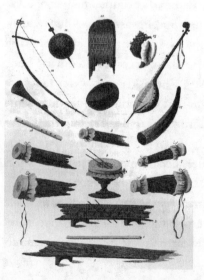

The engraving from the first edition of Stedman's *Narrative of a Five Years' Expedition Against the Revolted Slaves of Surinam* (1796) titled "Musical Instruments of the African Negroes," featuring the Creole-bania.

University of Minnesota Libraries, James Ford Bell Library

complained about the Creole-bania's rendering. Stedman's description notes that the Creole-bania has one short and three long strings. The engraving shows four pegs—three at the top of the peghead for the long strings and one on the side for the short string—but five lines crossing the skin head of the banjo, making it look as if there are five strings. In the engraving, the banjo's body is oblong, rather than the very round shape that almost all calabashes take on when they grow. The actual banjo Stedman brought back from Suriname has that almost perfectly round body. It also has a wooden neck that extends through the gourd and is flat at the lower end, but in the engraving the neck comes to a point, like a splinter of wood. The peghead is a blob shape, rather than the well-crafted carving of the actual instrument. Overall, the instrument Stedman possessed looks so little like the engraving that a person seeing both might not think they are the same instrument.

Other instruments are equally poorly rendered. A drum has a ragged open end and looks like it was made from a fallen tree, rather than having sharp, carefully carved corners. These drums were sacred instruments, and wouldn't have been poorly made. The skins that cover the ends of the drums are depicted as being held on with a single strop—construction that would not survive being played for one dance, much less many hours of a drummer beating his hands against the skin with great force. Surinamese drums are usually tightened with thick ropes that are tied or held in place with large wedges to make tightening the skin top easier.[17]

The engraver may have been working from Stedman's imperfect drawings, rather than the objects themselves, or from Stedman's descriptions, requiring him to visualize the instruments in his imagination, which may have been clouded by racist thought on the inferiority of enslaved Blacks. This is one reason why gaining knowledge from an artistic interpretation of an object is so difficult.

The final version of his book "was printed full of lies and nonsense," Stedman thought. He hated what it had become. But the reviewers and the public didn't care, and the book became a bestseller, translated into Dutch, German, Swedish, and Italian. And Thomson's pro-slavery changes could do nothing to eliminate the brutality Stedman had witnessed. One reviewer wrote that these accounts "will stimulate . . . speedy termination of the execrable traffic in human flesh." Even if Stedman didn't want to sign an anti-slavery petition or boycott sugar, his book showed readers that sugar was polluted with blood.[18]

XI

Albany, New York, 1803

Spring had finally come to the Hudson Valley. Leaves unfolded to absorb the sun's rays, and calves and lambs cried for their mothers. Toads no bigger than a thumbnail hopped and spring peepers chirped. The flowers bloomed and the people knew what this meant: "Pinkster comes indeed." In the spring of 1803, someone penned a poem for the celebration:

A PINKSTER ODE
For the Year 1803
Most Respectfully Dedicated To
CAROLUS AFRICANUS, REX:
Thus Rendered in English:

KING CHARLES [the African],
Captain-General and Commander in Chief of the
PINKSTER BOYS.[1]

The "Pinkster Ode" was signed "by His Majesty's Obedient Servant, ABSALOM AIMWELL, Esq." Absalom Aimwell wasn't the author's real name, but he was a real person.[2]

Absalom Aimwell was the pen name of a musician and writer who spent time in Philadelphia. He published a collection of songs in *The Philadelphia Songster* in 1789, a few poems including "An Eulogy on Whiskey," and a lecture and song dedicated to mechanics, working-class men like his father had been. This Aimwell may have been Andrew Adgate, an arranger of psalms and music teacher. But as similar as some of elements of the "Pinkster Ode" and the mechanic's lecture are to each other, Adgate could not have been the author of the "Pinkster Ode," since he died in Philadelphia in 1793. Either Adgate was not the earlier Absalom Aimwell, or someone else took Adgate's pen name for the "Pinkster Ode" ten years later.[3]

Aimwell crafted an almost 3,000-word poem about the Pinkster holiday in Albany, and he was educated enough to include references to the Bible, Greek mythology, the politics of the United States, and international geography. Even though Pinkster was celebrated by the Black population in the city and surrounding areas, it's hard to see Aimwell as anything other than a white man, given how restricted an education like his was at the turn of the nineteenth century, and how some lines in the poem display a belief in the inferiority of Albany's Black residents.

However, Aimwell was still the Black King Charles's "Obedient Servant," and declared:

O could I loud as thunder sing,
Thy fame should sound, great Charles, the king,
From Hudson's stream to Niger's wave

And so, Aimwell told the story of Pinkster in verse.

Good Pinkster comes with merry glee,
And brings a gladsome Jubilee.

Pinkster always promised to be an exciting and festive day. From the center of Albany, people walked up State Street to the top of the hill, while others came in from the surrounding areas like Watervliet and Rennsealarwyk. They waited for the King to appear: the man who would start the festivities and the man they paid homage to on this day.

The banner appeared, flying the colors of the King with his portrait. The people knew he'd follow on a cream-colored horse, and when he appeared, he was as regal as ever. The bright red coat he wore contrasted against his dark brown skin. His jacket reminded people of the British soldiers' uniforms, as it had been only twenty years since the end of the Revolutionary War. His jacket lapels were trimmed with bright golden lace, as was his hat. He wore yellow leather buckskins and blue stockings. This was the elected King, and at the beginning of the 1800s, the man who became the most famous Pinkster King was Charles. On this day, he was the most important man in town and would preside over Pinkster in Albany.[4]

Like the place names surrounding Albany, the word Pinkster was a vestige of New Netherland and the Dutch who had settled the Hudson Valley. It derived from the Dutch word for Pentecost, *Pinksteren*: the fiftieth day after Jesus's resurrection, when the Holy Spirit descended and came before the Apostles.

Though Pinksteren was a religious holiday, Pinkster blended it with pre-Christian rituals and African spiritual practices. In the northern hemisphere, Pinkster falls when days are lengthening, flowers are blooming, and summer approaches. In the Netherlands, the Dutch celebrated Pinksteren with fairs that featured food stalls, wrestling and boxing matches, performances by acrobats, exhibitions of animals and conjurers, and ring-dances done around a maypole with a *Pinksterkroon*, a Pinkster crown.[5]

What was happening in Albany was not a recreation of the Dutch festivities. People of African descent, whether enslaved or part of the growing free Black population, added their own customs to the celebrations, as Father Labat had seen with the Christmas calendas in Martinique. In the Hudson Valley in 1786, Scottish-born doctor Alexander Coventry wrote in his diary about giving Cuff, the man he owned, time off for Pinkster, since the holiday was for both Black and white people. "This is a holy day, Whitsunday, called among the Dutch 'Pinkster,'" and the festivities lasted two days, with "frolicking and dancing," Coventry wrote. In 1797, a white visitor found the people around the Hudson River celebrating Pinkster, where "every public house is crowded with merry makers" and "blacks as well as their masters" celebrate. John Williams, an emancipated Albany resident, remembered from his childhood that Pinkster was "partly pagan and partly Christian, like our Christmas day."[6]

In Albany, over 500 people were enslaved at the beginning of the 1800s, while the growing population of free Blacks numbered around 160. Many may have incorporated Christianity into their religious beliefs, either as members of the Dutch Reformed Church or as descendants of Catholics taken from Kongo. For Black Albany residents, celebration of Pinkster—the fiftieth day after Easter—could have been symbolic as well as religious. In the Bible, fifty represents freedom. Fifty days after Passover was a day when "ye shall do no servile work," and every fifty years there "shall be a jubilee unto you; and ye shall return every man unto his possession, and ye shall return every man unto his family." Passover and Easter don't always coincide, but Pinkster—celebrated on the same day as Pentecost, fifty days after Easter—was a temporary moment of jubilee.[7]

On Christian holy days, including Sundays, Easter, Pentecost, and Christmas, the enslaved were given a constrained measure of freedom to celebrate. In the 1650s, Governor Stuyvesant had banned the "planting of May poles" and "any noise making with drums or dispensing of any wine, brandy or beer" on New Year and May Day celebrations. In 1712, New York's colonial government passed a law that banned more than three enslaved people gathering at the same place, and restricted both when the "banger" player could gather at the African Burial Ground in Manhattan and when enslaved people in Albany could celebrate. So, even though the Pinkster gathering was illegal, like the Martinique calendas, the ban wasn't enforced and the celebration wouldn't be stopped.[8]

Rise then, each son of Pinkster, rise,
Snatch fleeting pleasure as it flies.

The Black community had been making preparations for at least a week. In town, drummers began to practice, making sure they'd be ready for hours of playing. On Pinkster Hill, so named because the holiday was celebrated there, men began putting up arbors of pine boughs woven together to form booths. The royal arbor for King Charles faced "a sort of Amphitheater . . . where the Guinea dance is to be performed." The arbors had been "filled up with seats, and stored with fruit cakes, cheese, beer and liquors of various kinds." With their "shrubby texture," they became almost like trees on the barren hill, rustling in the wind—the perfect place for the Holy Spirit to descend.[9]

> Now if you take a farther round
> You'll reach the Africs' burying ground.
> There as I rambled years ago,
> To pass an hour of love-worn woe;
> I found a stone at Dinah's grave . . .

Like the Common in Manhattan, Pinkster Hill was also known as an African burial ground. Aimwell was familiar enough with Albany to know that Dinah was buried there. Dinah (sometimes called Dean), together with two other enslaved people, Bet and Pomp (or Pompey), had been convicted of arson after a fire destroyed twenty-six houses in 1793. They were hanged in April 1794 and buried on Pinkster Hill. Like the Common in Manhattan, Pinkster Hill was a place for celebration, music, dance, and for remembering the dead.[10]

> There they find it all around,
> On the merry Pinkster ground.
> Every colour revels there,
> From ebon black to lilly fair.

Everyone came to Pinkster Hill. African Americans gathered on the hill, erected booths, played music and danced. The whites brought their families to watch the festivities, and a "motley group of thousands" from the city and county converged. For white children who came up the hill, the memory of Pinskter stayed with them well into adulthood.[11]

Now hark! The Banjo, rub a dub,
Like a washer-woman's tub;
And hear the drum, 'tis rolling now,
Row de dow, row de dow.
The pipe and tabor, flute and fife,
Shall wake the dullest soul to life . . .

The chief musician strikes the Guinea drum, while two other men, who wear cow tails and feathered costumes, play similar but smaller drums. James Eights, a white man who grew up in Albany, recorded his childhood reminiscences of Pinkster in the early 1800s. The most memorable musician for him was Jackey Quackenboss, who sat astride "a symmetrically formed wooden article" that reminded him of an eel-pot, with a "cleanly dressed sheep skin drawn tightly over its wide and open extremity." Eights remembered Quackenboss letting out the "euphonic cry of Hi-a-bomba, bomba, bomba in full harmony with the thumping sounds." The lyric is reminiscent of the song Moreau de Saint-Méry said was part of the Vodou ceremony in Haiti: "Eh! Eh! Bomba, hen! Hen!" The lyrics Eights remembered are even closer to the chorus that planter Drouin de Bercy heard during a Vodou ceremony in Haiti around 1814, about a decade after Eights's experience. Like Moreau de Saint-Méry, de Bercy was a white Creole in favor of restoring slavery to Haiti. He transcribed the Vodou song as "A ia bombaia bombé," which he translated as "We swear to destroy the whites and all that they possess, let us die rather than renounce this vow," although he didn't identify the language or who told him the meaning of the words. Eights didn't publish his recollection of Pinkster until 1857, so time and other experiences could have altered his memory, but it is possible that Quackenboss was singing the same chant de Bercy heard around the same time in Haiti. The revolution that kept Moreau de Saint-Méry from returning to Saint-Domingue had brought other former residents of the colony to the United States. One New York City resident remembered that Manhattan was "thronged with French people of all shades from the French colonies" as a result of the uprising in Saint-Domingue and the French Revolution. Whites from Saint-Domingue/Haiti brought enslaved people with them to the United States, including musicians—though the name Quackenboss suggests that Jackey was enslaved by a man of Dutch descent. In June 1794, the slaveowner Caradeau placed an advertisement offering a reward for Antoine who "Ran Away from Kensington, Philadelphia"; he spoke French "very well," spoke a little English, and "plays upon the banza." Quackenboss could have known people brought from Haiti, so his singing a song from there is possible to imagine.[12]

The "Pinkster Ode" mentions drums, pipes, flutes, fifes, banjos, and fiddles. A fiddler named Yat who lived in Glenville, New York, might have traveled to Albany for Pinkster or celebrated the holiday somewhere else in the Hudson Valley. In 1805, he had entered into a contract with his owners, John S. Glen and Glen's daughter Mary, stipulating that if Yat met the terms outlined in the agreement and paid the Glens ninety dollars, they would grant him his freedom in six years. As in London and Philadelphia, activists had been pushing for abolition in New York. In 1799, an emancipation law passed the New York legislature, stating that all children born after July 4, 1799, would be manumitted when they turned twenty-five if they were female or twenty-eight if they were male. This law did not apply to Yat, his wife, Mary, or his two children, who were all born before 1799. It wouldn't be until 1817 that New York set July 4, 1827, as the day that would end slavery in the state.

Sensing that the complete abolition of slavery was likely coming to New York, the Glens made their contract with Yat. He could see Mary every third week and they gave him days off: "Christmas Three days New Years two days Easter two days and for Pinkster Three days." This suggests that Pinkster was as important a holiday as Christmas. The Glens demanded control of Yat's fiddle, stipulating that they had the instrument to give as they wanted except on holidays, when it was Yat's. On Pinkster, Yat would have taken his fiddle and could have gone to Albany, perhaps playing a melody alongside Jackey Quackenboss beating the drum.[13]

Charles, the king, will then advance,
Leading on the Guinea dance,

Moving o'er the flow'ry green,
You'll know him by his graceful mien;

King Charles enters the amphitheater outside his arbor, a "dancing ground, where the parties perform and around which the spectators are assembled." One viewer's description of the dance in Albany sounds much like the calenda Father Labat saw in Martinique a hundred years earlier. Men and women take to the amphitheater, usually in couples, approach each other, and embrace. This dance, the viewer thinks, is "most lewd and indecent," with movements that "must cover even a harlot with blushes to describe." While some white observers called this a Guinea dance and others "real Congo dances," the dances on Pinkster probably weren't exactly the same as African dances. Most of the enslaved and free people of African descent who gathered on Pinkster Hill had been born in New York, and had created their own traditions based on what they learned and saw growing up.[14]

"This day our Bosses make us free. . . .
Let us with greatful hearts agree
Not to abuse our liberty."

Here, too, the white power structure dominated the lives of people of African descent, but allowed them enough freedom to head off potential uprisings, enough freedom to have Pinkster celebrations. But the whites wanted the Black population not to "abuse this liberty," as Aimwell put it in his poem. Three years after it was founded, the New York Manumission Society, which helped push through the 1799 gradual manumission legislation, created a committee to "consider the ways and means to prevent the irregular behavior of free Negroes." Black people could have freedom from bondage, the Manumission Society thought, but complete freedom was undesirable. "Free Negroes" shouldn't admit enslaved people into their homes; they should moderate their drinking; and they shouldn't fiddle or dance. In this view, freedom and Pinkster could not coexist.[15]

And sing a little, and laugh a little,
And fiddle a little, and foot it a little,
And while you swig the flowing cann,
Always be an honest man.

The same moral boundaries that were placed on free Blacks were also placed on whites who enjoyed Pinkster too much. The dancing, the music, and the drunkenness were not fit activities for a religious holiday. The same year that Absalom Aimwell wrote the "Pinkster Ode," a white observer wrote anonymously in the *Daily Advertiser* that the holy days of Pentecost have "degenerated into periodical seasons of dissipation" and that only "a certain class of whites" attend. It is not just the Black residents who act "without reproof and without reserve." Whites, too, find their "restraints are flung off, and nature, depraved nature, undisguised and without a veil, on every side is exhibited." Just as James Alexander warned in the *New-York Weekly Journal* in 1736, these Black festivities could be tolerated but when whites got involved, everyone needed to be careful. And yet, as bad as dancing, music, and drunkenness might be, the white residents of Albany couldn't seem to stay away. They wanted to engage with this exciting, yet foreign, culture. By viewing African American celebrations from a distance, whites could engage with activities thought untoward but feel that they were not actually sinning themselves.[16]

A year after the "Pinskter Ode" was published, the Albany Common Council set out to "regulate the amusements of the Negroes" on Pinkster. Their aim wasn't to change how the Black residents celebrated, but rather to separate white and Black revelers. They declared that "no white persons shall . . . erect or put up any Boothe or Tent within the said City near to or where the Negroes shall erect or put up theirs, nor shall any white persons expose for sale any beer, Cyder, mead, spirituous liquors, or cake, crackers or any other kind of Refreshment at the place or places where the Negroes shall meet to carry on their said amusements."[17]

Separating whites and Blacks, or limiting the extent to which white residents could participate in Pinkster, didn't stop whites from celebrating. In 1811, the Common Council passed another ordinance effectively banning

Pinkster. Now, it became illegal for anyone to set up booths and tents, sell alcohol, parade, or march during "days commonly called pinxter."[18]

Pinkster didn't just happen in Albany. It was celebrated in New York City, Long Island, and even New Jersey. Even before it was banned in Albany, it seems to have started becoming a deracinated and commercialized exercise in nostalgia in New York City. The last act of a theater performance held on Monday, May 21, 1804, was "PINXTER MONDAY; or HARLEQUIN's FROLIC," which promised to offer "The celebrated FRICASSE DANCE, with other Pantomime Tricks and Drolleries." The fricassee was a comical imitation of a French country dance in which the dancers would stop to slap their thighs, a description not unlike Father Labat's of the calenda. And like the performance of *Jeannot et Thérèse* in Saint-Domingue, the "Pinxter Monday" performance seems to have used African American culture and dance for comic effect, although whether the performers were whites in blackface isn't known.[19]

If anyone in the audience had wanted to see a true Pinkster celebration, they could have witnessed one in the city the day before, which was Pentecost. Then, "boys and negroes might be seen all day standing in the market place, laughing, joking, and cracking eggs," while later "the grown up apprentices and servant girls, used to dance on the green in Bayard's farm in the Bowery." If Pinxter Monday was an imitation of Pinkster festivities, it was an early hint at what would become the US's most popular form of entertainment by the mid-1800s.[20]

As useful as some lines of the poem are in providing an image of Pinkster, many more employ racist stereotypes of people of African descent. The poem is lighthearted about Pinkster, especially compared to the disparaging 1803 newspaper account, yet it depicts the Blacks in Albany as entertainment for the white audience.

The poem also has words of warning about interrupting the celebration. Aimwell brings the banjo to the fore:

But should the rubble, wrong and rude,
Dare on your dancing lines intrude,

Then beat the banjo, rub a dub,
And send the rogues to Beelzebub.

If someone interferes with the dancing, perhaps someone who isn't welcome, the banjo will send them to hell and the devil. The white intruder
being overtaken by evil spirits was what Moreau de Saint-Méry warned
of during the Vodou dance in Saint-Domingue. Do the lines of this poem
imply that the banjo has such extraordinary supernatural power? Or does
it just make for a nice rhythm?

But now the sun declining shows,
The day is drawing to a close . . .
Except a few whose nerves are strong,
They join the revels all night long. . . .
Now let us sing, long live the king. . . .

As the day ends, King Charles and his entourage parade down the hill
to the streets of Albany, where they knock on doors and demand tribute
from the white residents who were "glad to bestow something to get rid
of him."[21]

The jubilee is temporary. No matter where Pinkster is celebrated, the
next day the Pinkster King wakes and is still enslaved.

INTERLUDE

THE STRUM STRUMPS, THE CREOLE-BANIA, THE WATERCOLOR FROM
South Carolina: I knew these instruments and images when Pete and
I walked into the Rijksmuseum in Amsterdam in 2017. Otherwise,
I don't think I would have suggested that our last stop of the day
be the rooms of art from the Dutch colonies. We hadn't gone there
earlier because I wasn't yet obsessed with this history and knew little
of Hans Sloane, John Gabriel Stedman, or John Rose, and the people of African descent they came into contact with in the Americas.
Pete had seen the Creole-bania in 2004 at an exhibit at the Musical
Instrument Museum in Brussels, which also featured his own banjos. And when we visited Berlin in 2015, I convinced him that he
should see another banjo from Suriname, dubbed the panja, at the
Ethnological Museum. But he wasn't convinced that these two Surinamese instruments shared the same lineage as the North American
banjo. Although he considered the instruments banjos, the Creole-
bania and the panja just look too different from the instruments in
Sloane's book and Rose's watercolor. The Surinamese instruments
have narrow necks and small calabash bodies, rather than the flat,
board necks and gourd bodies of the Sloane and Rose images and

a banza from Haiti rediscovered in 2003. How the Haiti banza was constructed—and how Pete imagined the Strum Strumps and the banjo in the South Carolina watercolor were constructed—seemed to more closely align with how the earliest wooden-rim banjos were constructed in the 1840s and how banjos are still constructed today.

None of this precluded the possibility that the room in the Rijksmuseum might reveal something new and interesting about the banjo's early history. But it did more than that—it ended up being the room where our game paid off. I found a gourd banjo player leaning on a tree in Gerrit Schouten's diorama, and Pete spotted a dance almost identical to that in the watercolor from South Carolina. In Schouten's diorama and Rose's watercolor, the female dancers each hold a scarf, with one corner with each hand. In both pieces of art, one woman holds the scarf low while the other holds it high. They raise their feet slightly off the ground, as if the artist wants to indicate movement. The two women face a single man. He bends at the hips as if lowering his torso closer to the ground. In Schouten's diorama, he holds a scarf, while in the Rose watercolor, he holds a staff. We didn't have the watercolor in front of us, so we couldn't analyze all the similarities at that moment. We bought the only book we could find on Schouten and the dioramas in the museum gift shop and, since it came shrink-wrapped, we decided to wait until we got home to Baltimore to open it.

The book, in Dutch, categorized Schouten's dioramas by theme. As I flipped through it, I saw dioramas of Paramaribo, plantations, Carib (Kali'na) and Arawak (Lokono) camps, and the one that had captured our attention in Amsterdam: Slavendans. The section on these dioramas, generically titled "Slave Dance," included full images and details from six dioramas made by Schouten between 1817 and 1831, and the engraving of Surinamese instruments from the Dutch translation of John Stedman's memoir. As Pete and I scanned the pages, a word kept jumping out to him: banya. Without knowing the word, he saw that it was a homophone of "bania," as in Creole-bania.

A detail of Gerrit Schouten's diorama of the waterfront in Paramaribo, showing a man playing a string instrument with a rounded body. *Aankoop met steun van het Johan Huizinga Fonds/Rijksmuseum Fonds, de Mondriaan Stichting, het Scato Gockinga Fonds/Rijksmuseum Fonds en de Stichting Dr Hendrik Muller's Vaderlandsch Fonds*

"What does this say?" he asked desperately. "What does this word banya mean?"

At the time, I didn't read Dutch at all, but with knowledge of English, Swedish, and German, I slowly read the passage out loud, trying to locate other homophones and words I might recognize.

"It's the name of the dance," I said finally. Our jaws both dropped.

To date, no one has conclusively discovered the etymological origin of the word banjo. In the 1948 book *Some Sources of Southernisms*, linguist Milford Mathews quotes a letter from African American linguist Lorenzo Dow Turner stating, "The most probable source of *banjo* is the Kimbudu (Angola) word mbanza, an instrument similar to our *banjo*." Trying to track down the banjo-like instrument to which Turner was referring is almost impossible, since the use of the word mbanza as the precursor to banjo always just circles back to Turner. No one has been able to confirm what he wrote to

Mathews. The *Oxford Dictionary of Music* has no entry for mbanza.
Central Africans play many instruments with similar names: the
mbenza (binza) is a whistle of the Bwa, the banja are clappers played
by the Mbuti, the bangili is a horn of the Sere, and the banga is a
wooden whistle played by the Lese. The instrument with a similar
name and a similar physical form to the banjo is a nine- to thirteen-
string zither called the banzie or banzu played by the Azande,
Mangbetu, and Bwa. However, although zithers are stringed instruments, they have strings of the same length and lie flat on a table
or a person's lap when played, meaning they are functionally very
different from lutes.[1]

This idea that the word is of Central African origin also poses a
quandary with respect to the African instruments that are most similar to the banjo. While banjos are distinct from any known African
instruments, the plucked lutes and playing styles that seem most
closely related to the banjo are from West Africa, a large region that
spans from Senegambia to Nigeria. Central Africa has a much stronger tradition of harps.

Since Turner's letter was written, many others have tried to
unravel the linguistic mystery of the word banjo. In the 1980s,
Michael Coolen spoke with Wolof musicians in the Senegambian
region of West Africa who insisted that banjo and banjar were
European words, although master xalam builder Abdulai Ndiaye of
Senegal said banshaw was an old Wolof word used for non-Wolof
guitar-like instruments. A banjo researcher friend, Schlomo Pestcoe,
tried to decode the name Creole-bania, believing that understanding
the word bania could reveal something about the banjo's origins in
Africa and the origin of the word banjo itself. Before his death in
2014, he wrote on his blog, *Banjo Roots,* "Clearly 'Bania' must have
been a generic term for music instrument." John Gabriel Stedman
never explained where the name Creole-bania came from and he
never mentioned the banya dance, a clue that might have helped
Pestcoe. In *The Banjo: America's African Instrument*, Laurent Dubois

offers many possible points of origin for the word, but notes, "If the term 'banjo' ultimately gained traction, it is probably precisely because it resonated with possible meanings in different languages spoken by different groups." He also points out that there was a dance in Suriname known as the banya and, like Pestcoe, suggests "that on some level that term [bania] simply meant 'musical instrument' or perhaps 'an instrument to which we dance.' "[2]

After seeing Gerrit Schouten's dioramas and understanding that this was the banya dance—a dance that was very similar to the dance in the most iconic piece of art showing an early banjo—and that banya (dance) and bania (instrument) were homophones, I thought they had to have connections to each other, despite the distance between Suriname and South Carolina.

"If the dance lasted multiple days, then the celebration was called a banyaprei, a banya play," art historian Clazien Medendorp writes in the book on Schouten's dioramas. I knew that no one had connected Schouten's dioramas to Rose's watercolor, and that perhaps by learning more about the banyaprei, I could learn something about the dance in the South Carolina watercolor, which might, in turn, tell me something about the music and instruments that accompanied the dance, including the banjo.[3]

Like the fictional Alice, I had a moment of idle time and when I saw something curious and out of place, I jumped down the rabbit hole without thinking how I would get out. But that was OK, because research holes can be wonderlands. Sometimes, I spend days looking into one small fact I can't corroborate, wondering why I see it repeated over and over again, before recognizing that it's all right that I can't substantiate it. Sometimes we can't know everything. Other days, I feel like I'm engaging in a historical conspiracy theory. "Why hasn't anyone made this connection before?" I ask, before wavering back and forth between "I must be wrong," "I MUST be wrong," and "Because they've missed the clue!"

That was how I felt when I read Medendorp's book: in

Schouten's dioramas, I'd found a little golden key. That key opened
a door that led me to an understanding of Schouten's art, the banyaprei, and the banjo in Suriname. It also opened up a world where
everything wasn't as it seemed, where what I thought I knew about
banjo history—what we collectively knew about banjo history—
had to be reevaluated.

2nd Movement

•

"And you got to leave evidence. And your children got to leave evidence. And when it come time to hold up the evidence, we got to have evidence to hold up."

—Gayl Jones, *Corregidora*

"All of my father's text and songs, which I had decided were meaningless, were arranged before me at his death like empty bottles, waiting to hold the meaning which life would give them for me."

—James Baldwin, *Notes of a Native Son*

XII

Paramaribo, Suriname, 1816

In Suriname, the sun begins to sink every day at the same time no matter the point in the year. The reds and oranges that stream across the twilight signal the end of the time of working, of taking care of the crops in the fields, of crushing the sugar cane, of harvesting the coffee beans, of steaming the wood to make barrels. A deep darkness takes hold for hours. Then the morning comes, and the work begins again. The cycle of light and dark never changes, and the work only changes with the seasons, the heavier or lighter rain, the planting or the harvesting.

But one of these nights is different. The overseer or plantation owner has given permission to the enslaved to have a party, a dance. If it is a special holiday, like New Year's Day, the enslaved men and women might wear the finest clothing they have. Sometimes, the overseer or owner might invite outsiders to watch these festivities, which are sometimes called plays. Such an invitation might have been how soldier John Stedman saw the dance of the mermaid, or how, thirty years later, Gerrit Schouten saw the banya dance that inspired his art.

Within a short distance of Paramaribo, Schouten could have visited nearly a hundred plantations if he'd wanted to. Somewhere on one of these properties, people gather under a thatched roof, where there is space for dancers, musicians, and a chorus. A pole extends upward from the middle of the dance floor.

The musicians place their drums on the ground. The drums Schouten sees look similar to the drums engraved in Stedman's *Narrative*: a long, large drum with a skin head at one end held down by cords and wedges, and a smaller drum that sits upright. Unlike whoever made the engravings in Stedman's book, Schouten sees how well-crafted and sturdy the drums are.

Next to the drummers, a man blows into a wind instrument, which looks like a simple horn without finger holes. Another musician takes a seat, getting ready to play what Stedman called a bent, a bow held in the teeth with a string that the musician plucks or hits to create a melody.[1]

While the musicians wear no more than a draped piece of cloth, perhaps anticipating how much they'll sweat as they play for hours, the dancers are exquisitely dressed. One man wears a blue tunic with a red sash and a yellow-and-blue-striped cloth draped like a cape. Another wears a red sash around his waist, like the King in the Saint-Domingue Vodou ceremony, but with small pieces of fabric hanging at the front and back. The women wear skirts of patterned cloth with a second piece of cloth wrapped on top, creating two layers that recall the formal gowns of 1770s Europe. Wrapped around their heads is another piece of fabric, tied it in the back.

Every part of this—from the dance itself, to the music, to what the men and women wear—is a balancing act of permission and restriction, allowance and suppression. As early as 1698, the government of Suriname regulated dances by the enslaved, as the French had done with the calenda. In 1718, one Dutch visitor commented that the enslaved in Paramaribo gathered on Sundays at the waterfront or on the savanna to *baaljaren*, a version of the Portuguese and Spanish word *bailar*, to dance. This dancing was "prohibited because they could communicate with each other too easily, passing messages by means of their songs." A hundred years later, these dances were still considered dangerous, and were only allowed to take place with the permission of a plantation owner or manager.[2]

Laws may have specified what the enslaved could and couldn't do, but

One of Gerrit Schouten's Slavendans dioramas. He made at least six of these intricate papier-mâché banyaprei dance scenes between 1817 and 1831. *Rijksmuseum, Object number NG-2005-24*

that doesn't mean people followed those laws. Gerrit Schouten can see that in what the women wear as they dance. Strands of red, blue, and white beads hang around their necks and wrists. In the evening light, their golden rings and chains glimmer as they move around the dance floor. Like the dance, this adornment was only semi-legal. In 1777, an act stated that enslaved people were not allowed to wear "any gold or jewelry unless permission [was] granted for small golden earrings, necklaces or armbands with little golden lockets."[3]

He noticed bare feet. By not wearing shoes, almost everyone is following another part of the 1777 edict: no enslaved people "may wear stockings, shoes, [or] decorated hats." But one man is wearing stockings, shoes, and a hat. He stands regally behind the dancers in a suit of red with a

black three-cornered hat, looking like an eighteenth-century British soldier. He is the Kownu, the King.[4]

Now that everyone is in place, the dance can begin. The most finely
dressed of the women steps to the center of the stage. She is the leader
and designates the songs and dances that will follow; sometimes she is
called the trokiman, sometimes the Afrankeri. She might sing a prayer
before they start to dance, a prayer that allows them to start dancing, like
the "Bomba hen!" song that Moreau de Saint-Méry heard about in Saint-
Domingue. She might sing:

> Mama Aysa of the earth,
> in coming here we come not unannounced to you.
> Oh good mother,
> in coming here we come not unannounced to you.
> We've been in prayer at home,
> before we came to you.[5]

Then, she begins a new song. She sings a line and the chorus repeats
it, her lines becoming a story told to the sounds of the music. The lyrics
of the song trigger images, thoughts, and feelings. They call to the spirits, the gods, the ancestors, different rhythms and different songs calling
to different deities. The drummers look to the trokiman for cues about
what song is coming, what melody or line she will sing next. Although
certain people, like the woman leading the singing, have certain roles,
there is no division between spectator and participant; at some point,
everyone will join in.

As the women dance, they bend over, move toward and away from one
another, their feet barely lifting from the ground. A man might join in the
dance, facing a woman and moving toward her and back again. Someone
else enters the dance floor and waves a kerchief.[6]

Sometimes, another percussionist joins the orchestra. The kwakwa
mayoro takes his seat in front of a small table, a table small enough that it
might be mistaken for a footstool. Stedman called it the qua-qua; others
write out the name as kwakwa or call it the kwakwabangi. The musician

plays a fast rhythm that produces short, hard beats as the sticks strike the plank.[7]

The musicians tap their feet in time with the music and allow their bodies to enter the rhythm. It almost looks as if they are dancing, too. The ensemble is joined by rattles, which the female dancers hold in their right hands, tapping them against their left hands as they swing their bodies, pressing the soles of their feet into the ground as they turn and slide on their tiptoes. Some women who don't have rattles carry strings of nutshells.

People drink rum and molasses water and offer the drinks to the spirits and ancestors. If the spirit enters someone, it is now the spirit who sings and dances. The drums send these spirits back to where they belong at the end of the ceremony. The dance might last for hours, all night, or for days, new dancers and singers joining in. This is the banyaprei.[8]

Others had captured the banya in writing before Schouten framed the dance in his papier-mâché dioramas. Albert von Sack, who stayed in Suriname from 1805 to 1807, wrote that "their dances vary according to the different negro tribes," referring to the different places of origin, "though all consist principally in the muscular movement of their heads, and arms, turning of their bodies, accompanied by very quick steps, keeping in time very exactly to the music." J. D. Kunitz, another European who wrote about Suriname and its inhabitants, commented in 1804 that the enslaved were allowed dances throughout the year, but the plantation manager forbade the Water Mamma Dance, since it put people into a frenzy.[9]

Belgian artist Pierre Jacques Benoit wrote that the men and women dancing dressed in "oriental luxury," by which he might have meant their loose fabrics, sashes, and headscarves. The people danced to three types of instruments: the drums, a tambourin which is described as identical to the kwakwa, and "a kind of guitar." He wrote, "The guitar, which serves as a violin, is a half calabash attached to a stick, and on which is stretched a skin and four cords with guts. It is played hitting the string in time with the hand"—a description that immediately conjures the Creole-bania. He thinks that the choices of adornment, the dances, and the music originate in Africa but are "still really a national song of Kaya Paramaribo," using

The image of a du that accompanied P.J. Benoit's 1839 book *Voyage à Suriname*. Like the musician in Gerrit Schouten's *Waterkant van Paramaribo* diorama, the male dancer with his back to the viewer wears a headband with feathers, which may come from traditions in Kongo. *John Carter Brown Library, Brown University*

the Surinamese word for the streets of Paramaribo. It is so unusual to him that, he wrote, "Every description of it that you would want to make, would fall short."[10]

Schouten's diorama provides incredible detail, but it can only capture a single moment in time, a moment without sound or movement. The details he includes—from the jewelry to how the drumheads are tightened to the shoes of the man dressed in red—show he cared and had knowledge about what he was seeing, but how much could he decipher? He was both familiar with this culture—more familiar than someone like Stedman could ever be—and yet still an outsider.

Gerrit Schouten was born in Paramaribo to Hendrik, a white, Dutch-born poet and publisher who went to Suriname in government service and whose father had invested in plantations, and Suzanna Hanssen, the daughter of a white planter, Samuel Loseke, and his Black wife, Bettie van Hannibal. Bettie's grandmother Nanoe had been freed from slavery in 1713, and, through marriages to European men and an ability to earn their own income, women in the family had become prominent in Paramaribo. Suzanna had been educated in the Netherlands, learning piano and many languages.[11]

John Gabriel Stedman was friends with Hendrik Schouten during his sojourn in Suriname. He rode through the streets of Paramaribo in Hendrik's chaise, saw his "excellent collection of drawings," and visited his cabinet of curiosities. As an intellectual, Hendrik may have used his collection as a status symbol, just as Stedman would later use his in a modest attempt at fame. Stedman never wrote about what he saw in Hendrik Schouten's cabinet in Paramaribo, but it may have included music, books, drawings and watercolors, poems, and items Hendrik had collected in Suriname. At some point after 1796, Hendrik may have added a new tome to his collection of books: John Gabriel Stedman's *Narrative of a Five Years Expedition Against the Revolted Negroes of Surinam.*[12]

Gerrit Schouten was born in 1779, and grew up with this cabinet of curiosities, the theater performances his father put on, his mother's piano playing, and the writings of his father, including the first poem written partially in Sranan. His father could freely move in white circles, but Gerrit could not. Although the maternal side of Gerrit's family had been free of enslavement for five generations and his mother and grandmother had both married white European men, he was considered a free person of color. He was subject not only to social prejudices but to legal constraints as well, similar to what free people of color experienced in Saint-Domingue. Until 1799, for the first twenty years of his life, Schouten was subject to a curfew simply because he had African ancestors.[13]

Schouten never formally attended art school and never had the opportunity to travel to Europe for an education, as his mother had, but he learned advanced art techniques including color theory, multiple-point perspective, and forced perspective, perhaps by using the drawings and books his father had collected. His art looks like that of schooled European artists from the same time period. As an adult, he produced professional-quality watercolors of plants and animals for European collectors. No other Surinamese-born artist had ever reached this level. He also made dioramas for plantation owners, or to be bought by visitors as souvenirs. They would have been perfect for a cabinet of curiosities.[14]

Schouten's art demonstrates that he knew much more about Surinamese culture than a European visitor. In 1811, German landscape artist Louise van Panhuys arrived in Paramaribo with her husband, Willem. From his previous wife, Willem had inherited Nut en Schadelijk, a coffee plantation once owned by Stedman's friend Mrs. Godefroy. Gerrit Schouten befriended Louise van Panhuys, and perhaps because of their mutual profession and interest in floral watercolors, they spent time together. While Schouten's dioramas are full of texture and movement, bringing to life the scenes he portrayed, van Panhuys's two watercolors of enslaved men and women dancing to drummers are stiff. The dancers stand with both feet on the ground and arms firmly at their sides and the drummers rest both hands on the drum heads: choices that don't evoke movement. However, the man sitting on the drum with another drummer sitting beside him, and the woman in white with a red headscarf holding a small rattle, signal that she saw some of the most important elements of the dance.[15]

The lack of movement in van Panhuys's watercolors may be a reflection of her limited skill as an artist. Pierre Jacques Benoit had described the banya dance as a "grand party of the slaves," which he called a du. The book he published about his time in Suriname also included prints based on his drawings. The print of the du evokes movement and sound: some women raise their hands in the air as if shaking their rattles, other women bend their knees to crouch closer to the ground, while a man kicks up his feet and bends his torso back. Others hold their hands widespread, as if about to clap them together.

In Schouten's dioramas, the dance takes place under a thatched structure, drummers sit both astride and next to their drums, and, as in John Rose's watercolor from South Carolina, there is a large ceramic vessel on the right-hand side of the stage. In all except one of the dioramas one drum is left unplayed, with a piece of cloth draped over it. The three made between 1817 and 1820 feature a man in a red (or red and blue) soldier's uniform, the Afrankeri or female lead singer at the center of the stage, and two women holding scarves and a man dancing with his right leg planted and his left foot in the air—the same exact configuration of dancers as in the South Carolina watercolor.

In the later dioramas, the number of dancers increases, but they still hold and wave cloths. These pieces of fabric have particular messages and sayings attached to them, meanings that outside observers like Stedman, Benoit, and other Europeans never understood. The Afrankeri is still central, while the Kownu stands to the side of the dance floor. The red of his outfit could represent blood, denote Kongo royalty, or reference the water gods. In 1700s' Jamaica, Edward Long had thought the yell of "John Connu" during Christmas festivities referred to John Conny, but it may also have referred to the Kownu, the King, the leader of the celebration.

Schouten's status as a free man put him outside the culture of the people he portrayed in his dioramas. He made at least six dioramas on the Slavendans theme, with no two the same. Still, we don't know how many dances he saw. The dioramas could show amalgamations of typical dances he witnessed, or an actual dance that he sketched and then artfully crafted into a scene made of paper, glue, and paint. He probably didn't take part in these dances, but he was clearly familiar enough with them to create the realistic details that made his dioramas something people wanted to buy.[16]

Schouten never included a banjo in his Slave Dance dioramas. The only time he depicted a banjo is when he crafted a gourd-bodied instrument for a man leaning against a tree on the Paramaribo waterfront.

XIII

New Orleans, Louisiana, 1819

Benjamin Henry Latrobe's plan was to walk along the bank of the Canal Carondelet in the northwest section of town, where the city limits of New Orleans had been extended in 1804. He left his boarding house in the oldest part of the city, where brick buildings surrounded the cathedral and the Place d'Armes, and walked away from the river. When he'd arrived in the city a month earlier, in January 1819, by way of the Mississippi, he found that the city had "an odd look." Evidently, even with a European design, the city wasn't quite up to the standards of the British-born architect. Latrobe found the main plaza by his boarding house run-down, lacking the grandeur of a prominent central square. He found it disappointing that New Orleans didn't have more fine arts and cultural amenities. Yet every day of the week, he could see the market bustling with people from all over: men from the northern states, Spaniards who either remained from the time when the city belonged to Spain (barely a decade and a half earlier) or were temporary visitors to the port, Indigenous people who had originally inhabited the land and were slowly being pushed out, and both free and enslaved people of African descent. They came to buy and sell everything from oysters and large fish to sugar cane, oranges, and bananas. The noise was too much for Latrobe, and he wasn't afraid to judge Americans of any background, since he believed himself to be the relative of a French aristocrat. In reality, his family were middle-class clergy and he'd come to the United States after racking up extensive debts in Europe.[1]

After arriving in the US in 1795, he had designed the country's first Catholic cathedral, in Baltimore, had helped to survey Washington, DC, and had overseen the construction of the second Capitol building. When he lived in Philadelphia, he'd walked along the city's wharves, near the neighborhoods hardest hit by yellow fever outbreaks. In the summer months, the disease would sweep through cities across the country, producing symptoms that ranged from headaches and fever to organ failure. Some people thought yellow fever was connected to drinking water, and New Orleans had decided to build a system of waterworks. Latrobe was in the city to finish up the seemingly doomed project, which was already years behind schedule. Even worse, his son Henry, who had secured and managed the contract, had died in September 1817 of the disease.[2]

On this Sunday in February 1819, Latrobe walked farther from the river toward Lake Pontchartrain. As the brick houses gave way to wood, he could at least be happy that his feet were kept relatively dry on the brick and stone sidewalks. The sidewalks, the building materials, the grade of the streets: these were the things Latrobe would have observed as he walked. He was always walking, taking in the landscape and architecture and getting an intimate look at how the natural features of a place interacted with the built ones.[3]

Latrobe was surprised to find shops and theaters open on Sundays, and that "slaves and hirelings" didn't get the day off work. Sixteen years after Louisiana was added to the United States, Latrobe could still see the vibrant remnants of the city's French and Spanish colonial past. The majority of residents had African, French, or Spanish heritage. The municipal council also printed its ordinances in French, and the newspapers were in English and French. On a Sunday in this non-Anglo European culture, people went to morning Mass in the cathedral followed by a trip to the market around the levee next to the river—a day not unlike what Moreau de Saint-Méry had described in Cap François before the Haitian Revolution.[4]

Latrobe went to Mass on occasion when he was in New Orleans, though he wasn't religious. He acknowledged the existence of God, but after leaving the strict Moravian Church in which he'd been brought up, he didn't believe in organized religion. And so, on this Sabbath, he wandered the streets of New Orleans for his own enjoyment.[5]

If he had been expecting a quiet and somber walk during which to think, he would have been disappointed. This Sunday was the beginning of a holy week. On Wednesday, Lent would begin, and the days before could be festive, the excess before the feast on Mardi Gras. As Latrobe walked up St. Peter's Street toward the Common, he heard loud, resonant banging, a firm pounding on a hollow surface. The only thing he could think to compare it to was "horses tramping on a wooden floor." As he approached the Common, he saw hundreds of people assembled. He scanned the crowd and thought there must be at least five hundred, if not six hundred people gathered. All of them, he noted, seemed to be Black. "I did not observe a dozen yellow faces," he wrote in his diary, suggesting that people of mixed European and African descent, whether free or enslaved, didn't attend. He squeezed into a spot where he could see what was happening.

The people gathered in different circles and danced. In one circle, "a ring of a dozen women walked, by way of dancing" around musicians who sat in the center playing rhythm instruments. A player hit a wooden instrument in "the form of a cricket bat, with a long and deep mortise"—a hollowed-out part in the center that causes it to resonate. In the same group, a female musician played a calabash "with two short sticks." This may have been similar to the gourd drum that John Rose saw pressed between the musician's knees in South Carolina. The final percussion instrument was a "square drum" that looked a little like a stool, not unlike the qua-qua John Stedman saw in Suriname. The qua-qua had a wooden top, but Latrobe's sketch suggests this instrument had a skin top, more similar to the gome drums of the Akan.[6]

Latrobe, while fascinated, did not appreciate the music. "A man sung an uncouth song to the dancing" in one circle, he wrote, "which I supposed was in some African language, for it was not French, and the women screamed a detestable burden on one single note." It didn't occur to Latrobe that they could have been singing in a language neither African nor European, but a blended one like Gullah or Kreyòl.

In another circle, women sang a song "consisting of two notes," which reminded Latrobe of "the negroes working in our cities [who] respond to the song of their leader." Inside the circle, two female dancers shifted slowly, their feet and bodies hardly moving. In their hands, they held "each a coarse handkerchief, extended by the corners," just like the women in Rose's watercolor and Schouten's dioramas.[7]

Two years before Latrobe saw these dances in New Orleans, the German traveler Johann Ulrich Buechler also went to a spot "behind the city," probably the Common. Buechler wrote that here, the enslaved could feel unencumbered and have fun. Buechler saw a sea of bright colors and vivid fabrics. The men wore outfits that reminded him of an Indian or Asian manner of dress, with "Turkish turbans of different colors: red, blue, yellow, green and brown." They wore matching scarves around their waists, but otherwise they were naked. The women dressed in the newest fashions of silk, organza, and percale fabrics. He too saw that they danced in circles, forming a ring, and while he thought that they danced in a wonderful manner, he also described their movements as "ape-like." He called this in German a *Schauspiel*, a play. Like the banyaprei, this could mean that people had fixed roles and the dances progressed in a specific order. Or, it could mean that the dances were more like a performance than a social dance.[8]

On the Common, two drummers, one sitting atop a drum "about a foot in diameter" and the other holding a drum between his knees, like the drummers Moreau de Saint-Méry described in Saint-Domingue, accompany the women dancing with scarves. The drums didn't surprise Latrobe, but something else caught his eye. "The most curious instrument, however, was a stringed instrument, which no doubt was imported from Africa," he wrote. In all of his travels throughout the United States, from Richmond to Baltimore to Philadelphia, he had never seen anything like it. The musician playing it was "a very little old man, apparently eighty or ninety years old."[9]

Latrobe made a quick sketch of the instrument in his diary. The body is round, and Latrobe thought it was made of a calabash. In his drawing, the calabash looks like it has been cut down the middle. He includes a bridge holding up two strings, which Latrobe wrote were fastened with two pegs. Those pegs are at the top of the instrument, at the headstock or peghead, and sit behind the carving of a seated man. Both of the instruments Hans Sloane included in his book have two clearly visible long strings, but the Creole-bania has a short string as well, as do descriptions of other banjos. Did Latrobe miss the short string, or did this instrument only have two long ones? The peghead of the Creole-bania also has a carving, but not of a seated man.

For all of this detail, Latrobe's drawing is rather hard to decipher. Latrobe is very careful when it comes to the carved man and the pegs, but the construction of the banjo's body is less clear. In a side view, we see that the top of the body is clearly flat; on the flat top Latrobe drew a circle surrounded by smaller circles. This could be the skin soundboard poorly drawn, the smaller circles being tacks that hold the skin down, or Latrobe could be indicating holes in the skin, like the holes in a violin. In Saint-Domingue, French botanist Richard Tussac described banzas with sound holes in skin soundboards. But Latrobe drew and described another instrument as "a calabash with a round hole in it, the hole studded with brass nails," and his illustration of that instrument is similar to the soundboard of the banjo, which suggests that the skin of the banjo was held on with brass nails. Although Latrobe was an architect and painted watercolors, his drawings of landscapes are usually much better rendered than his drawings of people and objects.

To anyone who has read Father Labat's account of the French Antilles, Stedman's *Narrative* of Suriname, or Moreau de Saint-Méry's book on Saint-Domingue, both the dances in New Orleans and the banjo seem familiar. But the whole scene felt foreign to Latrobe. This is not surprising, since his attitude toward the cultures of people of African descent was consistently uninterested and condescending. "I have never seen anything more brutally savage and at the same time dull and stupid, than this whole exhibition," he wrote after observing the dances in New Orleans, which evokes the words Moreau de Saint-Méry used to describe the music of the enslaved on Saint-Domingue.

If Latrobe had read any of the accounts of the banjo in the Americas, he would have immediately recognized it or called the instrument by name. Instead, he said it was "imported from Africa," which wasn't an unusual idea at the time. Latrobe had worked and corresponded with Thomas Jefferson, who wrote, "The instrument proper to them is the Banjer, which they brought hither from Africa." Latrobe generally called everyone that he saw singing, dancing, and playing music "African." They spoke "in some African language" and "the allowed amusements of Sunday have, it seems, perpetuated here those of Africa among its former inhabitants." But he didn't really know what "African" meant.[10]

The last enslaved people to arrive in New Orleans from Africa were predominantly from the Congo River area, the Loango Coast, and Central Africa, while many who were born in Louisiana could have been of Senegambian descent, Senegambians having been the first and largest group to arrive in the colony. Latrobe's assessment of the people he saw as "African" is simplistic, but so is saying that one group of people predominantly influenced the culture and dances of New Orleans.

The banjo Latrobe saw illustrates the blending of cultures in New Orleans. The body was a calabash, he says—like that of the Creole-bania that Stedman collected. Calabashes may be used in the construction of Kilba, Hausa, and Toubou lutes, while Senegambians would have been more familiar with instruments made of gourds. But it isn't like the round-necked lutes from Senegambia, eastern West Africa, or western Central Africa, as it seems to have a flat fingerboard, with strings held on by tuning pegs. European lutes and guitars have flat fingerboards and tuning pegs; so do lutes from eastern parts of Central Africa and Mozambique. In the year before the end of the international slave trade, two vessels carrying captives from Mozambique landed in Louisiana.[11]

An unusual feature of Latrobe's banjo is the intricate carving on the peghead, of a seated man. The decorative arts of the Akan and Baule feature sculptures of men and women seated, with their faces forward and hands on their knees, very much like this carved figure. In Akan culture, a seated person represents calm and power against disorder. People from these cultures could have been present in New Orleans. But nowhere in Africa is there an analogue to what Latrobe saw.[12]

It's lucky that Latrobe wrote down anything at all, given his attitude, because his is the first known mention of the banjo in New Orleans. For almost a hundred years, since the founding of the city, others had observed similar dances, often at the back of town in the place that would become known as Congo Square, but none of them mentioned the banjo. Perhaps that is because Latrobe had arrived at a time of transformation in New Orleans.[13]

Antoine Simon Le Page du Pratz, who arrived in Louisiana from France in 1718, wrote about his time as one of eight hundred men who planned to settle in the colony. Within a year of the French settlement, 450 West Africans who'd been taken from Ouidah arrived aboard the *Aurore* and the *Duc du Maine* and were sold to colonists like Le Page. They were the first of thousands of people of African descent who would be sold to work first on rice and tobacco plantations and later in the indigo and sugar fields around New Orleans.

As in Martinique and Saint-Domingue, French colonial administrators applied the Code Noir in Louisiana, which meant that enslaved people were given Sunday off from work. Le Page wrote that slaveowners ought to provide a small plot of land where enslaved people could grow their own vegetables and encourage them to tend that on Sundays, "when they are not Christians." Otherwise, he warned, some three or four hundred people will gather "under pretense of Calinda or the dance," which he, like so many other colonists and colonial authorities, considered dangerous. Le Page thought that at these meetings, "they sell what they have stolen . . . and commit many crimes" and might even "plot their rebellions."[14]

Even though all enslaved people were supposed to be baptized, Le Page didn't believe many of those in Louisiana to be Christians. He wrote, "They are very superstitious," and have items called gris-gris that are so important "they would believe themselves undone, if they were stripped of those trinkets." In West Africa at the end of the eighteenth century,

Muslim holy men traded gris-gris, amulets with verses of the Quran that served as protective charms.[15]

The Spanish government and the Catholic Church didn't like the Sunday dances in New Orleans, either. In 1765, Spain had taken over control of Louisiana, after Louis XV gave the colony to his cousin Carlos III. No longer French, New Orleans didn't have to abide by the Code Noir. In 1786, Bishop Cyril complained about the enslaved people who during "the vespers hour assembled in a green expanse called 'Place Congo' to dance the bamboula and perform the rites imported from Africa by the Yolofs, Foulahs, Bambarras, Mandingoes, and other races." In response, Governor Miró forbid *los tangos*, or dances of the enslaved, before vespers were over. In 1795, the next governor ordered that to prevent plots "for running away, and excesses of other kinds," no one could hold "any Dances, or meetings whatsoever of slaves belonging to other places," meaning that enslaved people could not travel to dances. And if slaveowners wanted to hold "Dances, and amusements of their own slaves," they could "take place upon Sunday only, [and] shall always cease before night."[16]

Under Spanish law, enslaved people had the ability to petition for and purchase their own freedom. They could sell items at the Sunday markets on the outskirts of town where the dances were held or earn money for work—if their owner allowed it. During Spanish rule, a little more than a quarter of the city's enslaved population was able to buy their way out of enslavement.[17]

The change in colonial power also changed trade regulations, including the trade in human beings. In 1782, the Spanish stopped levying taxes on enslaved people brought to the colony, which meant that traders no longer had to record how many people were being sold. During Spanish rule, only two ships bringing human cargo directly from Africa are documented, while sixty-seven ships arrived from the Caribbean, including Jamaica, Martinique, Saint-Domingue, Guadeloupe, and Dominica. After 1792, Governor Carondelet banned imports of people from Africa and the Caribbean, another impact of Boukman's uprising in Saint-Domingue. So, in the ten years before Louisiana became part of the United States in 1803, no enslaved people arrived from Africa or the Caribbean, unless they were smuggled in.[18]

With the change of government, laws and demographics shifted dramatically once more. The enslaved could no longer easily purchase their freedom, and ships began arriving again from Central Africa and Mozambique. Between 1803 and the ban on the international slave trade in 1808, over 1,600 people were kidnapped from Africa to be enslaved in Louisiana, and ships brought at least 1,300 from the Caribbean. White residents of the United States moved to Louisiana, bringing their enslaved people with them, while both whites and free people of color arrived from Saint-Domingue during the revolution, sometimes bringing with them people they owned. All of these arrivals—free and enslaved from Africa, the Caribbean, and the US—shifted the culture of the city.[19]

Like Latrobe, many people of European descent felt that this new state was unlike the rest of the country. In May 1808, traveler and writer Christian Schultz ventured to the area near Bayou St. John, farthest from the river. He wrote that what he saw was not just dancing, but that the "Africans, collected together to perform their worship after the manner of their country." Like Latrobe, he noticed drums of various sizes, "three or four of which make a band." He didn't see people wearing turbans or scarves, but said they wore outfits "ornamented with a number of the tails of the smaller wild beasts," perhaps not unlike the tails worn by the dancers Hans Sloane saw in Jamaica. On two consecutive Sundays around the same time, Irish traveler and writer Fortescue Cuming walked around the city and reported that "On our way to the upper fort we saw vast numbers of negro slaves, men, women, and children, assembled together on the levee, drumming, fifing, and dancing in large rings," likely referring to the area in the northern part of the city known as the Common and, later, Congo Square. The next Sunday, he "found upwards of one hundred negroes of both sexes assembled on the levee, fiddling, dancing, and singing." A German visitor saw what he described as curious dances, while another commented on the general dancing on Sundays, and still another wrote that the dances "rocked the city." These accounts mention drums, fifes or perhaps flutes, and fiddles, but no banjos.[20]

Why hadn't the banjo been observed in New Orleans before Latrobe saw it in Congo Square in 1819, although many white people had observed the Black dances? Someone may have written an earlier account of the banjo that is still waiting in an archive to be found by an intrepid researcher. However, there is also the possibility that the banjo was new to New Orleans. The old man Latrobe saw may have called it a merry-wang, and have arrived on the *Jeune Sofie* from Jamaica in 1786. He may have called it a banjer, and come to New Orleans with an owner who relocated from Maryland after 1803. Or he may have arrived as property of a slaveowner fleeing Boukman's revolt, with the banza of Saint-Domingue becoming the banjo of Congo Square.

The majority of whites who left Saint-Domingue during the revolution went to places where they would be allowed to keep their slaves. Most went to Cuba, but others crossed the border to Santo Domingo or sailed to Jamaica or to US states that permitted slavery, including South Carolina, Virginia, and Maryland. In these new places, the enslaved people introduced their ways and customs to and were influenced by the existing cultures of the people they met. In 1809, those who went to Cuba were forced to move again, after Napoleon invaded Spain and the French were no longer welcome in the Spanish-held colony. New Orleans became a refuge not only for these slaveowners, but also for free people of color. By 1810, over nine thousand people had arrived in the city from Haiti, almost evenly distributed among whites, free people of color, and enslaved Blacks, doubling the city's overall population. In 1810, a third of the enslaved people in New Orleans had spent some part of their lives in Saint-Domingue. The Haitian culture mixed with that of New Orleans, a culture that now included the banjo.[21]

⌀

Twelve years after Latrobe visited New Orleans, Frenchman Pierre Forest saw a gathering on the lush green shores of Lake Pontchartrain. Here, three miles outside the city, Black residents gathered on Sundays, arriving by foot or barge along the bayou, or maybe even by steam-powered omnibus. While, in 1819, Latrobe noted that most of the people in Congo Square were dark-skinned, in 1831, Forest thought "the sight of the mixing of so many different colors" produced a "curious effect." Groups formed, each with its own flag "perched at the top of a pyramid-shaped pole." Men and women danced "with extraordinary speed and lightness," and Forest thought the dance was "more of a pantomime than a regular dance." He didn't explain what he meant by this, but it could be that the dances had parts and segments, roles like the banya dance in Suriname.[22]

"*Lisette quitté la pleine,*" "Lisette, you've left the plain," the song about a lost love started. Forest found it familiar enough that he could write down the French-sounding lyrics, although he didn't know the translation. "*Dempi mo perdi Lizette, Mo pas souchié calinda, Mo pas bram bramba boula,*" the singers continued. This was an adaptation of a Haitian song, developed from a poem written by a white Frenchman in Saint-Domingue in the mid-1700s. Moreau de Saint-Méry had copied down the poem, recording lines that mentioned the calinda dance and the bamboula drum: "My steps, far from Lisette, stay away from the Calinda; And my sash fitted with bells, languishes on my bamboula."[23]

Around this same time, in the countryside outside New Orleans, Theodore Pavie saw what he called Creole and Congo dances. By this time, even a visiting Frenchman knew what a banjo was. After dark, people gathered around a fire and someone tuned a banjo, "a rough guitar, mounted on a calabash with catgut" and began "to prelude as on a Moorish mandolin." Another man turned over a copper kettle and struck "a prolonged roll on it," the sound rising and disappearing into the woods. The banjo player signaled, and the dance began. Sometimes, the movements were fast, the dancers spinning around and clapping their thighs and hands with the rhythm of the drum. Then, they might stop suddenly "in an attitude of surprise and pleasure" and form a circle, and the dance would continue. The dancers followed the musicians, with young women and old men singing songs with "sad and plaintive" melodies that Pavie thought originated in Africa.

In one evening, Pavie saw this dance, another he thought looked like quadrilles, and "the Creole dance," which was danced "in a circle around the fire." When an overseer arrived and yelled, "Dance the dance of the Congos," three older men tuned their "banjas" while three others began drumming. The movements of this dance were more militaristic, Pavie thought, as the men snapped their fingers above their heads.[24]

There was no doubt in Latrobe's mind that the banjo was a Black instrument; and Pavie thought the dances and songs he heard were from Africa. Louisiana seemed to have a culture of its own: a mix of European, African, and Caribbean elements, not unlike the banjo itself. Whenever the instrument had arrived in Louisiana, it would soon transform again.

XIV

Haiti, 1841

When Victor Schœlcher arrived on the island in 1841, the people who still called this land Saint-Domingue might have been being derogatory or defiant, refusing to accept that France had lost control of the colony and that it was now the Black republic of Haiti—a recognition of the name used by the Arawak natives who had inhabited the island before Christopher Columbus arrived in 1492. This nation without slavery had existed for almost forty years. Schœlcher hoped his time here would further not only his understanding of a place no longer reliant on slave labor, but also his goal of bringing the abolition of slavery to France.

Schœlcher still remembered the first time he saw the selling of people as a regular practice. In 1829, ten years after Latrobe's visit to New Orleans, Schœlcher found himself there. At just twenty-three years old, it was Schœlcher's first trip away from France. His father, a porcelain manufacturer, had sent his son to Mexico on business, but Schœlcher took time to stop in the Crescent City.

New Orleans had no designated market for the sale of human beings. Instead, the slave trade was conducted at dozens of locations throughout the city. Schœlcher would have been able to see people sold across the street from the Louisiana State Bank, a convenient place if the buyer needed a loan for his purchase. He could have seen human beings sold along the waterfront, at the levee where earlier visitors had witnessed enslaved people dancing and celebrating, or at hotels, private homes, and yards.

Schœlcher saw a woman being sold in the middle of a square. She was poorly dressed, yet looked more like a statue than a person. Schœlcher remembered her as being "indifferent to her fate," but it's impossible to know what she was feeling as she stood there, except that resisting was unlikely to set her free. People walked past as buyers stood around. The auctioneer began to yell, "Come on, gentleman! 200 dollars for the pretty negress, a good laundress!" The bidding went up. "220 dollars, gentleman! She is still young, very healthy . . ."[1]

"It is a painful picture that will never leave my memory and which still saddens me," Schœlcher wrote after returning home. He had left Europe "without a preconceived idea about slavery." But this scene and the other realities of enslavement that he saw in New Orleans and Cuba changed him. He wasn't willing to think that slavery was a necessary evil or that slave labor was the only way that sugar plantations could operate. He wasn't willing to accept a narrative about people of African descent being inferior or destined for slavery. He saw it for what it was: brutal and inhumane. His trip to New Orleans had started him down a path of researching and writing about abolition, trying to prove both that people of African descent had culture and that they could be educated if they weren't enslaved—a radical idea when he traveled to Haiti in 1841.[2]

To support his ideas, Schœlcher read books by European travelers to Africa and histories of African countries. He noted technical advancements in metalwork and agriculture and government structures in Africa similar to European ones. As someone interested in music, Schœlcher was especially interested in musical instruments, and had read about instruments like the kora, a twenty-one-stringed harp of the Mandingo. He also researched the economics of slavery and studied the gradual abolition plan that the British colonies had put in place in 1834. At first, Schœlcher didn't support blanket abolition, favoring gradual manumission instead, but by the time he arrived in Haiti, he had come to believe that the total and immediate abolishment of slavery was necessary. His plan was to visit Haiti and see the progress of the country a generation after the revolution; to go to Dominica, Jamaica, and Antigua to observe complete emancipation; and to go to the French Antilles and Cuba, where slavery was still in practice.[3]

Schœlcher knew that using Haiti as an example of abolition wasn't without controversy. "The name alone sums up all the bad that the enemies of abolition say about the African race by awakening the idea of the Haitians' misuse of their independence," he wrote. For one, he didn't support the independence of French colonies. People knew about what had happened in Haiti, if not from the people who had come to their cities, then from accounts like that of Michel Étienne Descourtilz. A white Frenchmen who had married a woman with land in what was then still Saint-Domingue, Descourtilz had traveled to the colony in April 1799, trying to figure out what to do with their plantation. His 1809 book *Voyages d'un naturaliste* told of his capture by Lieutenant Jean-Jacques Dessalines and being forced to work as a doctor for the Black troops led by General Toussaint Louverture. The general had wanted landowners like Descourtilz to return and make their plantations profitable, thus providing a source of tax revenue for the state. But Descourtilz found that now-free people had no interest in working for him or other landowners. He also wrote about the "barbaric persecutions against the whites" and the "bloody theater of the massacres," creating a narrative that placed Haiti's status as a Black republic in a dark light.[4]

Despite the widespread negative depiction of Haiti, Schœlcher still thought it important to visit the country. He wanted to see this semi-mythical place for himself. Would there be disorder and barbarism, as many people in the French colonies had warned him? It had taken an armed uprising, a civil war, tens of thousands of people dead and displaced, and the destruction of plantations and wealth to arrive at emancipation. And yet, Haiti was also home to abolition's greatest triumph: the revolutionaries had put into practice what other countries around the same time had only talked about.

During the week of Carnival and the celebrations leading up to Lent, Schœlcher enjoyed the festivities. People wore masks, women wore hats, while men dressed as devils with horns on their heads or as generals in brightly colored garments with gold accents. One of the curiosities he saw was companies of men dressed like "savages." They had a drum six or seven feet tall, which they beat with sticks as they sang and danced. They were dressed in an unusual costume made up of pieces of striped or checkered cotton cloth tied around their bodies. Each of these groups had a name, a flag, and a king. The king wore a turban made of feathers and had a "rich costume," including a satin coat embroidered with gold and silver sequins. Schœlcher thought the companies very African. He learned that each group was made up of "people descended exclusively from one or another African nation," a fact that made them proud.

As an atheist, Schœlcher didn't positively portray any type of religion or spiritual belief, including the power of wangas and gris-gris for protection. He may have also downplayed Vodou as a religion, since Boukman's revolt began with such a ceremony, and Vodou had been accused of propelling the destruction of plantations and murder of whites. Schœlcher also may not have always understood what was religious and what was secular. The account he published two years after his trip, *Colonies étrangères et Haïti*, does not mention banzas, calendas, or other dances. And yet, somewhere on the island Schœlcher came across a banza and brought it back to France. He may have chosen not to write about music because it could contribute to a racist, pro-slavery view of people who were lazy and danced too much. Such a view would have echoed the published version of John Stedman's *Narrative* of Suriname. But Schœlcher was a music lover, and was trying to prove that people of African descent had a vibrant culture. That makes it surprising he never mentioned the banza.[5]

The pro-slavery writer Descourtilz, by contrast, mentioned the instrument many times in his book, expressing the racist views that Schœlcher may have been trying to avoid. Descourtilz also knew that if people were going to read and believe his book, he'd need to include engaging scenes and anecdotes about what he saw and experienced.

The banza, Descourtilz writes, is an instrument with five strings that "you pick like a guitar." Later in his natural history volumes, he describes its construction: "the Blacks prepare [the banza] by sawing one of these calabashes or a large gourd longwise, to which they adjust a neck and sonorous strings made out of fibres of aloe plants." Once, while passing by a hut, Descourtilz saw a woman practicing the chica dance, brushing her foot against the ground to the "thin and monotonous sound of the banza" her friend was picking. And while sometimes the banza might be played for a love song, too, he saw that it had a central place accompanying the calenda, just as Father Labat had seen in Martinique 150 years earlier.[6]

One day, Descourtilz writes, *une négresse creole* named Ursule came to him. Her friend François had just died and she was distraught. They were going to have a calenda, the "dance dedicated to celebrating funerals," which Descourtilz thought wild and indecent. She needed a sheep, which she might use for a sacrifice.

"The banzas, the bamboulas are already outside," she told him; they just needed the dancers and the procession. She left, tears filling her eyes, "her chest suffocating with sobs."

"François, he's gone!" she cried. "Poor François!"

Then, she began to dance intensely, before the ceremony itself had begun.[7]

The calenda took place at night, with people traveling all evening to get there, dressed in their best attire. In Saint-Domingue, the calenda had been restricted, but near Le Cap, the burial ground became a place of music and dance, similar to the African Burial Ground in New York City.[8]

Sometime in the eighteenth century, an unknown artist painted a calenda at Fossette, the burial ground outside Le Cap. Like the watercolor from South Carolina, this image shows adults playing instruments, dancing, and standing as a chorus. The bamboula player sits astride his drum. The banza player stands, holding the instrument across his chest, like the banjo player in the South Carolina painting. His right hand strums where the neck meets the body of the instrument, mid-stroke, while his left hand splays out, wide fingers pressing down multiple strings to form a chord.[9]

A man in blue pants dances, his legs bent, his heels off the ground. He faces a woman, who also bends her knees. She wears white, like everyone except the male dancer and one other woman. That other woman stands to the side of the dancers, wearing a white dress with a light floral

This eighteenth-century painting with the inscription "Île de Saint Domingue: Vue du Cap de la Fossette" shows a man playing a banza—similar in size to the one in the South Carolina watercolor—during a dance at the burial ground outside Le Cap. © *Etude Tajan*

print. Perhaps she is the leader of the dance, like the Queen in a Vodou ceremony or the Afrankeri in the banyaprei. A man stands beside her, wearing a white scarf tied around his head. He is the only man with a head covering, perhaps signifying that he is the King. The woman and the man clap their hands. A little in the distance, behind the action, stand two men and two women, as if waiting for their turn to dance. The ceremonies at Fossette could have been for all the loved ones lost. In the time before freedom, before Haiti, an average of two people a day were buried there.[10]

In his research into Haiti and its revolution, Schœlcher may have read about the banza in Moreau de Saint-Méry's or Descourtilz's books. He had also read about the kora, as well as the koonting, "a sort of guitar with

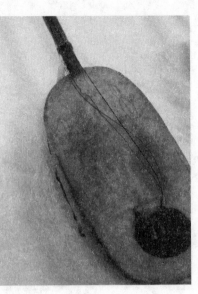

One of the kontings Victor Schœlcher
collected during his trip to Senegal in
1848. It is much smaller than the banza,
and has similar oval decorations drawn
on the skin soundboard. *Cite de la Musique*
(photo by Kristina Gaddy)

three strings," described in Mungo Park's book about his trip to West
Africa from 1795 to 1797. Park's basic description of a guitar-like instrument with three strings seems similar enough to a banjo, and perhaps
if Schœlcher hadn't seen a konting (as it is more commonly spelled) in a
museum, private collection, or an engraving, he might have thought that
the instrument he saw in Haiti was the instrument Park described. The
banza had four strings, three long and one short, and could reasonably
be described as guitar-like, since it was a plucked instrument about the
size of a small guitar. Schœlcher had read Park's book because he wanted
proof that Africans had culture, and what he saw or chose to see in Haiti
proved his point. Perhaps he thought that bringing the banza home to
France could prove that not only did the people of Haiti have a culture,
but that it connected back to Africa.[11]

The banza Schœlcher collected was a worn and oft-played instrument,
unlike the little-worn Creole-bania that Stedman had collected. Holding
down the skin head are not one but two sets of tacks, the visible, larger tacks
holding down a dark ribbon. One of the tuning pegs has been replaced and

The carving on the fingerboard of the banza that Victor Schœlcher collected in Haiti in 1841. He gave no indication from whom he got this instrument. *Cite de la Musique* *(photo by Kristina Gaddy)*

part of the neck has been worn down by the fingers of the banza player. It might have been played before the Haitian Revolution.

By 1848, Schœlcher could juxtapose the banza and a konting he had collected in West Africa after his American journeys. They were as different from each other as they both were from a guitar. The biggest difference is in their bodies, which make the sound resonate. Like a guitar, the konting Schœlcher collected has a body made of wood, in this case carved into an oblong shape. The banza's body is made from a gourd, which is less dense than wood and easier to hollow out. Although the banza and the konting both have a skin soundboard covering the top of the body, the banza's skin is held down by tacks and the konting's is held down by thin leather straps that wrap around the wooden body and form an intricate woven pattern. Although the bodies are not that different in size, the konting's slightly smaller body and much shorter neck also makes it closer to the size of a violin.

Both instruments have a combination of long and short strings, although the banza has four strings and the konting has three. How the strings attach to the instrument is also different. The strings of the banza wind around carved wooden pegs that go through holes in the top of the neck, usually called the peghead or pegbox if it looks like a box without a lid, as on a fiddle. The strings extend from the peghead, traverse the whole instrument, and then tie around the stub of the neck that emerges from the far end of the gourd or to a tailpiece attached to the neck. In contrast, the strings of the konting tie onto the neck with pieces of leather, and they extend from the neck only as far as a bridge that sits in the middle of the body, just above a hole cut in the skin soundboard.[12]

Another visible difference is in the necks. The banza's is broad, flattened like a board, while the konting has a narrow neck, rounded like a dowel. While the banza's neck extends through the body of the gourd, narrowing to a stick that exits where the flower of the fruit once blossomed, the konting's only extends halfway into the body, as far as the bridge.

These necks intersect with the bodies differently, too. The neck of the konting sits on the edge of the body and is held in place by the skin soundboard, while in the banza the flat neck bisects the gourd. The maker has cut off the top of the tubelike extension where the gourd was once attached to the vine and carved two parallel notches to hold the neck. While in the konting the neck is basically strapped down by the skin, the banza's neck would sit loosely in the notches if not for a wooden wedge that holds it in place.[13]

The neck-to-body construction on the banza is a small but important part of the instrument. Many African instruments like the akonting, konting, and n'goni have a neck that sits in a notch or directly on the body's edge, as in the konting Schœlcher collected. Others, like the gurumi, have a dowel-like neck and a gourd body where the top (rather than the side) of the fruit has been cut off, so the neck enters and exits through the sides (rather than going in the top and out the bottom) of the gourd. Although most West African lutes have rounded necks like the konting, some North and Central African instruments have both flat fingerboards and tuning pegs. However, African instruments with flat necks have carved wooden bodies, with the neck and the body essentially one piece.[14]

All three of these African construction styles put the neck on the same plane as the soundboard, which ultimately means that the height of the strings above the fingerboard is low from the far end of the fingerboard all the way to where the neck meets the body of the instrument. With the strings so close to the fingerboard, the player can slide his fingers up and down the neck, playing a wide range of notes at a rapid speed.

When the neck enters the top of the gourd, as on the banza that Schœlcher collected and, it appears, on the Strum Strumps and the banjo in the South Carolina watercolor, it is no longer on the same plane as the soundboard and the strings don't run parallel to the neck. Instead, the strings are at an angle: close to the fingerboard near the peghead, but pulled higher and higher off the neck as they approach the body of the instrument. This design makes the instrument harder to play and limits musicians to playing notes on the part of the neck closest to the peghead, where the strings can be pressed against the wood. And in fact on the banza, the finger wear on the neck is in one spot close to the peghead. Since on all three of these latter instruments, skilled craftsmen took the time and care to carve the peghead and decorate the neck with intricate patterns, they would have had the skill to construct lutes in the same method as African instruments if that was their desire.

What, then, was more important than playability? The answer lies in the way the neck intersects with the gourd. It can be thought of as a circle bisected by a line—and this symbolism was more important than the ease of playing the banza. This geometric figure, often called a cosmogram, depicts the earthly plane, represented by the circle, intersected by the vertical spiritual plane. It appears over and over in Vodou and other religions practiced by people of African descent in the Americas, including Christianity. Between the time of Descourtilz's and Schœlcher's trips to Haiti, slavery was abolished and the Code Noir became a thing of the past. Vodou rites no longer had to be practiced in secret or only when a slaveowner or plantation manager allowed. Ceremonies and dances had moved into ritual spaces called oum'phors, and spirits would enter this realm through a pillar called a poteau-mitan, which extended from the floor to the ceiling and allowed spirits to enter from their dwellings in the water below or the skies above. Again: the round ceremonial area, and the perpendicular line. The asson rattle, which a priest or priestess uses to summon spirits, also has this sacred geometry: a gourd or calabash bisected by the wooden handle.[15]

The Vodou drums are consecrated vessels, bringing and becoming the divine. Using the rattle, the drums, and song, the priest or priestess will first call to honor Legba, the spirit who guards the crossroads, who exists between the world of the living and the gods and the dead. Legba can open the pathway between the living and the dead, making way for spirits. Then, another spirit, or lwa, is summoned, which can enter the vessel that is the body of a practitioner or one of the govi pottery jars and glass bottles that sit next to the poteau-mitan. The practice of placing bottles on a grave is a Central African tradition brought to the Americas; they decorate Black burial grounds and memorials in the United States. Schouten made sure to include a large ceramic jar and glass bottles in his banya dioramas, and Rose showed a large ceramic jar and a glass bottle in his South Carolina watercolor.[16]

The banza, played at funerals where the dead and spirits were honored, wasn't just a musical instrument. It was a well of souls: a ritual object constructed as a cosmogram. The neck bisecting the gourd from top to bottom is like the poteau-mitan, the line that draws the spirits; the body of the instrument is a circle, the realm to which the spirits are invited.

The cosmogram also appears on the body of the gourd, the well itself. Four of the holes carved into the side of the banza Schœlcher collected are made up of two intersecting lines. Functionally, they are sound holes; the sound that resonates within the body of the instrument emerges through them. But the maker chose to cut them in a shape that honors Legba and represents the intersection of realms. The shapes of these sound holes are remarkably similar to the intersecting lines that surround the skin soundboard on the banjo in the South Carolina watercolor.

There is a fifth hole on the body, a triangle with one tip pointing toward the top of the instrument, suggesting an upward arrow which symbolizes a return to heaven. The peghead also looks like an arrow, although the very tip of the instrument may have been broken off above where a hole was drilled.[17]

The banza also has a decorative pattern on the fingerboard made of five pointed ovals. The largest one runs down the center of the finger-board. Two smaller ovals traverse this large oval, connected at the center of the large oval by their tips. Another two ovals extend downward from the top of the largest oval at 30-degree angles and connect to the horizon-tal ovals' outer tips. Look at it one way and the five ovals form both a cross and a triangle, the cycle of life and the ascension to the spirit world. Look again, and eyes stare back. In many African cultures, eyes symbolically protect through their vision. Look at it again, and three leaves hang. Fall-ing leaves symbolize grief when used in anaforuana, Afro-Cuban ritual drawings similar to the veve images drawn on the floor of the oum'phor or on drums in Vodou. "Twa Fey," or "Three Leaves," is a Vodou song for Simbi, spirit of the water.[18]

Schœlcher took detailed notes during his trip to Africa, but if he asked the maker or player what the carving on the banza meant, either he didn't record the answer or his notes don't survive. But whether or not he knew what it meant, it might have been the carving on the banjo that caused Schœlcher to collect the specific konting he did. On the skin soundboard of the Senegalese instrument someone drew pointed ovals with a line through the middle. These also look like leaves or eyes, and are similar to the eyes found on Mande decorative arts.

Even if Schœlcher didn't record who he got the banza from, he wrote on the skin head, "Banza, an imitation of an African instrument widely used by the black people of Haiti." Did he mean to say that this instru-ment was the same as the African instrument? That it was trying to be that instrument, but not quite succeeding? Schœlcher was a lover of music and collector of musical instruments, so he would have seen the similarities and differences between the konting and the banza. But did he understand the reason for the differences, the use of different materials and a different construction? He might have assumed that because he found the banjo forty years after the end of slavery in Haiti, its maker was trying to recreate an African instrument but did so at too far a remove to know what it should look like. Yet the construction differences are fastidious and purposeful. Through them, we see that the banza wasn't just an imitation of an African instrument, but part of an ongoing tradition of instruments called banjos in the Americas.[19]

XV

Suriname, 1850

As Brother Gustav Ferdinand Jansa rode down the river in Suriname, the forests and marshes made way for vast fields of sugar, coffee, cotton, and rice. The curves of the river contrasted against the straight property lines of the plantations, blocks of fields, and long rows of crops. The sugar was tall; its long blades of green made it look like an exotic grass. The thinner blades of rice rustled in the wind, and the coffee and cotton sat low and shrublike. As he passed the fields, he saw men and women, enslaved laborers, farming the crops. They loaded the goods onto small boats bound for Paramaribo and onto large boats bound for Holland.

Unlike most white men in the colony, Jansa wasn't concerned with the goods. His focus was on the people working. Each one was a possible convert, a possible name to report back to Germany. But their forced labor and their status as property made his job harder. Brother Jansa was a Moravian missionary and, by 1850, he had been in Suriname for almost a decade. The first missionaries of the Moravian Church, or Unity of Brethren, had arrived in Suriname in 1735, almost 120 years after the establishment of the Dutch trading post. The first hundred years of missionary work had been slow and hard, with few opportunities to preach to the enslaved. Even to set foot on a plantation, the Brethren needed permission from the owner. That proved difficult, since the owners were often absentee landlords—like Hans Sloane had been for his properties in Jamaica—collecting profits in Europe while an overseer and a lawyer managed the plantation. The Moravian Brothers had to write to each owner and wait for an answer. Though slow and cumbersome, the tactic worked: in the previous decade, the Moravian missionaries had expanded their preaching from just six plantations to 130—more than a quarter of all the forced labor camps in the colony.[1]

Brother Jansa had arrived in Suriname in the early 1840s during this period of growth. Not only were the Moravians the only missionaries in the colony, but the government and the plantation owners and managers had become more eager for the education the missionaries provided. The British, French, Danish, and Spanish colonies (except for Cuba) had all abolished slavery by 1848, and neither the slaveowners nor the Moravians thought the Dutch colony could hold onto forced labor much longer. "One of the principal causes of the extension of our Missionary work . . . [is] to prepare the Negroes for emancipation, which after the late events cannot possibly be much longer withholden from them," the Brothers in Suriname informed the Church headquarters in 1848.[2]

The missionaries regularly reported to headquarters in Herrnhut, Germany, where the Church leaders compiled the information and kept church members and other missionaries abreast of what was happening at their missions around the world. The Brothers wrote inspirational documents that showed the good work they were doing and even provided reading material for Moravian children, which replaced forbidden works like John Milton's *Paradise Lost*. In the late 1700s, these would have been the reports that architect Benjamin Latrobe read while growing up in the Moravian Church.[3]

The reports also offered the Brothers the opportunity to compare notes on the problem they all faced: getting people seemingly without religion to join the Church. Even with the permission of the plantation owners, theoretical support from the government, and more missionaries, getting the Gospel to the people was hard. Brother Jansa couldn't hold a service at his home base on the former Charlottenburg plantation; the government forbade enslaved people from assembling on plantations to which they didn't belong for fear of insurrection or escape into the jungle. So, day after day for the eight years since he'd moved to Charlottenburg, Jansa got into a boat provided by the Mission and rowers took him up and down the rivers, creeks, and canals to plantations on his route, where he attempted to convert the people in bondage.[4]

On a day in late 1849 or early 1850, Brother Jansa arrived at the Vaderzorg plantation along the Matapica canal. He thought that preaching here might be easier than in some of the other places he'd been, since the enslaved men and women spent fewer hours of the day working on cotton plantations than on sugar plantations. Jansa's primary obstacle was simply getting people to listen to him, since those of African descent, free and enslaved, already had their own religions, forms of spirituality, and customs. He was asking them to open their lives to Jesus Christ and cast out their old idols.[5]

His boat pulled up to the shore of the Vaderzorg plantation. A large two- or three-story white clapboard house loomed over the fields, with ornate woodwork over the windows and on the balconies. The planter and his family, if he had one in the country, lived here, tended to by enslaved people trained as domestics. Sometimes, in place of a wife, a planter had an enslaved woman, a Misi, to run his household. A cotton plantation had fewer buildings than a sugar plantation, since the raw product required less processing before being loaded onto a ship. There might have been a wood-working shop, where the valued *Timmerneger* built barrels, repaired tools, and prepared materials for new construction. Then there were the cabins where the enslaved lived.

Somewhere close to the cabins, perhaps just outside them, Jansa finds a place to deliver his sermon. The longer he has been coming to a plantation, the more people attend his worship service. After his sermon, an old woman comes up to him and says, "I will attend divine service in the future. Please take my name down. But, my house still contains many idols. I cannot remove them, I live in constant and great dread of them."

Jansa has seen this over and over in Suriname: idolatry. Worshipping of objects. How can the people take Jesus into their lives if they worship false gods? It's only recently that they have started admitting to him that they have these objects and asking him to do something about them.

Jansa follows the woman to her cabin and in a dark corner finds *gosee patoe*, ghost pots. He's learned that in these vessels the spirits of a person's gods dwell, just as the vessels in Haitian Vodou capture spirits and gods. Could these be the same kind of pots that Schouten inserted into his dioramas, or John Rose saw in South Carolina? Sixty years earlier, a visitor to Suriname learned of the priestess Dasina, who was reported to have a secret chamber in her house with "little idols in human and animal shapes," and when she cured a sick person, "she consults her pot and her figures which are her oracles," and gives the person "water that is in the pot to drink."[6]

To Jansa, these pots are the devil's work. He is "amazed at witnessing the infatuation, the deplorable darkness into which man, gifted with reason and understanding by his Maker, may fall through the deceitfulness of sin and Satan." While the woman may have been fearful of the spirits in the *gosee patoe*, Brother Jansa does not fear pots. He orders them to be brought out from the cabin and smashed. He thinks the old woman looks pleased.

"Leriman!—Teacher—Come!" another voice calls to Jansa. "I also have such things in my house!"

He goes to her, taking her idols and smashing them, throwing them in the water, or burning them. Like brutal slaveowner Thomas Thistlewood one hundred years earlier in Jamaica, Brother Jansa hopes that destruction of the idols will end belief in what the European men deem African religions. In homes across the plantations he visits, Jansa finds jugs and jars that hold spirits, carved wooden dolls representing gods, and ornamented sticks used to ward off evil visitors. The missionaries sometimes call them obeahs, but also give other names. John Stedman had seen obias in Suriname, too: cloth pouches with pebbles, shells, hair, and fish bones worn for protection, pouches that were called gris-gris in Jamaica and wangas in Haiti. Jansa calls them all idols.[7]

In front of another cabin sits another older woman with gray hair. She rests her elbows on her knees, her head in her hands. This may be one of the few times a week she can rest like this. Perhaps she is contemplating what Jansa is doing to the spirits all around her. Perhaps she is thinking that it is his god who is false.

"Mother! Have you also such idolatrous and sinful things hidden in your house?" Jansa asks her in Sranan. The Brothers had to know the local language in order to preach.

"No, I have none of them!" she replies firmly. Maybe she doesn't want to give them up to this man. Maybe she doesn't want him in her home.

He doesn't care what she wants. "Very well, if that is the case, whatever of the kind I find there, I shall consider belonging to me!"

Jansa enters her home, and the woman follows. Everywhere he looks he seems to find idols. And he feels it is his duty to remove them, even though the woman did not request a cleansing as the other women did. He starts grabbing them; she starts to protest. Jansa knows how much these objects mean to her. She "did all she could to prevent my operations, seeing that her idols were in danger, in whom she had trusted all her lifetime, and to whom her whole soul was wedded." But even understanding their importance does not deter him.

"I am conferring a blessing on you," he says. These profane objects prevent her from "attending divine worship, and from the knowledge of the true God." He doesn't tell us if she responds. He grabs the idols and removes them, while she shakes her head.

"Seek salvation! God can remedy the power of sin and Satan!"

Her lips stay sealed.

When Jansa takes the idols from another unwilling woman, she cries and screams, "overcome by grief and terror." He still believes salvation will be the result. This won't be the last time he roots out idols and destroys them although their worshippers do not want to give them up. These women, these worshippers, cannot tell us about their idols, practices, and religion. Their experience lives on only in stories and traditions passed to younger generations.[8]

The Brethren understood that the idols were part of a spiritual practice, just like the dances and music of their would-be converts. During these religious ceremonies, the followers spoke Sranan, but sometimes, at the end, people sang their own music and German hymns translated into

Sranan. According to the reports of Brother Cranz, the dances showed that "not every vestige of paganism in and around the town has yet disappeared." And so, to truly become Christians, Blacks must "no longer take part in the dances and other riotous amusements of their countrymen," as Brother Stanke wrote to the Mission Board. Brother Cranz considered the dances "frenzied" and "satanic." Brother Jansa thought they bordered "on a sort of demoniacal possession," and said that the people "dance until they fall down in convulsions," which may have been when the spirit entered someone. These were wínti-dansí, Winti dances, which one Sranan dictionary translates as "African idolatry dances."[9]

Did the Moravian Brethren consider these dancers "heathen" because they fully understood that this was part of the religious practice of many Afro-Surinamese, a practice that the missionaries believed interfered with a person's ability to devote themselves to Jesus Christ? Or was it because their dances and idols were so different from how a white European believed religion should look? In another report from Suriname, the missionaries seem to suggest that those who have converted to Catholicism have been allowed to keep their idols, as if Catholicism and Winti are not mutually exclusive. Catholics have things that might be mistaken for idols, too. How is a rosary—beads that provide protection through prayer—any different from an obeah except for the belief that imbues it with power? How is a statue of the Virgin Mary any different from one of the "dolls" Brother Jansa burned? Catholics would say they are very different, but not everyone might see it that way.

Jansa must have felt that some of these idols had value, at least as a curiosity or evidence of Surinamese heathen religions. After visiting the Vaderzorg plantation, where he destroyed the idols of the enslaved women, he kept a carved figurine. He described it as a small female idol made of light wood. He preserved other idols and religious objects, too.

♌

In 1857, Brother Jansa arrived in Holland with his wife for a break from their mission work, and for a higher purpose. He was traveling to Herrn-

hut to be ordained as a bishop. At some point, he must have made a connection with Leopold von Ledebur, the director of the Royal Cabinet of
Antiquities, Coins, and Art in Berlin. Von Ledebur took the post in 1829
and bought entire cabinets of curiosities containing man-made objects
from different cultures around the world, while placing paintings and
sculpture in a newly constructed museum building. In 1855, the Neues
Museum opened in Berlin to house the ethnographic collections. Perhaps
Brother Jansa had already heard about von Ledebur's interest in world
cultures and brought the idols to Germany in anticipation of giving them
to the museum. Jansa could also have learned about the museum once he
reached Germany, and sent items after he returned to Suriname. Or he
gave someone objects as a gift and that person gave them to the museum.
However it happened, by 1861, at least nine items that Jansa had collected
were in the Neues Museum's collection.[10]

The religious significance of eight of those items is clearly spelled out
in the collection notes. Item one is a whisk: palm fibers wrapped in red
cloth with cowrie shells and bells sewn on. It's given the name obia and
wards off evil spirits. Another whisk is called an aweya; it is made of palm
fronds, with a carved wooden handle, and is used to drive away evil spirits during the "idol worship" of the Blacks in Suriname. Another obia is
a necklace imbued with magic, made with bells, nutshells, and a small
carved figure; this one is "only worn by priests." Another necklace is made
of a cow horn and is used for "magic." There are two carved wooden
idols, one from the plantation Vaderzorg. Another item is a pantje, a red
square of cloth with a cross pattern sewn into the middle and adorned
with shells and bells, which serves as a priest's robe or apron. There is also
a priest's cap, intricately knitted with zigzag, chevron, and cosmogram-
cross patterns in white yarn with red cloth accents, as well as sewn-on
bells and cowrie shells.

The ninth item is a panja. A banjo. "Panja, 4-stringed string instrument, particular to the death ceremonies and to the song: Ananhitori."
Unlike Sloane, Stedman, or abolitionist Victor Schœlcher, Jansa clearly
understood the religious value of the banjo. And that is why he had to
confiscate it.

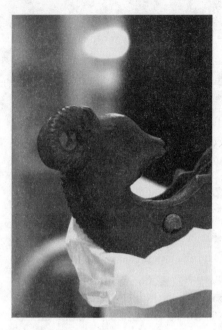

The carved peghead of the instrument Jansa collected. Its accompanying note says, "Panja, 4-stringed string instrument, particular to the death ceremonies and to the song: Ananhitori."

Staatliche Museen zu Berlin, Preußischer Kulturbesitz, Ethnologisches Museum (photo by Kristina Gaddy)

A detail of the S-holes carved in the side of the panja's calabash body. This banjo was collected by Brother Gustav Ferdinand Jansa before 1861.

Staatliche Museen zu Berlin, Preußischer Kulturbesitz, Ethnologisches Museum (photo by Kristina Gaddy)

Jansa obtained the panja seventy years after Stedman collected the Creole-bania, but the two instruments are remarkably similar. They are the same size, built with calabashes of similar diameter and necks of almost the same length. They both have four strings, three long and one short. The wooden necks are thin and long, the top flattened into a fingerboard where a player once pressed down the strings to sound notes. In both, the neck extends through the calabash, which was cut in half lengthwise not quite on the diameter. A skin replaces the area where the curve of the fruit once was, stretched tightly and pinned down with small wooden tacks. Both have S-shapes carved into the calabash body, holes that allow sound waves to emerge, similar to the f-holes of a violin. They both also have carvings where the strings end at the pegbox, though the Creole-bania's is broken-off and indiscernible. The panja's is carved into a ram's head, with a delicate nose, two eyes watching over the instrument, ears, and rippled horns. Both instruments were made by expert craftsmen who had the knowledge and tools not only to carve the wood but to create beading at the edge of the pegbox. These similarities suggest that the tradition of banjo-making remained relatively unchanged for at least two generations, an amazing fact given the decimation of human lives that cut off generations and their knowledge from each other during slavery.

Although the Creole-bania and the panja look different from the gourd-bodied, flat-necked banza that Schœlcher collected in Haiti, the construction of all three instruments is fundamentally the same. They all form a cosmogram, the intersection of the earthly and spiritual planes. On all, the side of the fruit is cut off and covered with skin, and the neck enters and bisects the fruit. Like drums, they are instruments that conjure spirits and, with their construction, might have been able to hold spirits, too. All three instruments are banjos; all three are wells of souls.

Brother Jansa must have thought he was doing a sacred act when he took the panja from its owner. He was saving the person from the idol worship that undermined Christianity. Regardless of his motivation, when Jansa took the panja, he also ended up preserving it.[11]

XVI

Paramaribo, Suriname, 1855

In contrast to the views of the Moravian Brethren, Hendrik Charles Focke thought that the Surinamese dances "banja and soesa are as much poetry as song, as much song as dance," and he wanted to tell people about their beauty.

Focke was born in Paramaribo in 1802 to a wealthy family. Like artist Gerrit Schouten, Focke's mother was a free woman of color and his father was from Holland. And like Schouten, the fact that Focke had African ancestors meant he was forced to grow up in a liminal space in Paramaribo, although this space was expanding. As the demographics of Suriname shifted in the 1800s, with a growing number of free people of color, so did the policies and laws related to race relations. In the 1700s, it was primarily white men who freed their slaves—especially enslaved people who were also their families, as John Gabriel Stedman had tried to do for Joanna and Johnny. By the 1800s, those who had been freed could purchase their family members' freedom. By 1850, the enslaved population in Suriname had decreased to the lowest level since the beginning of the 1700s, while the free non-white population continued to increase.[1]

Slowly, Schouten and Focke gained more rights. If someone had been born free, like Schouten or Focke, they were, by the dawn of the nine-

teenth century, supposed to have the same rights as someone the government considered white. The evening curfew that Schouten had to abide
by ended in 1799. Schools in Suriname began accepting free children,
no matter their background. Some could further their education in the
Netherlands, and study medicine or law. While Schouten never had the
opportunity to study in Amsterdam like his mother, Focke's mother, Wilhelmina, sent her son to the Netherlands, where he earned a law degree.[2]

Focke returned to Suriname, perhaps because he felt a sense of duty to
uplift and preserve what he must have experienced as Suriname's unique-
ness after his time in Utrecht, where he would have faced greater racism
than at home. After all, no matter how wealthy he and his mother were,
in other countries they were foremost people of color.

Although Focke was born in Paramaribo, he probably didn't consider
himself a *Krióro*, or Creole, since he defined that term as "the children of
our slaves." He probably didn't call himself *swart*, or Black, since he used
that word to refer to those he also referred to as *negers*, which generally
implied a person who was enslaved. Perhaps all he needed to be called
was Surinamese, and he had great pride in it.

He wanted to tell people about the worth of Suriname's unique creolized culture. In 1855, he wrote an article on "Music of the Surinamese
Blacks." He was interested in music and theater, and perhaps after his experiences abroad, he felt that in Suriname, the Black inhabitants had created
something worth documenting. He—like Brother Jansa and the Moravian
Brethren, the plantation owners, and, most importantly, the people who
remained enslaved—could feel that change was coming. Perhaps Focke
thought that emancipation would change the cultural landscape, and
he wanted to document it before that shift occurred. He may have also
wanted to acknowledge what the Blacks in Suriname had created as a way
to push back against the racism he surely experienced himself.[3]

In his writing on Surinamese music, Focke doesn't only call the banya
(he spells it banja) a dance or an instrument. For him, the banya was the
"typical, characteristic folk music of our Black inhabitants," the music created by those who had lived in Suriname for generations. He wanted to
defend it against the music of recently transplanted Africans, as he called

them. Focke may not literally have meant the people who were born in Africa, but those people who prioritized their African heritage over a Surinamese identity. By 1814, the US, Britain, the Netherlands, and Spain had all banned international slave trading, but people continued to be forcibly taken from Africa to Suriname until 1825. Focke's reaction to "the song of the transplanted Africans" was what one would expect from a white European visitor: he wrote that it "hardly deserves that name: the wild sounds seem more like accidental compositions of incoherent tones than a melody." He designated "Africans" into groupings such as Coromantis, Papas, and Loangos, and noted that different "tribes" had different music. Focke didn't think a "civilized ear" could recognize the variations between them. Since Focke didn't take the time to analyze them, we can't compare them to the banya music he did describe in detail.[4]

Focke offered his description of banya music with care and consideration, noting the nuances of the performance. He wrote about African American music as few other observers had.

He didn't offer the names of the best trokiman, or singing storyteller, or the best drummer he knew. He didn't describe any one performer in detail. Instead, for him, the dance was so ubiquitous among the Blacks in Suriname that it was almost as if specific musicians and dancers were interchangeable. The way he described the scene, it could have been anywhere in Suriname: in a courtyard in Paramaribo, on the outskirts of town, or at the houses of the enslaved on a plantation upriver.

When Focke sat down to write his article, he might have imagined the banya as he once saw it. If his mother had allowed it, the thirty-seven enslaved people she owned may have danced in her yard. Perhaps Pari, one of the oldest women Wilhelmina Focke owned, is the trokiman. Maybe Focke imagines Clara and William dancing, with Pari's daughters Helena and Ida joining in. Is Andries, who was born in the 1700s, playing the drum? Maybe Andries is too old and no longer has the energy required to drum for hours. But maybe he has taught Clara's son December to drum. Maybe neighbors that Focke doesn't know join in.

The drums Focke sees are like those in Schouten's diorama from forty years earlier. A man sits astride the long drum, playing with both hands.

Jacob Marius Adriaan Martini van Geffen's 1850s watercolor with the caption "A slave dancing the banja."

Rijksmuseum, Object number RP-T-1994-281-27

Focke notes that he hits "sometimes with the whole hand, either flat or rounded, hitting on the rim or in the middle"—techniques a drummer uses to create different pitches. He plays "with great skill and demonstrates an unshakable sense of rhythm." Another man sits next to him with a smaller drum, playing a rhythm with two sticks. Sometimes these smaller drums, which always sit upright, are played with the hands, too. This rhythm is "sharp and precise," playing the eighth notes of the music, a driving beat that would keep the song moving forward. When a drummer gets tired, another takes his place. A woman singer shakes a saka, a calabash filled with "pits, bones, and stones," with a stick bisecting the fruit to make a handle. With her shakes, she marks the eighth notes of the music. Another person might play the joro-joro, or "a string of shells split in half and strung together."[5]

Just as in the banya dances Schouten saw, a man and a woman dance opposite each other. Sometimes a third person joins in, to encourage, approve, or provide acclaim to the dancers with a few steps before returning to the bystanders. Those not dancing wave pieces of cloth "in a continuous undulating or swinging motion."

One woman steps to the front. As in Schouten's diorama, she is wearing the most vibrant outfit. In Jacob Marius Adriaan Martini van Geffen's 1850 watercolor, she wears a piece of red cloth over her shoulder and holds a string of shells between her hands, which she shakes to the beat of the drums.[6]

As the trokiman, the leader of the chorus and the dance, she sings out a line: "Arabi na' Pambo ben senni njoesoe: Soesoetei! No broko hatti o: alla joe kondre de na reti kabà." "Arabi and Pambo have announced: Society! Do not worry: your whole country is in order and rest." Each song is like this, says Focke: just a phrase, a poem. The chorus of female singers echoes the line, in unison, without harmonies or second voices. This song invokes Arabi and Pambo, Maroon leaders who created communities of free Blacks in the jungles of Suriname in the eighteenth century. The peace they signed with the Dutch, in which they agreed to refrain from attacking plantations to liberate more enslaved people, might be the "order and rest" the song refers to. It may also be a sarcastic political commentary, in that the treaty gave "order and rest" to the whites, while many more people remained enslaved. The conflicts between the Surinamese government and the Maroons didn't end with that treaty. Another banya lyric includes the line "Let's run away, o brother!" and during one banya dance, every enslaved person on a plantation decided to manumit themselves by running away into the jungle. So perhaps the lyrics to the Arabi and Pambo song had another meaning: don't worry, as long as the Maroons are here, you can escape into the jungle and be free.[7]

Although Focke transcribed the music he heard and placed the song into Western musical notation, the songs don't quite fit inside that rigid structure. Assigning notes to even beats often proves difficult with African-derived music, where stresses don't always fall on those divisions. The notes want to stretch out across the beats to which they've been assigned, and even across the measures Focke has designated. The song wants to be repeated, flowing over and over again with stresses here and pauses there that Focke can't capture. The song is also in a minor key, creating a darker, more somber tonality.

♫

Language, and precision of language, fascinated Focke as much as theater and music. While he was working on his article about music among the Surinamese Blacks, he was also working on a Sranan–Dutch dictionary—the first one ever compiled, even though the Dutch had been in Suriname for hundreds of years. Some people believed that what they heard Blacks in Suriname speaking was pidgin, a simplified version of a language which is used to communicate between two people or groups of people who don't speak the same language. Pidgins developed quickly on both sides of the Atlantic, not only as a way for enslavers, slaveowners, and plantation managers to speak to the enslaved, but for people from different African language communities to speak to one another. A pidgin becomes a creole language when it has native speakers and develops established grammar and unique vocabulary that may not be part of the language from which the creole was primarily derived. Although Dutch was the official language in Suriname, Sranan formed as an English-based creole with other European and African languages mixed in.[8]

Just as Focke was compelled to write about banya dances out of national pride, he likely thought that the changes coming to Suriname would alter Sranan. As enslaved people became free, their education, work, and prestige would come with learning Dutch. More Dutch words would be introduced into Sranan; people might even abandon Sranan in favor of Dutch.

In Focke's dictionary, the first definition for banya is "a sort of dance of the Blacks." The second definition explains why there is no banjo among the instruments accompanying it in the article he wrote; the banya is also, he writes, "An instrument (a zither of the Blacks) previously used for this [dance]." In C. L. Schumann's 1783 Sranan–German dictionary, banja is defined as "An instrument with gut strings, zither of the Blacks." Had missionaries like Brother Jansa erased the banjo from the banya dance because they saw it as a profane instrument and a dangerous part of the

Winti religion? Or had it fallen into more secular use, and was not used for banya dances any longer? Just as Focke's first definition doesn't expand on banya as a dance, his second doesn't expand on banya as an instrument.[9]

Focke mentioned the African dances in his article on Surinamese music, but failed to specifically mention wintí-dansí, which he defines in his dictionary as an "idol-worship dance." When he dismissed the African dances, he may have been referring to Winti dances, since his dictionary defines Winti as an African religion. Admitting that people in Paramaribo still practiced Winti might have undermined his argument about the cultural development of Suriname. Focke was very likely a member of the Moravian Church, the largest church in Suriname, and could have agreed with Brother Jansa that these idol-worship dances were improper and even dangerous. Since Focke doesn't address Winti dances directly, it's hard to see where Winti ends and banya begins. Could someone dance a wintí-dansí and a banya? Focke wrote that banya is folk music—that is, secular music. And although Focke doesn't include the definitions in his dictionary, there are many banya dances that are religious. The yorka-banya was done for the ancestors, yorka meaning ghost or ancestral spirits. The bakafutu-banya was connected to Winti and possession by spirits. Baka futu translates as "back foot," but baka is also the word for malevolent spirits in the Vodou religion in Haiti.[10]

The German-born August Kappler, who stayed in Suriname from 1836 to 1841 and returned in 1842, knew that dances could be both secular and religious: "They have many dances that I don't know by name, some of which are connected to their fetish-worship and are strictly forbidden by the government." On Sundays, around the plantation cabins, people would dance to the sound of drums and shovels beaten with pieces of iron. Those who sang also danced around each other, he wrote, while other members of the chorus stood, swaying on their feet. To the beat of the drums, a song leader would sing a verse that the chorus would repeat as others danced. Kappler didn't understand the songs, but he did understand that they had satirical content that made the dancers and spectators laugh. He also saw that dances on the anniversary of a death were more festive. People wore special clothes, baked cakes, and had fresh meat to eat. The biggest dances were those held at the New Year, when everyone received liquor and wine.[11]

Focke explained that he believed banya music was not only Surinamese but was "unique to Black creoles. This music seems to characterize the festivities of the Blacks, with only slight changes and differences, not only in this colony, but in French, British, and Spanish colonies, from Brazil to the US south." He thought the banya music was "substantially the same as the Bamboula of the French colonies and the Banjo of the southern states of North America." Although others called the bamboula and banjo instruments, Focke thought they were styles of music, and maybe dance. In Suriname, the banya instrument took its name from the dance, and perhaps there was once a banjar or banjo dance in North America.

♫

Brother Jansa returned to Suriname in the fall of 1858 to continue the Moravians' mission of bringing Jesus to all those who had not yet accepted him, and the mission was growing stronger. A year after Jansa returned, Brother Van Calker wrote that he'd heard a rumor that Winti priestess Hendrina de Parra wanted to "give her name," that is, relinquish her religion. The Brothers believed that "others will follow her example." According to Van Calker, she was a drummer for dances held on the outskirts of town and "for this occupation, she possessed a degree of skill, to which not everyone can attain, and was therefore a person of some consequence, so that her conversion is looked on by the heathen as a great loss."[12]

Jansa continued destroying idols, and—at least according to Jansa— women sometimes thanked him for it. But slavery was still hindering the Moravians' work. It "is so decided an obstacle to [a Christian life] . . . that its abolition as speedily as possible is much to be desired," the Brethren in Suriname wrote to Herrnhut. The enslaved had no right to go to church on Sunday and observe the Sabbath, no right to live with their spouse, no right to go to school and learn to read and write. For the enslaved, the worst part might have been the unspoken sense of imminent emancipation not yet fulfilled. In Suriname, a "peculiar state of feeling pervades the population, from the fact that emancipation is fully expected to take place, and yet is postponed from year to year," wrote the Brethren.[13]

The world was changing. Slavery was ending, industrialization had begun, and in the United States, the banjo was becoming something new. Focke may have known this. He didn't know of anyone collecting Black folk music in North America or the Caribbean, and, as a music lover, he thought this was a shame. He wanted to compare the Surinamese banya music he treasured to that of neighboring countries. The only comparison to his own efforts that he could think of was the work of Louis Moreau Gottschalk, a composer born in New Orleans who had just finished writing a suite inspired by his hometown. Gottschalk's music was composition, not transcription, and Focke admitted, "I cannot judge to what extent the basic melody in Gottschalk's Bananier is truth, imitation, embellishment, or pure invention."[14]

INTERLUDE

⌀

NOW, WHEN I LOOK AT THE WATERCOLOR FROM SOUTH CAROLINA, I
see a lineage of traditions extending backward and forward in time.
I imagine Mr. Baptiste, William, Lincoln and George, King Charles
and Jackey Quakenboss, Hendrina de Parra, and all the named and
unnamed musicians I've come across in my research. I hear choruses
of voices in minor tonalities, the undulating tones of drums, and the
melodies of a gourd banjo. I see people dancing calendas, banyapreis,
and Vodou ceremonies. I feel resilience and courage in the face of
great oppression.

Even though we don't know the year, the exact time, or the exact
place of Rose's watercolor, looking at every detail—and comparing
those details to other accounts and what scholars now know about
different African cultural traditions—brings the lives of the enslaved
in North America into sharper focus.[1]

The women dance with cloths. In Kongo, Yoruba, and other West
and Central African communities, people honor ancestors with cloth,
and perhaps because this tradition is so widespread in Africa, the
practice of waving a cloth while dancing is prevalent across the Americas. In Schouten's dioramas, women dance with a cloth held between

their hands, and in banyapreis performed today in Suriname, women dance with cloths held in both hands or by a single hand. Architect Benjamin Latrobe saw women dancing with cloths in New Orleans, as did government official Moreau de Saint-Méry in Saint-Domingue. The cloth the women wear tied around their heads in South Carolina could have meaning, too. In the banya, handkerchiefs are representative of events or proverbs, enabling dancers and actors to communicate without words during the play. The pattern on the cloth, or the way a headscarf is folded, determines the meaning.[2]

The man dances with a dowel. In 1730s' New York City, newspaper editor James Alexander saw "some [men] exercising the Cudgel, and some of them small Sticks in imitation of the short Pike." They could have been stick fighting, as calendas were sometimes described. In a dance with women, the men may have been using the staffs as conjure sticks to agitate spirits. Like the pillar of the oum'phor or the handle of the asson rattle in Vodou rites, the stick was a way for spirits to enter the earthly realm from above and below. It was a symbol of power, and the person who carried it had the ability to do magic. In the coastal regions of South Carolina and Georgia, sticks carved into the shapes of snakes, lizards, or alligators were used by conjurers. In St. Vincent, traveler Charles Day observed a man dancing with a magical stick during a Willy or Jumbee dance.[3]

A man stands, clad in a red jacket. In the Yoruba religion, the deity of thunder and lightning, Shango, is represented by the color red, but red is also closely tied to Kongo traditions. Kongo chieftains were wrapped in red cloth before burial, and in Kongo spiritualism "red represents the convergence of invisible forces with the lives of ordinary people." The Vodou King in Moreau de Saint-Méry's narrative wore a red crown, and the Kownu's costume in Schouten's dioramas is the red regimentals reminiscent of British soldiers' uniforms, like the King of Pinkster's clothes in Albany.[4]

Next to the man in red is a woman in white. In writing about the Gullah, historian Margaret Washington Creel notes the early presence of "Upper Guinea Africans of the Senegambia and Windward

Coasts," who almost universally belonged to the Poro and Sande
secret societies. Female Sande initiates wore white head ties, and
"the Mazowo (high priestess) always wore white." White is also associated with the land of the dead and the Yoruba deity of creativity,
Obatala. In the watercolor from Saint-Domingue showing a dance at
the burial ground outside Le Cap, almost everyone wears white. In
the banya, the Afrankeri or trokiman—the storyteller who explains
and defends high morals to the observers—can be distinguished
by the fact that she has the most elegant outfit. In other places, a
clean white outfit may have been the best dress a woman owned.
In Schouten's dioramas, the Afrankeri stands centrally in the scene
with her hands clasped but is not engaged in the dance, just as in the
South Carolina watercolor, the woman in white looks on but does
not dance.[5]

Historian Sylviane Diouf writes that "the Yoruba, the Congolese,
and the Angolans" had a "strong reliance on rapid drumming, call
and response, group singing, and short melodic lines." Latrobe, in
New Orleans, heard a man singing in a language neither English
nor French, to which a chorus of women responded. In Saint-
Domingue, Moreau de Saint-Méry heard women forming "a chorus
that responds to one or two principal female singers whose striking
voices repeat or improvise a song." In New York during Pinkster,
drummer Jackey Quakenboss cried out in time to the drumming,
"Hi-a-bomba, bomba, bomba," which was then called back by the
women who were not dancing. Sloane had Mr. Baptiste transcribe
lyrics in Jamaica: "Ho-baognion, Ho-baognion, Ho-ba, Ho-ba,
ognion, ognion," which when sung sounds more like, "Oh-Bania,
Oh-Bania, Oh-Ba, Oh-Ba, On-ya, On-ya," which might connect the
banya music to the oldest image of the banjo.[6]

In Rose's watercolor, the drum is not a long, hollowed-out log, as
in so many descriptions and images, but small enough to fit between
the percussionist's legs. Maybe it is made of a gourd—all that the
musician could get away with after the Stono Rebellion and the pro-
hibition of drums in the colony. He plays it with two sticks, similar

to the qua-qua Stedman saw in Suriname. Anthropologists Melville and Frances Herskovits saw the qua-qua as a central part of what they called Koromanti dances in Paramaribo in the late 1920s. *Quaqua* was also a Dutch word used to describe people from the Ivory Coast, although in her book on Schouten's dioramas, Clazien Medendorp writes that the quaqua drum is from Kongo. The drum was more than just a provider of rhythm for the dancers. In *Slave Religion*, Albert Raboteau writes, "Among the Yoruba and Son, the orisha and the vodun are called to take possession of their devotees by the songs and the drumming of the cult group, each of the gods having his or her own songs and rhythms." Historian Mary Turner notes that missionaries in Jamaica found that "drumming and dancing were intertwined at the religious practices they were determined to root out." In *Creole Religions of the Caribbean*, Margarite Fernández Olmos and Lizabeth Paravisini-Gebert write that "consecrated drums and the polyrhythmic percussion they produce, along with clapping, the spoken or sung word in repeated chants and dance (rhythms and dance are coded to the identities of the gods that are summoned in ceremonies and rituals), produce an altered focus on consciousness that beckons the supernatural entities and communicates between worlds."[7]

A terra cotta jug sits in the corner of Rose's watercolor and every one of Schouten's banya dioramas. Brother Jansa knew of vessels that held spirits and gods, which he heard called *gosee patoe*. In Haitian Vodou, the priest and priestess can summon the gods and spirits to enter the oum'phor, but once the spirits arrive, they need a place to reside. Followers can be "mounted" by a spirit, but the spirits can also enter a govi, a terra cotta pot that serves as their home. Pots are one of the minkisi containers in Kongo spiritual practice, "material conduits through which the living were assisted by the dead." Each nkisi—which Robert Farris Thompson explains can be "leaves, shells, packets, sachets, bags, ceramic vessels, wooden images, statuette, cloth bundles, among other objects"—contains medicine and a soul. In Central Africa, ceramic bowls and jars are used for preparation of medicine and to induce spirits.[8]

The banjo: wood, gourd, skin, and tacks constructed in a specific way, representing the Kongo cosmogram or dikenga. The cosmogram is also "the voyage of the soul" through four phases of life: birth, the peak of life, death, and the afterlife. Visually, this can be represented by two intersecting lines or two intersecting lines within a circle, but it can also be represented by actions. In the South Carolina Lowcountry, there is a tradition of passing a baby over a casket. At the New York African Burial Ground, "more than 90 percent of the remains . . . are oriented to the west," symbolizing a voyage to the next phase of life.[9]

We don't know whether the people gathered to dance in South Carolina would have called this a calinda, a banyaprei, a Congo dance, or something else entirely. We do know that the banjo was a central part of these dances and rituals from South America, through the Caribbean, to northern parts of North America.

The South Carolina watercolor is filled with meaning. It tells us not just about the time and place in which it was created, but also illustrates the commonalities between the cultures of African descendants across the Americas. Although the dances in the watercolor and Gerrit Schouten's dioramas are nearly identical, it wasn't until I started reading about the component parts of the banya and understanding how those related to African and African American spiritual beliefs that I felt better able to understand early accounts of the banjo. What John Rose observed in South Carolina wasn't just one dance that happened a single time, but a tradition that extended at least as far south as Suriname and at least as far north as New York. When I learned that the man in the red jacket in Schouten's dioramas was the Kownu—the King—and de Kownu could have been the origin of the word Jonkonnu, and also that King Charles wore a red coat and a man had been buried in the New York African Burial Ground in a red coat, I felt like a conspiracy theorist.

Facts and accounts I discovered helped me figure out the history and cultural context of the banjo—that wasn't a conspiracy. But slowly, things I saw and experienced outside my research on this

book became connected to much deeper meanings, much deeper histories. In researching an article about a ghost story from Maryland's
Eastern Shore—where banjos have been documented since the mid-
1700s—I found a reference to the belief that witches could "turn people into horses and ride on them" and that one man "died from the
effects of such a trip, the clay being found under his finger and toe
nails." In *Tell My Horse: Voodoo Life in Haiti and Jamaica*, Zora Neale
Hurston explains that in Vodou, the god Guede "manifests himself
by 'mounting' a subject as a rider mounts a horse. . . . [the person
mounted] is the horse of the loa [Guede] until the spirit departs." A
person who has unwillingly become a horse must go to a hougan, or
priest, to get rid of the spirit.[10]

I watched films produced by Val Lewton, including the 1943 *I
Walked with a Zombie*, directed by Jacques Tourneur. A young nurse
arrives on a Caribbean island to take care of a sugar planter's wife
who seems to be in a sort of walking coma. Vodou plays a central
role in the plot. The practitioners wear patches of cloth for protection at ceremonies, like the patches of cloth Moreau de Saint-Méry
heard about in the Vodou ceremony on Saint-Domingue. Late at
night, the nurse hears drumming coming across the sugar fields,
and the drums seem to be able to control the behavior not only of
the Black worshippers but of the white landowners too. That power
imbalance was a fear of whites for as long as slavery existed in the
Americas and was why drumming and dancing were banned.

I live in Baltimore, where for the last six years almost a person a
day has been killed. The victims in over 70 percent of these murders
are identified as Black, and across the city families and friends set up
memorials for someone they've lost. They put out balloons and flowers, and bottles, which I had always assumed were just the deceased's
favorite drink. Schouten made sure to include glass bottles in his
banya dioramas, and bottles are common grave decorations among
the Gullah of South Carolina. American material culture expert John
Michael Vlach writes that many "grave goods in Afro-American

cemeteries . . . are associated with water or can be interpreted as water symbols." In Haiti and Suriname, bottles can capture spirits.[11]

My mother immigrated to the US from Sweden the year before I was born, and my father's family have lived in Virginia and the Carolinas since the 1700s. I know that as a white woman growing up in the US with this background, more cultures exist outside my world of experience than within it. However, in this country, and in other countries colonized by western European nations, I have been told that my narrow slice of European-derived culture is the one worth learning about. We don't often acknowledge that our folklore and ghost stories may have origins in African and African American culture. We don't see Vodou as a legitimate religion, derived from religious practices in what is today Benin, combined with other religions and spiritual practices from Africa and further syncretized with Christianity in Haiti. Instead, we see zombies and witchcraft. And when I saw a bottle as part of a memorial, I didn't think: this could be a part of an African American tradition that dates back hundreds of years here in the Americas, preceded by similar traditions in Africa. Our schools don't teach us this history.

These experiences I've told you about, reader, may not be as connected as I think they are. I might be seeing deep references to Black history and culture when there are none. Witches turning people into horses might be part of European folklore. Jacques Tourneur and Val Lewton were not Vodou practitioners, so what did they really know about the religion? That bottle of Crown Royal I saw on the street might have been a victim's favorite drink. But what I realized, once I had seen Gerrit Schouten's diorama, was that I had to open my eyes to the reality that Black history and culture have been so suppressed and misunderstood by white culture that I wouldn't see connections unless I looked hard. But why had they been suppressed? How had we lost all this information? Why was it that an instrument constantly described as "Black" and "African" came to be thought of as a white instrument? The story can't stop here.

3rd Movement

•

"We are all born into histories, worlds existing
before us."

—Sarah M. Broom, *The Yellow House*

XVII

New York City, 1840

On a cold night in January 1840, people in Lower Manhattan crowded into the Bowery Circus. They had been promised a variety show. Mr. Glenroy would ride bareback on his Arabian horse around the ring and Mr. Bacon would also showcase his horsemanship. There would be a strong man, a clown, and gymnastics exercises done by the whole troupe. If the entertainers were lucky, ladies would crowd the box seats, where they'd paid fifty cents to sit, smiling and waving handkerchiefs during the performance. If the performers were unlucky, the crowd in the pit, where seats cost only twenty-five cents, would get rowdy.[1]

Sometime during the show, between two of the acts, Joel Walker Sweeney stepped on stage. His striped pants, checked vest, billowy white shirt, and tied cravat were his distinguishing look, but even without the outfit, people noticed the instrument in his hands, the instrument that made him famous. He strummed and sang:

Now white folks, I'd hah you to know
Dare is no music like de old banjo.
And if you want to hear it ring.
Just watch dis finger on de string.

Then came the chorus, which the crowd might sing along to:

> Oh, Jenny get your hoe cake done, my dear.
> Oh! Jenny get your hoe cake done, love!

The audiences loved Sweeney and what the *New-York Daily Herald* advertised as "his Etheopian melodies upon the banjo." They didn't mind that he blackened his face with burnt cork and imitated Black language, clothing, and music for his act. They probably preferred it that way. Dick Pelham was on the same bill with his dance-and-music "Negro extravaganza." Even though Black performing artists could have been hired, these performances were meant as white interpretations of Black culture for fellow whites. Sweeney and Pelham were two early Blackface Minstrels, performers who capitalized on the easy-to-see-through illusion of Black culture.[2]

They were creating a craze, an American popular music phenomenon, even though what they were doing wasn't necessarily new. White audiences could have seen impersonations of Black song and dance in London done by Charles Dibdin, in Saint-Domingue at *Jeannot et Thérèse*, or in New York forty years earlier on Pinxter Monday, just to name a few performances. In 1819, architect Benjamin Latrobe didn't know what the instrument he saw in Congo Square was, but around the same time, the banjo started to become a symbol of Black culture. Not long after that, it became a standard subject in songs that were presented as authentically Black. Dibdin referenced the banjer in his songs, which were published in England and reprinted in the United States in the late 1790s. "The Bonja Song," published sometime in the late 1810s or early 1820s, used one of the many names for the banjo with the lyrics, "Me want no joys, no ills, no fear, but on my Bonja play."[3]

None of these performances or songs were as popular as "Coal Black Rose," published and performed in New York in the late 1820s. The song made it all the way to Texas, where someone, more than seventy years after the fact, remembered a white judge named Robert McAlpin Williamson singing the song adapted for the banjo. Although Blackface musicians performed these songs as they traveled with circuses across the country, the publication of sheet music meant that people could learn and play the repertoire anywhere that roads and boats brought goods—from the East Coast to the Appalachians to the Mississippi River.[4]

The sheet music for "Coal Black Rose" included a guitar part (along with a piano part), lyrics about the banjo, and an illustration of a heavily caricatured Black man holding a banjo. Although the instrument was probably only an estimation of what a banjo looked like rather than a careful, true-to-life rendering, the instrument is small, like the banjo Hans Sloane saw in Jamaica 150 years earlier, and has a rounded back, suggesting it is a gourd banjo. The man in the drawing is not holding the instrument across his lap, like the man in the South Carolina watercolor, or high on his chest, like the man in Gerrit Schouten's diorama. Instead, the banjo is placed phallically between the man's legs, creating a stereotyped image of an oversexualized Black man. The popularity of "Coal Black Rose" was followed by T. D. Rice's "Jump Jim Crow" in the early 1830s, "Zip Coon" in 1834, "Sitting on a Rail" in 1836, and "Jenny, Get Your Hoe Cake Done" in 1840. All were catchy, earwormy songs sung by professional Blackface performers as part of theatrical acts and during interludes in circus performances.[5]

Blackface was mockery. The character of Jim Crow was supposed to be a slave on a Southern plantation, ragged and rough, while Zip Coon was a well-dressed dandy, a foolish Black man trying to be higher than his station. Perhaps white New Yorkers coming to the performances on the Bowery imagined Zip Coon as one of the free Black men in the city. In the Jacksonian era, the white working class was concerned about their freedoms and rights, and creating stereotypes of Blacks on stage helped to justify racial inequity and pro-slavery sentiments. In 1837, on a stage in Baltimore, T. D. Rice told the audience, "I effectually proved that negroes are essentially an inferior species of the human family, and they ought to remain slaves." Although Blacks might be allowed to buy tickets to a separate section in the third tier, this entertainment was not for them.[6]

Paradoxically, Blackface included flattery. Sweeney, Pelham, and their fellow Blackface Minstrels did their best to promote themselves by saying that they played on a "real banjo" or sang a "celebrated Negro melody."

Rice claimed that the song and dance steps of Jim Crow came from a Black man working in a stable he'd come across while on tour. All of these performers could have seen Black dances in New York markets or heard of the old Pinkster celebrations in Albany.[7]

The dialect they used was also meant to be authentic. Although the Blackface performers may not have been from the South, they could have heard Black English vernacular from any of the working-class Blacks in New York City, or they could have gleaned an exaggeration of it from newspaper articles, novels, and other printed documents where writers transcribed what they thought of as Black speech. On stage, the performers were trying to create characters, but in order to be good performers, they had to make their characters seem true to life. These dialects, although derived from creole languages that had their own syntax and grammar, were also used for comic effect, conveying an image of uneducated Blacks. Characters became caricatures.[8]

Joel Sweeney's relationship to the banjo was bound up in a mythology of authenticity, made up partially by himself, partially by others. This much is true: Sweeney was white and grew up in central Virginia, and he learned to play the banjo from an enslaved man. He might have been playing in the early 1820s as a teenager. Some said his first banjo was made of a gourd with four strings, like the ones people of African descent were playing, and that he eventually made one by attaching a neck to a wooden hoop and adding another long string, thus creating the five-string, wooden-rimmed banjo. Others said that joining the neck to a wooden hoop or "rim of a sugar box" was already common among Black players. Other white men had heard people play the banjo and may even have played one, but most of the accounts of the banjo by white people express a derision similar to that of Maryland lawyer James Hollyday or brutal slaveowner Thomas Thistlewood.

This much is also true: by the late 1830s, Sweeney was traveling from Richmond to South Carolina as a professional banjo player, finally making his way to New York City in 1839. While Sweeney seems to have had a fixed costume by this time, the accounts of where he got his banjo from or what it looked like are contradictory. During one show in 1837, Sweeney played "on a real Banjo, made by himself," but fellow Blackface Minstrel performer William Whitlock received a banjo from Sweeney that same year apparently made by someone else. While the banjo on the "Coal Black Rose" sheet music is clearly supposed to have a gourd body, Sweeney's instrument on the 1840s' sheet music covers of "Jenny Get Your Hoe Cake Done" and "What Did You Cum From" isn't quite round, like a wooden-rim would be, and has frets, which guitars had at the time but banjos didn't. The engravers making sheet music covers didn't have to be accurate; the illustration just needed to make people think "banjo" when they saw it. Sweeney was the first performer to make the banjo synonymous with his act, but he wasn't the inventor of the banjo, probably wasn't the first white person to play a banjo, and may not even have been the first white person to use a banjo on stage as a prop of Blackness. And he wasn't necessarily the person who made the banjo one of the most popular instruments in the United States during the mid-1800s.[9]

Another story steeped in mythology goes like this. Musicians Dick Pelham, William Whitlock, Dan Emmett, and Francis Brower had their realization as they were sitting in the North American Hotel. It wasn't surprising that they were there, at the corner of Bowery and Bayard in New York City. They were circus performers and the hotel was across the way from the Bowery Circus. Performers would stop in to get food or just to relax after a show. And maybe that's what they were doing, hanging out before or after a performance, or just going to where the action was.[10]

Emmett and Brower had performed together at the Franklin Theater with a man named Pierce, before Emmett and Pierce began performing at the Circus as a duo. That didn't last long, and Brower hadn't found a new partner. Maybe the four musicians sitting in the North American Hotel knew that playing together had been more successful than playing solo. They came up with the idea of creating a bigger act: Whitlock on banjo, Emmett on both fiddle and banjo, Pelham on tambourine, and Brower on the bones. They had rhythm and melody, and Pelham and Brower were also good dancers.

They grabbed their instruments and crossed the street. At the Circus, they found Uncle Nat Howes, who could book them for a show. Instead of playing a tune, they started making a racket with their instruments, playing all at once, as discordantly as they could manage. They hadn't practiced, or at least that's what they'd later claim, and were just hoping Howes would book them to shut them up. Instead, he said, "Boys, you've got a good thing. Can't you sing us a song."

That's how the story went if Emmett told it. Whitlock said they were in a boarding house with the instruments lying about when they decided to play a song together. Then they went and performed on the Bowery.

However it happened, the result was the same. Emmett dragged his bow across his fiddle's strings and began singing; the others knew the song and started a chorus. They were surprised: the thump-thump of the rhythmic banjo combined with the melody from Emmett's fiddle and singing and the tackety-tack of the bones in Brower's hands, finished with the lower, resonant drum of the tambourine that matched the notes of the banjo. Yes, this configuration really would work. They had a new group, and on February 6, 1843, they would present the "First Night of the novel . . . Ethiopian band, entitled the Virginia Minstrels."[11]

They, again, billed themselves as authentic. But they were all white, none of them were from Virginia, and the entertainment they were performing wasn't new. More than that, even as the Virginia Minstrels took the stage as a foursome with banjo, fiddle, tambourine, and bones, they were recreating what could have been heard in Black communities from New York to Suriname. The bones produce a sharp clack, not unlike the sound made by the qua-qua. The fiddle offers a melody line, like song. The tambourine is a simpler version of a drum, with all its tones. And the banjo is the banjo, a Black instrument.

Just two months after their first performance in New York, the Virginia Minstrels performed in Worcester, Massachusetts, advertising "songs, refrains, and ditties as sung by the southern slaves at all their merry meetings such as the gathering in of the cotton and sugar crops, corn huskings, slave weddings, and junketings." Emmett was born in Ohio, Brower was from Baltimore, and Pelham and Whitlock were

New Yorkers. Although they may have witnessed and participated in exchanges of Black and white culture in Manhattan or on Long Island, had they seen any of these "merry meetings" during their trips south? There wasn't a strong likelihood they could have heard a song at a corn husking or a slave wedding. And did they mean "junketing" in the sense of junket as a festive social affair, or had someone gotten the word confused with Junkanoo, the parade celebration seen both in Jamaica and in North Carolina?[12]

♫

Here is another story. In 1842, Charles Dickens stumbles around the streets of Five Points in New York, not impressed with the ball he was given upon arrival, not impressed with anything in the city, really. His guide has brought the party to a saloon, which Dickens calls Almack's but which people in the district call Pete Williams's place. He's greeted by the Black landlord and landlady, "whose head is daintily ornamented with a handkerchief of many colors."[13]

"What will you please call for?" asks Williams. "A dance? It shall be done directly, sir."

Dickens learns that this means there will be a "regular break-down."

Two musicians sit on stage, a fiddler and a tambourine player, and begin to play, while "five or six couples come upon the floor, marshaled by a lively young negro, who is the wit of the assembly, and the greatest dancer known." Two of the young women wear scarves around their hair, like the landlady. Each man pairs with a woman, and they begin to dance. They continue until they've been "so long about it that the sport begins to languish." Then, the young dancer "dashes to the rescue," joining in. The fiddler smiles and picks up the pace, sensing a new energy, a change in the atmosphere. The landlady smiles, Williams looks proud, even the room seems brighter to Dickens. Then:

> Single shuffle, double shuffle, cut and cross-cut: snapping his fin-
> gers, rolling his eyes, turning in his knees, presenting the backs of

his legs in front, spinning about on his toes and heels like nothing but the man's fingers on the tambourine; dancing with two left legs, two right legs, two wooden legs, two wire legs, two spring legs—all sorts of legs and no legs.

He doesn't look like he's even tired, Dickens thinks. The young man out-dances his partner and "finishes by leaping gloriously on the bar-counter, and calling for something to drink." Applause erupts across the room.[14]

Charles Dickens—like Sloane, Labat, Alexander, Hollyday, This-tlewood, Stedman, Moreau de Saint-Méry, "Absalom Aimwell," Rose, Latrobe, Jansa, and even Schouten and Focke to a certain extent—is an interloper. How similar are the dance steps that Dickens sees in New York to what these men saw going back almost two hundred years? Change the setting from a basement in Manhattan to a sugar plantation on Mar-tinique, where Father Labat described men and women dancing across from each other as they leaped and twirled. Change the fiddler and the tambourine player to the banjo player and drummer of Congo Square. Change the young dancer who livens up the dancing between the cou-ples to the third dancer who jumps into the banyaprei, brightening every-one's steps. Like so many outside observers, Dickens doesn't record the song they played or the name of the dance if it has one other than "break-down," and he doesn't even write down the name of the dancer who has entranced him.

But Dickens isn't really an interloper. This is a new period in history. Pete Williams was a successful businessman who welcomed both whites and Blacks into his establishment to make money. He didn't put on Min-strel shows, but people knew they could see Black musicians and dancers showcasing their skill at his saloon. This was the story as Dickens told it in his *American Notes for General Circulation*, published in 1842. A reporter for the *New York Sporting Whip*, who in the manner of a gossip columnist got the details of where Dickens spent his time and referred to him by his nick-name Boz, wrote that Dickens went to Almack's, where about one hun-dred Black patrons were gathered, and danced "cotillions and quadrilles, to the popular airs of 'Sitch a gittin' up stairs' and 'Jim along Josey.'" Those were both tunes from the Minstrel stage, and they may have been played, or perhaps they were only what the reporter—who expresses racism elsewhere in the piece—assumed Blacks would be playing and dancing to. From there, the reporter wrote, Dickens went to where "Peter Williams keeps a ballroom underground," and danced all night. The *Sporting Whip* reporter never mentions a fabulous young dancer, while Dickens seems to conflate the two taverns owned by Williams.[15]

Dickens's account of his experience would launch a young dancer's career. In December 1842, a reporter for the *Sporting Whip*—who may or may not have been the earlier reporter, as the pieces were not signed—went to Almack's looking for the dancer, who would have been just twelve years old when Dickens saw him. Now called "Boz's Juba"—a callous name for a free Black child—he was already earning money from dancing.[16]

"He took his station upon the floor, and we never saw such dancing before . . ." the *Sporting Whip* reporter wrote. "Talk about your Diamonds, why they are no comparison to the dancing we witnessed there." On the Minstrel stage, a white teenage dancer who billed himself as Master Diamond claimed to be the best "Negro dancer," dancing as authentically as Sweeney played the banjo. In January 1843, the *Sporting Whip* announced a dance contest between Diamond and Young Juba. Soon, he'd be billed as Master Juba, which like Master Diamond served as a pun on his mastery of dance and the fact that he was young enough to be an apprentice. As Blackface Minstrelsy took off, Juba would perform on stage with white men, their faces darkened with burnt cork.[17]

Five years later, in England, promoters made the most of the fact that the dancer traveling with G. W. Pell's Ethiopian Serenaders was "Boz's Juba." Although the whole troupe received accolades, the press and the audiences were as taken with Juba as Dickens had been. He was noted as "a youth of color . . . only eighteen," "small in stature, though tightly, trimly built, with an abundance of muscular power." Audiences in London were told they "should not miss the opportunity" to see the "agility, rapidity of movement, and strength, which is possible for a pair of human legs to be made to exhibit," and that Juba's "Plantation Dance" was especially noteworthy. But it was the Irish press who declared that however good "European mimics"—that is to say, white Blackface Minstrels—tried to be, they were nothing compared with Juba. In Dublin, the *Freeman's Journal* wrote that "no man—much less youth—of European birth and habitude could . . . achieve the wonders of simultaneous muscular exertion" as Master Juba.[18]

Juba wasn't the only Black Blackface performer, and even though Minstrel shows had become incredibly popular, not everyone was taken with Blackface Minstrelsy, even when the performers were Black. The same year that Juba performed in Dublin, Frederick Douglass offered his own review of Gavitt's Original Ethiopian Serenaders in his newspaper, the *North Star*. The troupe, "said to be composed entirely of colored people," still wore burnt cork, and "their lips, too, were evidently painted, and otherwise exaggerated." Instead of sounding like Black singers, they sounded like white performers doing a bad job of imitating Black performers. With the exception of B. Richardson, a great dancer, they "were a poor set, and will make themselves ridiculous wherever they may go," he wrote. Douglass admitted that readers might question why he even went to a Minstrel show and why he was reviewing it, knowing that it "seemed to feed the flame of American prejudice against colored people." He offers an idea: "It is something gained, when the colored man in any form can appear before a white audience," and perhaps if they "represent the colored man . . . as he is . . . they will then command the respect of both races."[19]

Whether or not the Virginia Minstrels invented the Minstrel Show, or Joel Walker Sweeney was the creator of the first five-string, wooden-rim banjo, or Dickens saw Juba at Pete Williams's dance hall, this is also true: within a matter of months of the Virginia Minstrels' first performance, there would be an explosion of Blackface Minstrel groups and Minstrel music everywhere. The troupes had names such as Christy's Minstrels, the Kentucky Minstrels, the Alabama Minstrels, the Southern Minstrels, the Congo Minstrels, the Ethiopian Minstrels (not to be confused with the Ethiopian Serenaders), and the Original Virginia Minstrels. For all of them, a banjo or two was an obligatory accessory. The places in New York where the troupes performed would be called African Opera Houses, and the performers would tour the country and the world. Shops in Boston, New York, Philadelphia, Baltimore, South Carolina, and London would sell sheet music written by white men displaying banjos on the cover, and soon, anyone could walk into a store and buy a banjo.

XVIII

New Orleans, Louisiana, 1850

The singing hasn't started yet, but soon, anyone walking the streets of New Orleans's Vieux Carré will be able to hear it. On a hot night in early July 1850, Leonora approaches the home of Betsey Toledano, among the large brick buildings with wrought-iron balconies and squat clapboard-sided homes in the oldest part of the city. Leonora is owned by a man named Gricot, and if he hadn't given her a pass, she wouldn't have been allowed out this late. At 9 p.m., a cannon was fired at the Place d'Armes near the Mississippi River to mark the beginning of the evening curfew for the enslaved. But as in so many other places and in so many other times, this gathering can't be stopped by limits placed on the movement of people of African descent. For Leonora, coming to priestess Betsey Toledano's home for a Vodou ceremony is worth breaking the law.[1]

Inside, Leonora gathers with other women in one of the rooms that has become a ritual space, called the oum'phor in Haiti. The walls are decorated with images that to an outsider would look like Catholic saints, like St. Peter and St. Michael. In Vodou, St. Peter, who guards the gates of heaven, becomes Legba, who guards the crossroads between the living and the dead; St. Michael is Ogun, the Yoruba god of war and iron who favors the color red. Sometimes Leonora and other Vodou practitioners pray to St. Michael, but it is Ogun that descends and takes over a devotee's body. St. John the Baptist, too, is a spirit in his own right, celebrated with a feast in June.[2]

On the ground in Betsey Toledano's home, other worshippers have laid out vessels for the ceremony: earthenware bowls and basins containing small pebbles, gravel, paving stones, or a large flint stone. One of the bowls is an offering to Ogun, also the spirit of thunder and lightning, in hopes that he will not send a bolt upon the house. There are also vases and goblets holding liquid, more offerings to the spirits and ancestors. White cloths are laid on the floor, with candles and offerings of food.[3]

To begin the ceremony, Toledano sings out a line and the followers repeat it back. They may have gathered to celebrate a special occasion or to petition the spirits on behalf of a particular person. This determines what words Toledano chooses to sing. Her voice and those of the chorus carry up and out of the house into the street.

The police in New Orleans have been on high alert all summer for Vodou ceremonies. Early in July, the Third Municipality police received a tip that "there had been nightly gatherings of both sexes, black and white" on Bernard Street at the home of a man named Fostin. Captain Mazarat entered the house and found twenty women dancing around "the Pythoness of the temple [the priestess] in what is termed among the initiated the Wanga." In New Orleans, wanga was a dance, but in Haiti the word was used for protective charms, and in Jamaica merrywang meant banjo. Fostin's room was arranged for the purposes of Vodou ceremonies, with "banners, bannerets, wands, images, snakes," and even a carved wooden figure, which the police confiscated. The *Planters' Banner* noted that they arrested "a dozen free women of color," one enslaved woman, and "five or six [married] white women," the word "married" signaling to the reader that the white women were not low-class or prostitutes.[4]

Once again, the police hear the singing and barge in, arresting Toledano, Leonora, and another enslaved woman called Darkey. Everyone else escapes. Reporting on the earlier arrests in the Third Municipality, the *Weekly Delta*, a paper surprisingly sympathetic to the Vodou practitioners, questioned "[t]he right of the police to interrupt these ceremonies." Toledano appeared before the court asking the same question.[5]

The *Weekly Delta* described Toledano as "a stout and intelligent free colored woman." She had been born in New Orleans around 1810, and lived
on her own. The newspaper didn't report whether or not she invoked
her constitutional right to practice her religion freely, without the inter-
vention of the government, but she forcefully contended that "she had a
perfect right to hold the meetings of the Vodou Society in her house." She
was the priestess of the society and women came to her house for religious meetings. "The society was a religious African institution, which
had been transmitted to her, through her grandmother, from the ancient
Congo Queens," the newspaper reported Toledano telling the court.
The ceremonies might be mysterious, but they were not immoral. She
explained what the bowls meant, how they could protect her home from
lightning. She showed the court her necklace of seashells and glass beads,
which her grandmother had given her. With this necklace, she—like the

A ritual space depicted in P. J. Benoit's *Voyage à Suriname*, where the priestess Benoit
calls the Mother of Serpents serves as a diviner. Carved wooden figures are around
the room. He wrote that "jugs and calabashes" were on the ground. *John Carter Brown
Library, Brown University*

boy Father Labat wrote about in Martinique—could bring down a rain shower whenever she wanted to, she said.[6]

In Suriname, Brother Jansa destroyed idols because they interfered with Christianity, but in New Orleans, police couldn't take objects and arrest Betsey Toledano for the same reason. What they could charge her with, however, was "encouraging unlawful assemblages of slaves." Toledano's arrest was reported in papers across the country. Whether enslaved people should be allowed to gather had been an issue for the New Orleans government since before Latrobe visited the city in 1819, since before the city was made a part of the United States. As in New York, gatherings of enslaved people had been outlawed because they could provide opportunities to plan and foment rebellion. Now, the mixing of free and enslaved people caused even more fear. Vodou leaders were often free women of color. The followers and power they gained from their position further challenged white male authority.[7]

During the Vodou-scare summer of 1850, the newspapers didn't report that the police confiscated instruments. Banjos and drums, the instruments that Latrobe had seen in dances at Congo Square and Theodore Pavie saw outside the city, were no longer classified as parts of these dances. They were secular, not religious. In the city, banjos appeared on stage in the hands of the Original Virginia Minstrels (musicians who were not in fact the original Virginia Minstrels) and other troupes, in the music store of H. D. Hewitt, and, sometimes, accompanying the Congo dances.

On a Sunday afternoon in 1843, a *Picayune* reporter went to a public "black ball" taking place in the courtyard of a home in the Third Municipality, in the neighborhood of the Bayou St. John. The leader of the musicians was strumming "a long-necked banjo, the head of which was ornamented with a bunch of sooty parti-colored ribbands." Was the body of the banjo a gourd, or was it a wooden-rim like Sweeney's? One of the percussionists played a butter firkin, a wooden tub "covered with a tightly drawn sheep skin"—basically a wooden-rimmed banjo without the neck. He beat it in time with his fingertips. Another "beat the jaw bones of an ass with a rusty key," offering a sharp clacking rhythm, and others "beat most vehemently an old headless case that lay on its side, ballasted with iron nails." As they played, people sang a chorus. Three dancers took to the floor, one man and two women. Their feet moved, but their bodies seemed to float around the space. The man both danced and added to the music, wearing "a pair of leather knee caps from which were suspended a quantity of metal nails." As he moved to the music, the nails jingled.[8]

The reporter called this the Congo dance—the same dance Pavie had seen almost ten years earlier. The dance may have come from Haiti, where there are religious and secular versions of the dance, and even one called Congo Creole, to complicate matters further. The dance—whether in a public performance like the one the reporter saw or at a private affair— wasn't the same as a dance Betsy Toledano and her followers would have done during their ceremony.[9]

Dances, music, and religion didn't seem to be exclusively Black or white in New Orleans anymore. Toledano had white followers, and white reporters could attend a Congo dance. Maybe it was the time, the exact midpoint of the century; maybe it was the place, a city that had always been multicultural; or maybe it came down to shifts in the population and the fact that slavery, while still a solid institution, was being questioned more or more. The banjo, too, wasn't just a part of Black culture anymore, but it wasn't fully part of white culture, either.

ॐ

To return to New Orleans in early April was wonderful, when the brutal heat and humidity of the summer hadn't yet set in but the warmth was welcome after still-chilly spring days. On the Mississippi River in 1853, a steamer slowed as it approached the city, a delayed late-night arrival when the city lights would have been glimmering and reflecting off the water. Louis Moreau Gottschalk was happy to be back in the city and hear the music of his childhood, which had inspired so much of his recent success.

Gottschalk was born there in 1829, but had left for France to study music days before his eleventh birthday. The songs of home lived so vividly in his mind that when he fell sick with typhoid fever in 1848, the delirium blurred the boundaries between memory and reality. The songs of the Crescent

City crossed the ocean to the countryside outside Paris and seeped into his mind, repeating in his feverish brain. As the fever began to fade, he wrote a composition with a melody based on "Quan' patate la cuite," a song his sister Clara also remembered from their childhood. His maternal grandmother and Sally, the enslaved maid of the Gottschalk family, had both been born in Saint-Domingue and had sung songs for him and his sisters. His mother's family had taken Sally with them when they left the colony during the Haitian Revolution, going first to Jamaica and then New Orleans, and Sally had cared for Moreau, as the family called him. Gottschalk named the piece "Bamboula," and followed it with the compositions "La Savane," "Le Bananier," and "Le Mancenillier": his *Louisiana Suite*.[10]

In Paramaribo, Surinamese writer Hendrik Focke had managed to hear "Le Bananier"—either he played it from the sheet music published shortly after Gottschalk first performed the piece in 1849 or he heard someone else play it. Focke had wondered about its provenance. The *Louisiana Suite* existed somewhere between a rendering, a reimagining, and wholesale creativity. Gottschalk was not, as Focke was, dabbling in the study of human cultures. He was a composer, remembering songs— music that was already a blend of France, Haiti, and New Orleans—and creating something new.

"Bamboula" begins with four low chords pounded on the piano, evocative of the deep beats of the bamboula drum Moreau de Saint-Méry had seen in Saint-Domingue. Focke considered the bamboula the dance of the French colonies, and a visitor to Martinique in the early 1800s wrote that the bamboula was a dance to "bid farewell to Carnival." Wherever the name originated, the word could refer to the drum or the dance, and was tied to the musical culture of people of African descent in French colonies, as Louisiana had been. To his "Bamboula," Gottschalk adds a melody line that dances around, improvising on the song he heard in childhood. Even the composition's name was supposed to evoke exoticism and nostalgia. He wrote it in 1848, the year Victor Schœlcher, collector of the banza, drafted the decree that would free people held in bondage in France and the French colonies.[11]

In "La Savane," Gottschalk again turned to a melody from Louisiana, "Pauve Piti Lolotte." A version of this song, along with "Lisette quitté la pleine"—the song Pierre Forest heard in Louisiana in 1831—was published in the 1811 pamphlet "Idylles et Chansons, ou Essais de Poésie Créole, par un Habitant d'Hayti," suggesting both were known in Louisiana and Haiti. Gottschalk used the song only for inspiration, changing the key, slowing it down, and adding his own variations and flourishes.[12]

Gottschalk chose "Song of the Blacks" as the subtitle for his "La Bananier" and based the work on "En avan' Grenadie," which a company of free Black men had supposedly sung during the Battle of New Orleans. Gottschalk's song has the qualities of a march, with short, staccato notes and a melody in a major key that sounds Western European. At times, Gottschalk kept the melody with one hand on the piano, using the other hand to run up and down the keyboard like a frantic bumblebee or adding those runs to the end of a melodic line.[13]

The final composition of the Louisiana suite is "Le Mancenillier," the manzanilla tree, and it includes melodies from the Haitian "Chanson de Lizette," the Black Creole song "Ou som souroucou," and similar songs from Louisiana and Martinique, "Ma mourri" or "Tant sirop est doux." Gottschalk's piece begins with a simple melody, one that is easy to sing along to. The composition moves forward, becoming more complex, as Gottschalk blends the melodies with his runs that feel almost improvisational. He then returns and repeats the now familiar melodies.[14]

As a virtuosic piano player and composer, Gottschalk could have remembered these songs from his childhood in Louisiana, whether he heard them on the streets or from Sally or his grandmother. In New Orleans, whites went to Black dances on plantations and in ballrooms, and white women went to Black Vodou priestesses like Betsey Toledano for spiritual counsel. Gottschalk imbues this exchange between Black and white, African-derived and European-derived, into his classical music.

Gottschalk's compositions were incredibly popular in France and soon were being played by touring artists in the United States. His father wanted him to capitalize on this popularity, so the twenty-three-year-old traveled to New York in January 1853, with his grand piano below deck. There,

P. T. Barnum, the circus magnate who had managed the banjo player William Whitlock and the dancer Master Diamond, offered Gottschalk the
extraordinary sum of $20,000 a year plus expenses to tour the US. "My
father had his [unjust] prejudices against Barnum," Gottschalk would
later write, so they turned him down, saying no to a salary almost one
hundred times the average of a laborer in New York and an amount that
would have significantly reduced their money worries.[15]

Gottschalk toured on his way to New Orleans. In Cincinnati, Ohio, he
played to "thunders of applause," and in Louisville, Kentucky, he played
two concerts at Mozart Hall, where the Blackface troupe Well's Minstrels
had performed two weeks earlier. On solo piano, Gottschalk played his
own compositions as well as selections from operas like Lucia di Lam-
mermoor. He also understood popular music and the appeal of American themes to his audience. During his second concert in Kentucky,
he "charmed the audience by a beautiful improvisation of 'Old Folks at
Home,'" a recent Stephen Foster hit. The audience responded enthusiastically to Gottschalk, letting out "shouts and hog calls."[16]

Both Louisville and Cincinnati were on the western frontier and linked
the north and the south. Free Blacks, enslaved people, and poor whites,
including Irish immigrants, were building canals to connect east to west,
and north to south. It was in Cincinnati that Stephen Foster worked as
a shipping clerk in the 1840s, hearing songs he would transform into his
Minstrel melodies. In the 1838 Tales and Sketches from the Queen City, Benjamin Drake wrote of an unnamed Black man "extracting sweet music from
his gourd banjo" playing "Sittin' on a Rail," a tune that appeared on the
Minstrel stage. Drake also wrote of white Cincinnatians "listening to the
songs and banjoes of the slaves." Citizens there defended the freedom of
a man known as Black Bill after he was accused of being a runaway slave,
adding that his "ability to play the fiddle and banjo" made him "indispens-
able at dances." Thus, Cincinnatians knew the banjo as an instrument
played by whites on the Minstrel stage and by Blacks at dances.[17]

In France, Gottschalk had been American, but in the United States,
his background as New Orleans-born and French-raised made him seem
foreign. The audience craved themes that spoke to what it meant to be

American. Gottschalk would use the sound of the banjo as a symbol of Americanness in his piano performances, first in his medley of Stephen Foster's hits and later in a composition of his own.

When Gottschalk arrived in New Orleans, he headed for his grand-mother's house, feeling immediately at home. He wrote that "[his] old negroes, old friends of my childhood" greeted him, referring to the peo-ple still enslaved by his family. They hugged him in "the most touching spectacle of affection." How they actually felt is impossible to know.[18]

Just as they had in Ohio and Kentucky, audiences in New Orleans showered Gottschalk with praise. On stage, his delicate frame looked even smaller next to the piano. But as he began banging out the chords of "Bamboula," the physicality of his playing filled the space at the Odd Fellows' Hall. After every piece the audience applauded with verve until he returned to take a bow. They strewed bouquets across the stage. Gottschalk thanked them for the warm welcome, perhaps feeling as though he really were home—not an American in France or a Frenchman in America, but a white Creole in New Orleans.[19]

That summer, after leaving New Orleans, Gottschalk began composing a piece he'd call "The Banjo." One correspondent for the *Picayune* heard the sounds of a "banjo imitation" in "Bamboula," and others probably heard the instrument echoed in Gottschalk's Foster melodies, all before Gottschalk composed a piece that was specifically meant to imitate the banjo. He wasn't the first classical musician to use the banjo as inspiration for his compositions, either. In the 1820s, A. P. Heinrich traveled to Ken-tucky and wrote "The Banjo Quickstep" and "The Log House," which was printed with a banjo on the cover.[20]

Still, this was a departure for a classical composer. Years later, in 1864, Gottschalk described his "The Banjo" as a "melody for the negroes!" Here he is being facetious. He doesn't mean that it is a melody for the Black pop-ulation or from Black people; he's referring to the criticism that his work isn't real classical music.[21]

The subtitle to Gottschalk's "The Banjo" was "Grotesque Fantasie, An American Sketch." The word grotesque probably meant ugly or carica-tured, and, by the mid-1800s, the word was often used to describe Black appearance, especially in relation to dance or music. As with the titles of his *Louisiana Suite*, Gottschalk was placing the song within the context of Black performance.[22]

If his inspiration for this piece, like his *Louisiana* pieces, was the interplay of Black and white cultures in the United States, was there a specific source for the melody that dominates the composition? He could have heard Black banjo playing in New Orleans during his childhood and upon his return in the spring of 1853. He had also heard Blackface Minstrels playing banjo upon his return to the US. He wrote about the troupe Buckley's Serenaders for the *Morning Times*, and he'd played Stephen Foster's tunes on stage. But if he used a Creole song or one he heard from a Black banjo player, he didn't reveal it, and the source hasn't been identified.

In "The Banjo," Gottschalk plays with Blackface Minstrel tunes of the era, with their big major chords and simple ascending and descending melodies. The basic melody of "Banjo I" (Op. 15) and "Banjo II" (Op. 82) seems to be "Johnny Boker," a song published by Joel Walker Sweeney. But at one point, Gottschalk makes a cheeky turn with a melodic phrase that sounds like it comes from the melody of the lyric "I came from Alabama with a banjo on my knee, I'm g'wan to Louisiana my true love for to see" from Stephen Foster's "Oh, Susanna!" Foster frequently plagiarized his own songs—and apparently Gottschalk didn't mind stealing from Foster either—and that melodic passage also sounds similar to Foster's "Ring, Ring, de Banjo!"[23]

Sweeney and Foster didn't necessarily write these songs. The melodies could have been inspired by or copied from Black musicians in central Virginia or Cincinnati. The problem in tracing the origins of Blackface Minstrel songs is that it becomes almost impossible to disentangle what the performers might have heard and where they found their material. As Focke asked, was it truth, imitation, embellishment, or pure invention? Blackface performers wanted to be authentic, so they said they learned their material from Black musicians, and that may be true. But because of the immense popularity of Blackface Minstrelsy, many more people—including Gottschalk—were going to hear these tunes at performances and learn them from sheet music, rather than from someone like Black Bill.

XIX

Washington, DC, 1857

If James Buchanan's inauguration in March 1857 had been set in a novel written by one of white artist Eastman Johnson's abolitionist literary friends, it would have taken place on a cold and rainy day, with strong gusts of wind. But this wasn't a novel, and a warm sun shone down on the formal ceremony to swear in the fifteenth president of the United States.

On the steps of the Capitol, Buchanan addressed the crowd, supposedly the largest the city had seen. He did not skirt around the biggest issue facing the country, the issue that was central to his winning the presidency. As a pro-slavery Democrat, he told his supporters, "Congress is neither 'to legislate slavery into a Territory or State nor to exclude it therefrom.' . . . It is a judicial question which legitimately belongs to the Supreme Court of the United States, before whom it is now pending, and will, it is understood, be speedily and finally settled." Congress had already decided that the states had the right to decide whether or not to permit slavery, and that the federal government did not have the right to intervene. While many had thought abolition would be coming to the US soon, Buchanan's election seemed to put that possibility farther away, perhaps even out of reach.[1]

The case Buchanan was referring to in his inaugural address was *Dred Scott v. Sanford*. Scott, an enslaved man, had sued for his freedom on the grounds that his owner had taken him to a free state, and as a resident of the free state he couldn't be enslaved. Just two days after Buchanan's inauguration, the Court decided that Scott had no right to sue because he wasn't a citizen of the United States. The decision, written by Maryland justice Roger B. Taney, used the founding documents of the country to show that "neither . . . persons who had been imported as slaves nor their descendants, whether they had become free or not, were then acknowledged as a part of the people." Because people of African descent had never been considered citizens, the court declared, they could not be considered citizens now. Thus, Scott and all people of African descent had no rights in the court.[2]

For people of African descent living in the United States, free or enslaved, this week in March 1857 would have been devastating. White abolitionists saw themselves farther from their goal, and if the courts, Congress, and the president all agreed that slavery could continue, what could they do?

Eastman Johnson chose to make art. It had been almost a decade since Johnson lived in DC. When he moved to Boston and then Europe in 1848, he'd left off doing quick charcoal-and-chalk portraits for Washington personalities to study art in Düsseldorf. He then traveled to Paris and on to The Hague, where he found he was "deriving much advantage from studying the splendid work of Rembrandt and a few other of the old Dutch masters." With news of his mother's death, Johnson returned to the United States in 1855, and while he could use the skills and knowledge he'd gained in Europe to paint a multitude of subjects, the art world, like the musical world, wanted to see American themes. During a brief sojourn around Lake Superior, Johnson had sketched and painted the Ojibwe, trying to capture what he perceived as the disappearing way of Native life.[3]

He arrived in Washington, DC, to a changed landscape. The Washington Monument stood halfway finished in the midst of a vast expanse where the only building standing was the recently completed Smithsonian Castle. Johnson's father, Philip, had just bought a new brick row home on F Street, a few blocks from the White House, one of the expanding residential sections of the city.

Johnson also saw an American subject that hadn't changed much since he was last in DC, a subject that seemed both pressing and important: slavery. While the British and French colonies had abolished slavery, the practice was still legal in the US, Dutch colonies like Suriname, Portuguese colonies, Cuba, and Brazil. And despite what Buchanan and his supporters wished, the debates about slavery and its expansion into new states hadn't been settled. Even in the nation's capital, abolitionists were active. Though enslaved people didn't make up a large part of the city's population, abolitionists found the continued legality of slavery in the nation's capital unbearable. In 1853, Solomon Northup, a free Black man born in New York who had been a farmer, laborer, and fiddler, published his account of how he had been abducted on a trip to Washington and then sold, once again putting a face, a name, and a story to what was happening in the city. Supporters of slavery believed that abolition in Washington would be like a crack in the dam.[4]

In the early summer of 1857, Eastman Johnson visited George Washington's former home, Mount Vernon, thinking he would portray the scene of the first president meeting the Marquis de Lafayette. Many artists would have seen it as a handsome manor, an estate with sweeping grounds, important white people, an American aristocracy gained not through inherited titles but hard work and conviction. When he came to the house, Johnson realized that such a view omitted the people doing the hard work to make the property run; that view meant imagining that enslaved men, women, and children weren't part of the scene. Johnson saw those people and put them at Washington's home.[5]

Johnson's painting *The Old Mount Vernon* moves the focus onto a Black man sitting in the doorway of a cabin, on the threshold between the verdant open grounds and the darkened slave quarters. To the man's left, a wooden fence has rotted and fallen apart. To his right, a child stands alone. The white clapboard building with no windows is placed in the foreground, larger and more present than Washington's desirable home, as if daring the viewer to see that this plain building and its residents are more important. The breaking-down isn't just in the physical surroundings but in the man's body, slumped over with his hands on his knees. Johnson also painted six versions of the kitchen, in which an enslaved woman sits in front of the hearth with children next to her. Here, plaster falls off the lath and bricks crumble. Johnson places people of African descent at the center of these paintings, free of caricature, not only acknowledging their presence and existence but seeming to point to their importance, while also suggesting that slavery as an institution causes decay.

Johnson seems to have had a clear view of slavery, even though he'd had both pro-slavery and abolitionist influences in his life. He grew up in Maine, which had seceded from Massachusetts and become a separate state in 1820 during the Missouri Compromise. This new free state counterbalanced Missouri's admission to the union as a slave state. He had exposure to abolitionist ideas from writers Ralph Waldo Emerson and Henry Wadsworth Longfellow. But Johnson's father worked for the pro-slavery Democratic Party, and Johnson didn't need to leave his family's social circles in Washington to see slavery. In the fall of 1857, his father would marry Mary Washington James, a relative of George Washington and the owner of a Black twenty-one-year-old woman and two young children. When the couple married, an agreement ensured that James's property would not transfer to Johnson—property that included the woman and children. The F Street neighborhood where Philip Johnson lived was a known pro-slavery neighborhood; Jefferson Davis, future president of the Confederate States of America, lived just a few blocks away. This was the reality of slavery in the capital as Johnson saw it: human bondage was everywhere, tacitly approved, even if it happened to be hiding in interior yards.[6]

In fact, the inner courtyards of his father's F Street home provided the scene for Eastman Johnson's next major painting with a slavery theme, a painting which would become one of his most lauded works.[7]

A well-dressed white woman peeks through an opening from the adjoining yard, quietly entering a place she wouldn't normally go. This yard is a picture of neglect and decline: the broken rafters of the wooden building's mossy roof are collapsing, plaster peels off the walls, and an upper window is broken. She—and we—see a scene that is usually hidden, behind the new brick row home that Johnson has obscured with a tree. In the painting, there is only a sliver of blue-white sky, maybe suggesting that there is a small hope of freedom. Two young Black girls turn to see the woman coming into the yard, where children and adults, men and women, seem to be at an idle moment in their day.

A lighter-skinned Black woman talks to a man, who has an ax at his feet. She doesn't raise her eyes to meet his but looks at the corn stalks in her hand instead. At the center of the yard, a man sits on a stepladder, strumming a banjo. A boy looks up, as if longingly, at the musician. Another child dances to the music, both his hands held by a dark-skinned Black woman who squats down. A girl lies next to them. On the second story of the wooden house, a woman and child look out of the window, the action unfolding beneath them. Each person is fully rendered, with individualized facial expressions, postures, clothing, stylistic choices, and a range of skin tones, some reflecting the reality of the rape of Black women by white men at some point in the family's history.[8]

In the manner typical of genre painters, Johnsons paints groups of a few people interacting with one another. He used his skill to structure the composition of this complex painting, organizing the people well across the canvas and creating the right depth of field for each figure in relation to the others. This rendition of "Negro life" also presents a changed expression of Black cultural life compared to the art of John Rose or Gerrit Schouten. While their works feature the dance as a central scene of action, Johnson's painting is made up of vignettes, where the people are all occupying the same space but not engaging in the same activity. The banjo player concentrates on his music and doesn't notice the woman and the boy dancing; the woman and man talking to one side focus on each other. The girls at the edge of the yard focus on the white woman coming around the corner, who may be looking toward the banjo player and drawn by his music. But the banjo player is not playing for a specific occasion or a dance, and the woman and the child dancing are not doing so as part of a ceremony or celebration. Nor does the banjo look like the banjo in Schouten's *Waterkant* or Rose's watercolor. Without realizing it, Johnson depicted what the banjo had become, both physically and culturally.[9]

In 1858, Eastman Johnson moved to New York, but he probably traveled back and forth between Washington and his studio while working on the painting, which he would title *Negro Life at the South*. He often painted studies of places that would become the background in his works, where the people were figures yet to come. Then, separately, he would paint studies of models, before refining the figures and adding them to the canvas of his final work. He used the yard and slave quarters of his father's house as the background for *Negro Life at the South* and his sister as a model for the white woman peeking in. He painted at least two studies in oil of the banjo player and the admiring boy.[10]

On his travels between Washington and New York, Johnson would have had to stop in Baltimore. There was no north–south rail connection across the city's harbor, so passengers had to get off at President Street Station on the east side of the harbor and walk or take a carriage to the west side to board a train at the Camden Street Station to continue their journey, or vice versa. In the waterfront neighborhood of Fells Point, just east of President Street, young enslaved men caulked ships in the same shipyards where Frederick Douglass had labored before escaping to freedom. As in Washington, slave labor was a reality, though freedom could be found across the Pennsylvania line, forty miles north. Douglass had escaped after boarding a train north dressed as a free Black sailor. By 1820, free Blacks in Baltimore outnumbered the enslaved. Black residents had their own churches and schools, owned businesses, and worked as doctors, midwives, teachers, bricklayers, and sailors, among other professions.[11]

The boats in the harbor brought French plums and Malaga figs from Europe, sugar and bags of coffee from the Caribbean, and oysters and tobacco from just across the Chesapeake Bay. This city was a crossroads, representing the northernmost city south of the Mason–Dixon Line, a city in a state built on the wealth of tobacco plantations, and the departure point for the new Baltimore and Ohio Railroad.

A few blocks north of the water was the heart of the city's entertainment district. Walking between trains, Johnson could have wandered up to Baltimore Street, where the rural south and industrial north were

One of Eastman Johnson's most famous paintings, *Negro Life at the South* (1859), featuring a Black banjo player with an instrument made by William Boucher, Jr., in Baltimore. *Oil on linen; 37 x 46 in. (94 x 116.8 cm). Robert L. Stuart Collection, gift of his widow Mrs. Mary Stuart, New-York Historical Society, S-225.*

coming together in the music industry. At the shop of William Boucher, Jr., Johnson could buy a banjo. If he didn't buy one there, he found one somewhere else, since he used a Boucher banjo for *Negro Life at the South*, the two studies of the banjo player called *Confidence and Admiration*, and a later work titled *Musical Instinct*.

Boucher was a white German immigrant whose father, William E. Boucher, Sr., was a singer, organ-maker, and instrument dealer. William, Jr. moved to Baltimore and began making fiddles and drums. When he realized there was an exploding interest in banjos, he began building those, too. By the mid-1840s, he was making banjos and entering them into competitions at the Maryland Institute Mechanics Fairs.[12]

The banjo in Johnson's paintings is a classic Boucher. The wood is a rich red-brown, while the skin that covers the top of the rim is a mellow white-yellow. Like the banza from Haiti, the neck is basically a flat board. Even though the banjo is less than seven inches long on Johnson's canvas, he includes the carved decorative ogee below the short string peg and the S-shaped peghead, which evokes the side profile of a fiddle pegbox as well as early Romance Era guitars. The ogee and the S-shaped peghead became trademarks of Boucher's instruments. The body is no longer a gourd but a wooden rim, a hoop often about twelve inches in diameter.[13]

Unlike the banjo in Rose's watercolor or the banza, Boucher's instruments were industrial objects—not an invention, but an innovation made for the sake of commercialization. Boucher designed his banjos to be mass-produced, responding to demand created by Blackface Minstrel performances. No two gourds or calabashes are the same, no matter how expert the grower, so a banjo-maker would have had to fit the neck and the fruit together in a unique manner each time. There was no easily repeatable process. With a wooden rim of uniform diameter, the process could be repeated over and over again in the same way. Like gourd- and calabash-bodied banjos, some early wooden-rim banjos had skin heads tacked on, including the one that Johnson painted. But tacks didn't allow musicians to tighten a skin that had a dull sound or one that had sagged in humid conditions. Boucher claimed to be the first banjo maker to use metal drum hardware to tighten the skin heads, a system similar to the ropes and wedges used by Surinamese drummers to tighten the skins on their drums. He also took shortcuts to make the banjos look more expensive than they were, such as painting a pattern on the neck or rim to suggest higher-quality rosewood.

But even with these changes, Boucher wooden-rimmed banjos retained a construction element from earlier gourd and calabash banjos. His instruments generally reflect the neck-to-body construction of the early banjos we still have—the Haitian banza, the Creole-bania, and the panja. That is, the neck butts up against the outside surface of either the fruit or the rim, narrows to pass through a hole in the body, then traverses the inside of the body and butts up against the inside surface of the gourd or calabash or rim before narrowing again to pass through a second hole. This design is unique to banjos. On violin-family instruments and guitars, for example, the neck stops at the outer edge of the sound chamber and is mortised into a block inside the body. Boucher may have taken this element of his construction from a gourd banjo, if he happened to have seen one, or he may simply have copied it from another wooden-rimmed banjo he came across at the theaters on Baltimore Street where Minstrels performed. His method of making banjos combined the old and the new, the white and the Black, tradition and innovation.[14]

By the time Eastman Johnson painted *Negro Life at the South*, the banjo was everywhere. It had been on stage not just in New York and London, but in Japan in 1854 when Admiral Perry visited. It had been in the hands of white men with their faces painted black, and Black men who painted their faces even darker black. Southern slaveowners like banjo player Joel Sweeney's neighbors knew about Minstrel Shows, as did abolitionists like Frederick Douglass. In 1855, a Boston publisher put out *Briggs' Banjo Instructor*, noting that "there had never yet been published a complete method for this instrument." The book made learning banjo music accessible to middle-class white people and provided "plantation melodies which the author learned when at the south from negroes" and specifics about how to play and tune a five-string, wooden-rimmed banjo.[15]

When Johnson's painting was first exhibited in 1859, critics were impressed by his skill. "Conceived with great spirit, and painted with Dutch fidelity," the editors of *Harper's New Monthly Magazine* wrote when it was shown in New York at the National Academy of Design Annual Exhibition. Some viewers recognized an abolitionist message. The anti-slavery *New-York Tribune* called it "a sort of 'Uncle Tom's Cabin' of pictures," referring to Harriet Beecher Stowe's best-selling abolitionist novel, the scene "presenting a sad picture of Southern Slavery."[16]

The care Johnson showed for his subjects didn't translate for all viewers as it did for the *Tribune* writer. While the magazine *Crayon* also found Johnson's skill praiseworthy, this was "notwithstanding the general ugliness of the forms and objects." The painting hadn't even left the show

before understanding of the work shifted. William P. Wright bought it for
$1,200 for his personal collection. Wright was a cotton broker, a supporter
of Justice Taney and the Supreme Court's decision in the Dred Scott case,
and someone who denounced abolitionists.[17]

Even if Johnson had painted *Negro Life at the South* with the idea of ele-
vating the lives of the enslaved and condemning slavery as a decaying
institution that should no longer exist, the stereotypes that people like
Wright saw led them to believe that it supported their pro-slavery cause.
The man flirts with the woman and she responds with a coquettish look,
and a viewer sees an overly sexualized slave like the man on the cover of
"Coal Black Rose." The banjo player only cares about his music, and as in
"The Bonja Song" he has no worries. The image of the woman dancing
with the boy posits long-standing traditions passed down through generations, uncorrupted by any current reality, including the reality of enslavement. This idea of "happy slaves" was what pro-slavery advocates latched
onto when they saw the painting. A tobacco company used a lithograph
of the painting with the title *O Carry Me Back to Old Virginny* to promote a
product produced with slave labor. When displayed in Boston, the painting received the title *Kentucky Home* and later, *My Old Kentucky Home*, a reference to the tune written by Stephen Foster. As so often happens, people
saw in the painting what they wanted to see, and perhaps, like the plantation owners who bought Schouten's dioramas, someone like Wright
believed that the image of happy slaves denied his own complicity in a
brutal, dehumanizing system.[18]

As much as Eastman Johnson might have wanted the viewer to see
an anti-slavery message in *Negro Life at the South*, something about it was
ambiguous. And as the United States got closer to dividing over slavery,
there was no room for ambiguity. In 1860, Henry Ward Beecher, brother
of author Harriet Beecher Stowe, commissioned Johnson to paint a child
he'd christened Rose Ward (born Sally Diggs). Rose, dressed in a scarlet
jacket and black skirt, stares at a ring on her finger. Beecher had "sold"
Rose's freedom at the Plymouth Church in Brooklyn, in an auction that
was supposed to gain money, publicity, and sympathy for the abolitionist
cause. The ring on Ward's finger had allegedly been given in the auction:

it was her Freedom Ring. Beecher selected young, light-skinned women and girls for the auctions, people that a white person might look upon and think, "She looks just like me."[19]

Two years later, during the Civil War, Johnson traveled to northern Virginia after the Battle of Bull Run. He saw a woman, man, and child on a horse, and painted *A Ride for Liberty—The Fugitive Slaves—1862*. The work is full of urgency as the horse gallops into the night and the woman turns to look back, an allusion to the understanding that abolition was close, but not close enough.

~

Eastman Johnson might have believed in the power of art to promote abolition, and Henry Ward Beecher in the power of publicity. But when white nineteen-year-old Lucy McKim arrived in Union-controlled South Carolina in 1862, she realized that art, fake auctions, and sermons were nothing compared to seeing how the now-free men, women, and children had once lived. Her parents' home in Philadelphia had been a stop on the Underground Railroad and they had supported John Brown's raid, yet McKim still wrote home to her mother, "How lukewarm we have been!"[20]

Lucy's father, James Miller McKim, had been tasked to go to Port Royal as part of the effort to educate, house, clothe, and feed the ten thousand newly freed people on the South Carolina Sea Islands. Her father, white educator Laura Towne, and other abolitionists were figuring out how to set up schools to teach the freedpeople to read and write and begin new lives outside the confines of slavery. McKim had come as her father's assistant and was fascinated by all she heard and saw. And she believed that sharing the music she heard the Black people singing would bring out their humanity to whites.

Lucy went to a praise and a shout, religious ceremonies unique to the Sea Islands. While a praise felt more like a typical church service, a shout incorporated music and dancing. Those gathered pushed benches to the side of the small cabin and the best singer, one who could improvise new lyrics, might start with "Pray all de member," the first line to a common shout song. Other men would base him, singing back the chorus lines and interjectionals, "O Lord!" At the praises, attendees sang hymns that Baptists or Methodists across the South knew, but at the shout, they had their own songs, songs that the McKims had never heard before.[21]

Men and women form a circle and begin to do a shuffling walk. They hardly pick up their feet from the floor, moving forward almost with a jerk, a hitch. The dance brings sweat to their foreheads and as they tire, they step away and others join in. Sometimes they sing; sometimes they leave that to the lead singer and the basers, who may also provide body percussion by clapping their hands, patting on their knees, or stomping their feet.[22]

James McKim thought the dance was like "African worship." Another white viewer thought it like a "pagan performance." White teacher William Francis Allen thought it wasn't African but African American, an African tradition mixed with the Christianity of the United States. As in dances like the calenda and banyaprei, which could create possession by and communion with the gods, spirits, and ancestors, visible possession—the Holy Spirit descending onto worshippers—was often a part of the shout.[23]

Much had changed since John Rose painted people dancing eighty years earlier. In the 1780s and 1790s, one man noted that most of the enslaved in South Carolina were "great strangers to Christianity," and Sundays and holidays were used "for the purposes of dancing, feasting and merriment." That merriment wasn't irreverence; it was reverence for spirits, communicating with ancestors, and gatherings of a spiritual community. While the Great Awakening had swept through much of the British North American colonies and drew people into Protestant Christianity in the first half of the eighteenth century, the movement had little impact on the whites in the Sea Islands, and even less on African-descended people. It wasn't until the latter part of the Second Great Awakening that religious practices started to change in this area. Baptist and Methodist conversions and teaching began in the 1830s, taking hold in the 1840s to 1860s. Sometimes, a slaveowner allowed for a Praise House. If they didn't, people snuck into the woods to a Brush or Hush Arbor, designated by an upside-down pot, to gather for services which blended the older African and African American spiritual traditions with Christianity. Like those people who snuck away at night to dance the calenda, people here went to secret meetings, and not always only on Sundays. The preacher could speak of God and Jesus and teach the Bible, but worshippers could also dance in a ring as a way to commune with God.[24]

Lucy's uncle, Reverend John McKim, thought that many of the songs were from "old Camp meeting hymn[s] of the white Methodists" that the people of the Sea Islands had adapted. Lucy questioned this assertion: "Who can tell whether many of the quaint camp meeting tunes which [we] now obtain everywhere did not originate with the blacks?" Lucy and others heard people on the Sea Islands singing tunes from hymnals and the religious canon, but the Black worshippers also sang songs that were entirely their own, the spirituals.[25]

What was absent in the praise house was any instrument. For hundreds of years, drums, fiddles, banjos, and wind instruments were part of religious dances. Now, as a result of conversion to Christianity, there were none. What Rose had seen was a spiritual dance, and central to it was the banjo, just as the instrument was in Suriname and Haiti. But the banjo and the fiddle and Christianity didn't seem to mix. When Swedish author Frederika Bremer visited the United States between 1849 and 1851, she wanted to hear the music of the enslaved. In Augusta, Georgia, after an old enslaved man named Romeo sang her a "death-song," a young man "who was not so evangelical as the rest, came and sang with his banjo." Around the same time as Bremer's visit to Georgia, another man said twenty violins had been destroyed by Methodist missionaries in the state. Writing about her experience as a white girl on a plantation in Mississippi, Susan Dabney Smedes remembered that when the enslaved people joined the Baptist Church, they stopped playing instruments. The "most music loving fellow" told the preacher that he'd broken his fiddle and banjo and thrown them away.[26]

Traditions that seemed secular but which might have been spiritual practices couldn't be easily blended with Christianity and were disappearing, too. Harriet Jacobs had been born enslaved in 1813 but published her memoir as a free woman in 1861. As a girl in eastern North Carolina, she remembered that they rose "early on Christmas morning to see the Johnkannaus." Two men led the procession of dancers dressed "in calico wrappers," over which they wore a net that was covered in "bright-colored stripes." They wore cow tails and horns. Some men beat on "the gumbo box," which was a box made into a drum with a sheepskin cover, like the drum Latrobe saw in Congo Square. Others played triangles and jawbones. Like King Charles in Albany, they went around asking for money. Jacobs does not give a reason for the disappearance of the Junkanoos, but one man said it was the Black preachers who stopped the practice since it degraded the Blacks "in the eyes of the white people of the community."[27]

Lucy McKim knew that the Civil War and the end of slavery would fundamentally change the United States for the better. She also knew that collecting the songs created and passed down during slavery was important. Soon, that music might be gone.

McKim wrote down the songs she heard and put the melodies in Western musical notation. She felt it was hard to capture "the entire character" of the songs "by mere musical notes and signs." Just as Mr. Baptiste had tried to translate rhythms and expressions of Black Jamaican music into notation Hans Sloane could read, Lucy needed to capture "the odd twists made in the throat; and the curious rhythmic effect produced by single voices chiming in at different irregular intervals" for people who had never heard the songs.[28]

When she got home to Philadelphia, she arranged the songs for voice and piano and played them for friends, including William Lloyd Garrison and his son Wendell, during meetings held to talk about the events happening in Port Royal. She envisioned collecting and publishing a book of the songs. "They are valuable as an expression of the character and life of the race which is playing such a conspicuous part in our history," she wrote in *Dwight's Music Journal*, where she managed to get one song published. "The wild, sad strains tell, as the sufferers themselves never could, of crushed hopes, keen sorrow, and dull, daily misery which covered them as hopelessly as the fog from the rice-swamps."[29]

After the war and her marriage to Wendell Garrison, a friend connected Lucy to William Francis Allen. He had spent nine months on the Sea Islands teaching school with his wife, Mary. Allen could read and write music and had transcribed songs. His cousin, Charles Pickard Ware, who had spent time working on St. Helena Island, helped them. They compiled 136 songs from all over the South into *Slave Songs of the United States*, the first collection of songs of Black Americans.

McKim, Allen, and Ware were sharing the culture that had existed during the brutality of slavery and oppression for hundreds of years. One of the songs they received from St. Charles Parish in Louisiana had the title "Calinda," with the chorus "Dansé calinda, boudoum, boudoum." Dance the calenda, the song says—the same dance Father Labat saw in Martinique in 1694.

They had a hard time finding songs that they thought were secular, which Allen described as "of an intrinsically barbaric character," songs that "may very well be purely African in origin." Allen claimed that "all the world knows the banjo, and the 'Jim Crow' songs of thirty years ago," but he thought those songs—tainted by Minstrelsy—didn't seem authentic. Even though they wanted to put together a second volume of secular songs, they couldn't find enough, a problem that encapsulates the history of the banjo around the same time. On one hand, they may not have been able to find secular songs in Black communities because religious music had replaced them. On the other, secular Black music had been both coopted by white musicians on the Minstrel stage and used by professional Black musicians, removing the songs from any perceived folk tradition.[30]

Slave Songs was published just two years after the end of the war, in 1867, and within five years, white people were already writing about hearing fewer of the songs that had seemed ubiquitous in the early 1860s. At the same time, music traditions both secular and religious provided material for a growing number of Black professional musicians, from touring groups like the Fisk Jubilee Singers to songwriter James Bland.

Some of the selections in *Slave Songs* would become known around the world, sung a century later in the street marches of the Civil Rights Movement and on the stage of country music's Grand Old Opry, by white performers. Others still live obscurely in the pages of the collection—songs that someone heard, thought important enough to write down and preserve, hopefully to be revived and appreciated, reevaluated, and better understood one day.

CODA

𝒟

IT'S A WARM, EARLY FALL NIGHT IN SEPTEMBER 2019, AND I'M WALK-ing across a field in central Virginia on my friend Dena Ross Jennings's farm. I see the lights illuminating musicians and dancers, spectators and singers on the porch of a small house she's moved to the property.

Dena's not related to my partner, Pete Ross—at least as far as they know. Dena is Black but thinks that she must have some Scottish ancestry from which her surname stems. Dena is a doctor, musician, banjo maker, and the founder of the Affrolachian On-Time Music Gathering. She defines On-Time as "the style and influence of Black Americans on roots and traditional genres of music and dance found in early pieces and inspiring new works with dignity and respect."[1]

Tonight she held an outdoor concert, and now the jam has started. On the porch, I see a group of musicians, most of whom are Black, playing a fast-tempo, hard-driving tune on banjos, fiddles, guitars, a bass, a cello, rhythm bones, and a washboard. American traditional music is hard to define, since much of it has origins in commercial music, from Blackface Minstrelsy to "Hillbilly" and "Race" records of the 1920s—not sources people typically think of as traditional.

As I hear this music and think about the interconnected web of genres that we force ourselves to define and the centuries of lived experience that gave rise to it, I think of Dena Epstein, the white librarian who published *Sinful Tunes and Spirituals* in 1977. Her book was the culmination of more than twenty years spent documenting the history of Black music that many people claimed didn't exist. She went through thousands of books and sources, and laid the foundation for this book, Dena Jennings's event, and a broad recognition not only of the history of the banjo but of the landscape of Black music before the Civil War. It's hard to imagine us being here without her research and that publication.[2]

Scott Didlake was one of the musicians and luthiers inspired by Epstein. The title of my book comes from something he once said: "What you have in that sound chamber is like a well of souls. It's haunting. All the people and all that culture that went into that thing." He said there was something mystical about the banjo, but didn't know that it was a ritual object and could itself serve as a well of souls. When he was dying of Lou Gehrig's disease in 1994, he invited Pete to apprentice with him in Jackson, Mississippi. Like Didlake, Pete felt that the erasure of this history was an injustice that needed to be righted. At the time, there were only two other people making gourd banjos in the US. Pete's obsession with early banjos was deep and immediate and, through phone calls and letters, he met others who were interested in this early history. In 1997, he wrote to Epstein about the bangeau reference in James Hollyday's papers, which she hadn't included in the appendix to her book and he had tracked down at the Maryland Historical Society. (The only reason I know this is because the postcard couldn't be delivered and Pete keeps it tucked in our copy of *Sinful Tunes*.)[3]

At the end of *Sinful Tunes and Spirituals* Epstein writes, "Much work, however, remains. No one person could hope to examine every potential source for the history of black folk music." She was asking others to take up the mantle, and some did, but few of them were Black. This may have been not because they didn't recognize the banjo as Black, but because of the negative connotations from Minstrelsy that it carried.[4]

This isn't to say that Black people weren't or hadn't been playing the banjo since it entered the realm of popular white culture. "The banjo never left the hands of Black people, even when white banjo players were the norm in the public eye," my friend Valerie Díaz Leroy wrote in an email to a group of people who were reviewing an article about banjo history. "There is a common misunderstanding that the cultural practices of Black communities mirrored this popular perception," when, in fact, they didn't.[5]

In the late 1990s, people were talking about the continued tradition of Black banjo playing, mainly in internet forums like Tony Thomas's "Black Banjo Then and Now" group. In 2005, Thomas helped organize the first Black Banjo Gathering in Boone, North Carolina. If you know anything about the Black Banjo Gathering, you probably know that the event led Rhiannon Giddens, Dom Flemons, and Justin Robinson to form the Carolina Chocolate Drops. They met and learned from Joe Thompson, a fiddler from North Carolina who grew up in the Black string band tradition. The Chocolate Drops won Grammys, toured the US and the world, and had a platform to share a story of Black American music that had almost been obscured. And they inspired other Black musicians who had traditionally been cut out of or discouraged from playing American traditional music because "they didn't belong"—some version of which many Black musicians have heard in country, old time, and bluegrass circles.

If the Black Banjo Gathering provided the space for the first generation of a Black folk music revival to develop, Dena Ross Jennings is providing the space for the second. While I knew some of the story of how she started playing and building banjos, I didn't know why she created the Affrolachian On-Time Music Gathering.

Dena grew up in a strict Pentecostal household in Ohio, singing church music and even performing with her sisters on the radio. "I assumed that all Black churches sounded like our church. What I

didn't know is that my mom and her family had transplanted themselves during the Great Migration from Appalachian Kentucky." At
church, there was music, with upright bass, tambourine, and hand-
clapping. "I didn't realize that when my mom's family moved from
Kentucky, they unscrewed their whole culture including the church
like a lightbulb and screwed it in in Akron." The music from church
was what she knew, and it became an influence when she started
playing guitar and writing her own songs.[6]

During one performance in a coffeehouse after college, when she
was playing songs she'd written, Dena's friend Andy Cohen told her,
"You realize you're playing banjo tunes?" and she said, "What's a
banjo tune?" He pointed her to Black Appalachian string band music,
and, "For the first time, I heard recorded music that sounded like
the music I heard in church growing up. I always wondered why our
music didn't sound like Mahalia Jackson . . . it sounded like *Hee Haw*.
By the time I came along, the banjo was gone from our culture."

During a visit to Elderly Instruments in Lansing, Michigan, Dena
saw a recreation of an early wooden-rimmed banjo made by Jeff
Menzies. "I didn't know how to play a banjo, but I liked the way it
sounded." Through a stroke of good luck, she ended up taking a solo
workshop with Menzies in Ontario, after everyone else had canceled.
Three days into the workshop, she knew she had to do an apprentice-
ship with him. The next morning, she remembers, a place came up
for rent across the street, so she spent the next four years in Canada.

After Dena moved to the Virginia farm, she decided to put
together a festival and a retreat. Her goal for the retreat was to have
attendees "present that thing that you are thinking about, that thing
that you want to try, and you can do that in the safety zone of being
around people that at least have the same vision that you have."[7]

When I asked her what the future of her event looked like, she
told me, "I want a Thang in every state across the country," referring
to the nickname of her event, so that "all the people who can't travel
to central Virginia in September have some place where they can do
theirs." She also wants the festival at her farm to be "so big that we

can't contain it." She'll always have the retreat for a smaller, invited crowd. And her retreat is one of the places where event organizers, instrument makers and dealers, educators, and musicians can come together to talk about projects and research and use what they learn from one another to increase the recognition of Black music as central to American music.

As the musicians play at Dena's, I see my friend Lillian Werbin dancing while waving a white handkerchief up and down. Lillian is the co-owner and manager of Elderly Instruments, which was founded by her father, Stan, in 1972, and is the store where Dena came across Jeff Menzies's banjo. We're both on the planning committee of the Banjo Gathering, an event that has been an incubator for early banjo research and that her dad has been attending since its inception in 1998.[8]

Although Lillian has been around banjos all her life, it was her godmother, Rosemary Miller, who made the connection between Black American history and the banjo. Because Lillian is adopted and Stan and her mom are both non-Black, she says, "all of my lessons on Blackness were from Rosemary." And when Rosemary found out that Lillian's parents owned Elderly, she asked, " 'Do you know he understands your history?' She went on and on about the banjo, and it was the first time those worlds collided for me." Lillian learned more banjo history working at Elderly over a decade later, and she now feels a connection to the banjo: "A Black item thriving in white America, with a history that is unknown. I am a human representation of that instrument."

As the owner of an established music retailer, Lillian wants to create a more welcoming environment for other Black people in traditional American music. "I'm learning that it's going to be a hard road; the reputation of the entire industry is not welcoming," but in the retailer–dealer world, she says, "my presence changes the game." In addition to being on the planning committee for the Banjo Gathering and coordinating the Midwest Banjo Camp, she is on the advisory committee for the International Bluegrass Music Association's

Arnold Shultz Fund, which its website describes as being created to increase the "participation of people of color in bluegrass music."[9]

On Dena's porch, Valerie Díaz Leroy stands toward the back of the group, playing her banjo. Like Dena, Valerie played the guitar before she played the banjo. A friend once asked her, "Hey, have you played a banjo before?" and when she did, it felt so good that she wanted to get one. But as a "Haitian–Puerto Rican Boston gal," seeing the banjo next to the Confederate flag and knowing the instrument's association with rural Southern culture wasn't just off-putting; it was frightening. When a friend told her about the Suwannee Banjo Camp in Florida, she thought, "If I go there, I will get killed." She decided to go anyway, and learned about the African origins of the banjo and African American banjo playing.[10]

Then, in watching a documentary about banjo builders, Valerie saw Pete describing the banza that Schœlcher collected. Her first thought was, "There's a f—ing Haitian banza?" Valerie had felt a connection to the banjo before, but had not understood why this instrument called to her. "I didn't know, but I knew. I've been driven by emotion, not the technical side [of banjo playing]. It's mine, I'm part of the story."

In her work with music educators, Valerie wants them to use the banjo as an entry point into the history of Black music and to open a conversation about it "as music from a people, rather than notes on the page." She wants them to see that the history of a song that stems from Blackface Minstrelsy, combined with "the experiences of Black people and people of African descent, helps frame the 'why' of the removal of songs [from curricula], or the placement of the songs in higher grade levels, so students are able to analyze these songs as artifacts."

What she's managed to do in helping build a curriculum around the banjo for the National Museum of African American Music is to provide teachers with the tools to talk about stereotypes and appro-priation—from kindergarten to adulthood. She wants people to understand that as a popular art form, Minstrelsy "permeated everything [and] led to stereotyping and systemic injustices, that was such an accepted part of culture—and still is. I try to impress upon people that it's not just in the past but we are dealing with [it] today."[11]

Jake Blount drives the jam at Dena's with his fiddling. When we spoke, he told me that white people's knowledge and perception has to change as more Black people play the banjo. Jake plays what's called old time music, songs that stem from pre-bluegrass string bands and have both vernacular and commercial origins. He's played guitar since he was twelve. In high school, he was taken with the banjo playing in a band he saw: "I was talking to them and I said, 'I've never seen anyone play a banjo like that,' " referring to the downstroke or clawhammer style most old time banjo players use. The white banjo player explained that the style originated in Africa. "I started reading more about Black music history generally—I was more interested in spirituals and gospel—and then came to understand the role the banjo had played. And, specifically, where my family was from in the Chesapeake Bay region." He felt the banjo's long history in Maryland connected him to his ancestors, especially as his father grew up on a "farm [that] was part of the plantation where our ancestors were enslaved."[12]

Jake began playing the banjo in college, researched Black string bands, and recorded their songs, which became part of his first EP, *Reparations*. He felt that something had been missing from modern Black string band playing and wanted to showcase Black musicians from the early and mid-twentieth century, showing "how cool it can sound." He "just had this mind of, 'What can I do in the old time music community to bring this stuff back to the fore?' " Now a professional musician, in addition to putting songs and tunes from these more-forgotten Black and Indigenous players on his albums, he teaches the tunes in workshops, and the songs are making their way back into the canon.

I asked him how people react to learning about the neglected history of Black banjo playing. He mentioned the importance they place on "knowing the provenance of the tune," and so they are happy to learn it is from a Black banjo player like Nathan Frazier. He pointed out that this can be problematic, too. "The fact that this music was played by Black people back in the day almost gets used as a get-out-of-jail-free card for there not being any Black people around now [playing the music]. I don't even know if it's a conscious thought. I think there's a fetishism for the Black history of the music. And also an exoticism."

Knowing Jake had explored the subject, I asked him why he thinks there are so few Black banjoists today. "There's a thousand answers to that," but one of the reasons is because "the cultural tendency of Black people, especially in this country, is to look forward and not backward. And if you look backward, it's to look forward."

I'm oversimplifying it, but in old time especially, the idea is to play music recorded at the beginning of the twentieth century or by folklorists who found the "old timers." As Jake says, the old time scene needs "to be open to the sound shifting. That's just part of the deal." Black people don't have the same musical references as white people, and regulating the sound "isn't asking Black people to come back to the music. It's asking Black people to come back into the music specifically in the way white people want us to." And, he pointed out, that sound also has racist origins, even beyond the Minstrel Show. "They [white musicians] still have not engaged in [a] critique with where the sound they're aiming for comes from"—which, in many cases, is "Hillbilly" records. "We are imitating this old sound, which is really cool, but where does this sound come from and who are we excluding by limiting it to that?"

Hannah Mayree plays the banjo during the jam, but stops to talk with Pete and me. Later, I asked Hannah more about the Black Banjo Reclamation Project that they lead. The first time they took interest in the banjo was when a white person was playing at a squat house in Buffalo. "I was introduced to banjo through the not-mainstream white banjo players," mostly "nomadic, houseless" travelers, who busk all over the country. Hannah had grown up in a household with instruments and played guitar, but soon identified that "there was

something really different about it [the banjo], something I was connected to." They learned from Black and white players, but, "once I
became aware of the Carolina Chocolate Drops . . . I was like, 'It's a
Black instrument, with even deeper roots on the African continent.'"
Even if Hannah was learning that history one-on-one from other
players they met at festivals, being Black in predominantly white folk
music scenes meant that Hannah experienced racism. "Some of it was
a lot more overt, some of it was more subtle, but if you're coming up
to me with banjo jokes and racist comments, it continues patterns
of oppression related to the white history of banjo." Hannah asked,
"At what point is it going to start being not OK that you are the only
Black person? It creates further harm in many cases for people like
myself and doesn't foster a healthy environment to learn and grow.
Otherwise, a lot more African-descended people would already be in
these spaces." They began conceiving of ways to get more Black people playing banjo, "on my own terms, away from the white gaze and
judgment based on conceptions of what folk music is."[13]

At one festival Hannah met another Black musician, fiddler Carl-
ton Dorsey, also known as SeeMore Love. In 2018, SeeMore and
Hannah were putting together a music tour, and Hannah had the
idea of getting banjos from white people who didn't want or need
them and giving them to Black people who did. "[If we are] getting
a banjo from a white person and giving it to a Black person, that's
me doing something to change this dynamic that I've been dealing
with." On tour, Hannah collected and redistributed banjos. From
there, the project has grown to community events and building and
playing workshops, where Black people can "learn about it [the banjo
and its history] in a Black space." Collecting and redistributing banjos
is still the priority, since not all community members can afford an
instrument. Hannah and their collaborators have also been invited
to predominantly white music communities to perform and teach
workshops, to help musicians realize "racism [within their commu-
nity] was a problem they needed to address." Hannah doesn't want
to "keep perpetuating harm with the banjo" and sees the work of the

Black Banjo Reclamation Project as healing. "I am doing this because it feels good for me and heals me, and has been beneficial for me, and I can see that other people can benefit from it, too."

"I don't feel like there is one specific Black banjo community, although I feel deeply that transforming oppression related to the banjo is something that Black people in America have an opportunity to work towards at this time," Hannah told me when we spoke, and they couldn't be more right. Dena, Lillian, Valerie, Jake, and Hannah are five of the Black banjo players who live in the US and disseminate banjo music and history, although in different ways. There are other Black musicians, educators, and builders in the US, and those who are doing similar work across the Caribbean—from Jamaica, the Bahamas, Suriname, and Haiti, to Saint Lucia and Antigua and Barbuda. It's time we listen, learn, and support them and the many other Black people doing this work.[14]

In this book, I've tried to reveal what we know about the banjo, to undo an injustice of history created by white people. I've been able to answer some of the questions Dena Epstein's research left open, building on the work of other scholars and banjo enthusiasts. But I also know that there are many more stories to uncover.

In November 2021—after I had already written the above paragraph—Pete received an email from Alexandre Girard-Muscagorry, a curator at the Cité de la Musique in Paris. Alexandre is working on his PhD, exploring Victor Schœlcher's instrument collecting and abolitionist aims. He was searching through a database of French museum collections when an image struck him. Alexandre wrote to Pete, "I haven't seen it yet [in person] but . . . it looks very much like an ancient banjo (the profile of the flat neck, the gourd resonator, the spike, the shape of the sound holes, etc.). What do you think?"[15]

Pete clicked on the photo attachments and said, "Holy shit."

The construction of the instrument was exactly the same as the banza, with the flat board neck that enters the gourd through where it attached to the vine, bisects it, and exits through the pip. It had cross-shaped sound holes. The skin head was held on with cut nails.

It also provided proof for guesses that Pete had made about the banza's construction. The banza collected by Schœlcher didn't have a nut that would keep the strings close to the fingerboard near the headstock, nor a tailpiece where the strings could attach at the bottom of the gourd. Based on the image of the Strum Strumps from Jamaica and the watercolor from South Carolina, Pete had guessed that some sort of string held tight with a wooden wedge created a nut, and that the tailpiece would have been leather. This instrument had the string nut, the wooden wedge, and a leather tailpiece. When Pete and I went to see the instrument at the Musée des Confluences in Lyon, France, we knew it was a banjo. It had so many similarities to the banza—down to the finger wear pattern on the neck, suggesting the instruments were tuned the same and the musicians would have played songs in the same tuning. We have some leads about where it might have come from and how it ended up in Lyon, but nothing conclusive. It has a story; I just can't tell it yet.

I wrote this book because I came across new information I thought needed to be shared, but my real hope is that you, reader, find a mystery in it that needs to be solved, or realize you can provide an insight that I haven't, and that this work and research continues. As Dena Epstein wrote, one person can't look through all of the sources that might tell us something about the banjo or early American music, but maybe we've uncovered enough now that the banjo won't be seen as foolish or the butt of a joke, but as an instrument worthy of our attention and study, an instrument that reveals our American history.

Gratitude

My first thanks go to the people I interviewed for the Coda. I first publicly read a section of this book at the Thang—a section very similar to the opening you read. I am grateful for the support of all the Thangsters, but especially Valerie Díaz Leroy (and Willow), Lillian Werbin, Jake Blount, and Dena Ross Jennings. Thank you to Hannah Mayree for taking the time to be interviewed and for making sure I was asking myself hard questions. Thank you to Rhiannon Giddens for her foreword, but more importantly for spreading the banjo history gospel.

There are obviously many more Black banjoists and roots musicians whom I couldn't interview for the Coda. Buy their CDs and LPs, go to their shows, support them with your money. And learn more about the music equity organizations that they lead, including Imani Works, the Rhapsody Project, Decolonize the Music Room, and the Black Banjo Reclamation Project.

I couldn't have written this book without the support of the people behind the Banjo Gathering, which includes Lillian Werbin as well as Greg Adams (who asked questions about what I was writing and why) and Cullen Strawn. Our banjo research wouldn't be where it is today without the Gathering's founders and instigators—Peter Szego, Jim Bollman,

Hank Schwartz, Bob Carlin, Robert Winans, and Tony Thomas—who all wanted to know more about the banjo's earliest history and African origins. After my partner Pete Ross and I presented about Schouten's dioramas at the Banjo Gathering in 2017, it was Peter Szego who said, "Well, isn't this going to be a book?" Then, I hardly believed it could be.

Every time I found something related to the panja and Suriname, I wished I could email Schlomo Pestcoe. Schlomo's rediscovery of the panja was what started to shift what we know about the banjo and instigated my discoveries. His untimely passing in 2015 meant he left with many questions still unanswered.

The second place I presented this research was at the Legacy of Slavery and Indentured Servitude Conference at the Anton de Kom University in Paramaribo, Suriname, where I had enlightening conversations with Karwan Fatah-Black, Bridget Brereton, Wendeline Flores, and Hilde Neus. I am also thankful to the founder of Het Koto Museum, Christine van Rusel-Henar, who explained the continuation of the banya and Koto Misi traditions in Suriname today. Darell Geldorp kindly allowed Pete and me to attend a banya rehearsal of the NAKS Wan Rutu dance group.

I couldn't have written this book without the support of fellowships and institutions. Dr. Marguerite Ragnow welcomed me to the James Ford Bell Library of the University of Minnesota, where, on a William Reese Company Fellowship, I spent three weeks with the writings of John Gabriel Stedman and saw his drawings, Sloane's Strum Strumps engraving, and Moreau de Saint-Méry's travel atlas. The Robert W. Deutsch Foundation's Rubys Artist Award provided financial support and made me believe in this project as a book. The Inner Loop Literary Writer-in-Residence Program at the Woodlawn and Pope-Leighey House and the Logan Nonfiction Fellowship at the Carey Institute for Global Good both provided time for writing, creativity, and connection to places and other writers.

Thank you to everyone who answered an email where I had a random question, including Jessica Glickman and Randy Browne. Thank you to Mary Caton Lingold for providing an advance copy of her article on Mr. Baptiste and, more importantly, for uncovering more about him. I'm grateful to Laurent DuBois for reading a draft and providing feedback. If you've read this far, you know that Alexandre Girard-Muscagorry's email about the banjo in Lyon was transformative. I'm also grateful to him for reading the chapter on the banza and providing more insight into Schœlcher's instrument collecting. Thank you to Marie-Paul Imberti for inviting us to see the new banjo in Lyon, and for being excited to learn more about it and its provenance.

Publishing a book is an incredible team effort, and I'm grateful to the folks at W. W. Norton: Amy Cherry, Huneeya Siddiqui, Gabby Nugent, Michelle Waters, Amy Medeiros, Lauren Abbate, Ingsu Liu, and Allegra Huston.

Thank you to my writing friends for practical and emotional support: Rachel Dickinson, Neda Semnani, Stephanie Murphy, Memsy Price, Ginny McReynolds, Laura Laing, Randon Billings-Noble, and Ellie Bozmarova. Writing this book between the summer of 2020 and the winter of 2021 was made easier thanks to all of you.

To my dad, who carefully and thoughtfully read this manuscript and helped with translations. To my mom, Thomas, Benjamin, Matney, Sidney, and Ellis, for love and support.

And finally, to my muse, my handler, my fact-checker, my travel buddy, my partner, Pete Ross.

Notes

More images and illustrations related to this book, including color versions of the illustrations that appear in these pages, can be found at www.kristinagaddy.com /wellofsouls.

Abbreviations

TASTD: Trans Atlantic Slave Trade Database; https://slavevoyages.org/voyage/database.

NYABG: *The New York African Burial Ground: Unearthing the African Presence in Colonial New York*, vol. 2, *New York African Burial Ground Descriptions of Burials 1 through 200*, and vol. 3, *Historical Perspectives of the African Burial Ground: New York Blacks and the Diaspora* (Washington, DC: Howard University Press, 2009).

United Brethren: *Periodical Accounts Relating to the Missions of the Church of the United Brethren Established Among the Heathen* (London: Brethren's Society for the Furtherance of the Gospel Among the Heathen, 1848–63).

Prelude

1 The word enslave is a verb meaning to subjugate into slavery, and so the noun enslaver is someone who makes someone a slave. In this linguistic sense, John Rose is not an enslaver, since he was purchasing people who were already enslaved. I do not use the word slave outside of this context. Rose and others in this book are the owners of enslaved men, women, and children and responsible for their continued enslavement.

2 Although this piece of art is known as *The Old Plantation*, I will refer to it as John Rose's watercolor or the South Carolina watercolor. Rose did not indicate a name

for his work, and the name *The Old Plantation* creates a romanticization around what were, in essence, forced labor camps. See Susan Shames, *The Old Plantation: The Artist Revealed* (Williamsburg: Colonial Williamsburg Foundation, 2010), 17–18.

3 I use the term African American to refer to people of African descent in the Americas broadly, not just in the US. More often I use person of African descent or Black. While Black is in more common use today to describe anyone with African ancestry, in some colonial contexts, it referred specifically to people who were enslaved; those who had African ancestry but were not enslaved would use the term free person of color, which I also use. As of this writing, a fourth early banjo was uncovered in a museum in Lyon, France, which Pete and I examined in January 2022. Although we're confident it is a banjo, its provenance has not yet been established.

4 Peter O'Dowd and Serena McMahon, "Béla Fleck's Journey to Find Truth in Origins of the Banjo," *Here and Now*, January 25, 2021, https://www.wbur.org/; Charlie Weber, "Why These Four Banjo-Playing Women Resurrected the Songs of the Enslaved," *Smithsonian*, April 10, 2019, https://www.smithsonianmag.com/; John Jeremiah Sullivan, "Rhiannon Giddens and What Folk Music Means," *New Yorker*, May 13, 2019.

5 Saidiya Hartman, *Wayward Lives, Beautiful Experiments* (New York: Norton, 2019), xiii. Any speculations I have made about the lives of the enslaved people are based on research from a multitude of sources not limited to those on the banjo. I will make it clear when I am speculating, because I will never be able to speak for those who were deprived of a voice.

6 Edward Kamau Brathwaite, "The African Presence in Caribbean Literature," *Daedalus* 103, no. 2 (1974): 74.

I—The Atlantic Ocean, 1687

1 John Thornton, "Cannibals, Witches, and Slave Traders in the Atlantic World," *William and Mary Quarterly* 60, no. 2 (2003): 274.

2 Stacey Sommerdyk, "Trade and the Merchant Community of the Loango Coast in the Eighteenth Century," PhD diss., University of Hull, 2012, 102 and 205.

3 Filipa Ribeiro da Silva and Stacey Sommerdyk, "Reexamining the Geography and Merchants of the West Central African Slave Trade: Looking Behind the Numbers," *African Economic History* 38 (2010): 77–105; Frederik de Wit, "Totius Africæ accuratissima tabula," map, 1688, Library of Congress, https://www.loc.gov/resource/.

4 Sommerdyk, "Trade and the Merchant Community," 34.

5 Sommerdyk, "Trade and the Merchant Community," 38; Jessica Glickman, email to author, July 22, 2020.

6 "Voyage ID 9827," TASTD.

7 Glickman, email; Johannes Menne Postma, *The Dutch in the Atlantic Slave Trade* (Cambridge: Cambridge University Press, 1990), 233–34.

8 "Voyage ID 9827"; Stephanie Smallwood, "African Guardians, European Slave Ships, and the Changing Dynamics of Power in the Early Modern Atlantic," *William and Mary Quarterly* 64, no. 4 (2007): 682; David Richardson, "Shipboard Revolts, African Authority, and the Atlantic Slave Trade," *William and Mary Quarterly* 58, no. 1 (2001): 76.

9 David Galenson, *Traders, Planters, and Slaves: Market Behavior in Early English America* (Cambridge: Cambridge University Press, 1986), 68; "Voyage ID 9827"; Smallwood, "African Guardians," 680–84; Postma, *The Dutch*, 165.

10 Sommerdyk, "Trade and the Merchant Community," 128; Edna Greene Medford et al., "Disease and Health," NYABG, vol. 3, 78; Marcus Rediker, *The Slave Ship: A Human History* (New York: Viking, 2007), 5.

II—Jamaica, 1687

1 Hans Sloane, *A Voyage to the Islands Madera, Barbados, Nieves, S. Christophers and Jamaica, . . . In large copper plates as big as the life*, vol. 1 (London: B. M. for the author, 1707), 2.

2 James Delbourgo, *Collecting the World: Hans Sloane and the Origins of the British Museum* (Cambridge, MA: Belknap Press, 2017), 35.

3 TASTD; "America and West Indies: December 1687," in *Calendar of State Papers Colonial, America and West Indies*, vol. 12 (1685–88) and Addenda (1653–87), ed. J. W. Fortescue (London: Her Majesty's Stationery Office, 1899), 474–85.

4 John Taylor, *Jamaica in 1687: The Taylor Manuscript at the National Library of Jamaica*, ed. David Buisseret (Kingston: University of the West Indies Press, 2008), 300–04.

5 Delbourgo, *Collecting the World*, 40–41; Ben Hughes, *Apocalypse 1692: Empire, Slavery, and the Great Port Royal Earthquake* (Yardley, PA: Westholme, 2017), 2–3; TASTD; Galenson, *Traders, Planters, and Slaves*, 4. According to Merriam–Webster, the first known use of the word plantation was in the fifteenth century and it meant "a usually large group of plants and especially trees under cultivation," but also came to mean "an agricultural estate usually worked by resident labor." In the seventeenth-century Caribbean, that resident labor was enslaved people of African descent. I use the word plantation because that is what people at the time used and it is a term many people understand; however, the word can also conjure romantic notions of the Old South (à la *Gone with the Wind*), and I want to emphasize that there was nothing romantic about them. They were forced labor camps.

6 G. R. de Beer, *Sir Hans Sloane and the British Museum* (New York: Oxford University Press, 1953), 20; Hughes, *Apocalypse*, 22, 37–38.

7 Taylor, *Jamaica in 1687*, 240; Hughes, *Apocalypse*, 39; Long, *History of Jamaica*, 423–25; Frederic G. Cassidy, "'Hipsaw' and 'John Canoe,'" *American Speech* 41, no. 1 (1966): 49.

8 Paul Gerdes, "African Dance Rattle Capsules from Benin, Nigeria and Congo:

Plainting a symmetric, hexanedral shape," 2013, http://www.mi.sanu.ac.rs/
vismath/gerdes2013hexahedral/hexahedron.pdf, accessed July 2020. See African
ankle rattles at the Musical Instrument Museum Online database, www.mimo
-international.com. Sloane, *Voyage*, vol. 1, xlix.

9   Taylor, *Jamaica in 1687*, 270.

10 Sloane, *Voyage*, vol. 1, lii.

11 Ted Gioia, *Music: A Subversive History* (New York: Basic Books, 2019), 162. Instruments can also be fretted to a twelve-tone scale, which still limits the number of
notes.

12 Taylor, *Jamaica in 1687*, 269.

13 The instrument Sloane collected is about 22 inches long; Pete Ross, interview, July
2020.

14 Some historians determine these regions, taken from TASTD, to be Eurocentric.
However, they currently represent the best data connected to geographic regions
established thus far. For more, see Paul Lovejoy's "The Upper Guinea Coast and
the Transatlantic Slave Trade Database," *African Economic History* 38 (2010); Schlomo
Pestcoe and Greg Adams, "List of West African Plucked Spike Lutes," in *Banjo Roots
and Branches*, ed. Robert Winans (Champaign: University of Illinois Press, 2018), 47;
Roger Blench, "A Guide to the Musical Instruments of Cameroun: Classification,
distribution, history and vernacular names," July 31, 2009, http://www.rogerblench
.info/Ethnomusicology/Papers/Africa/Cameroun/Cameroun%20musical%20
instruments%20book.pdf, accessed August 2020; Roger Blench, "The Morphology
and Distribution of Sub-Saharan Musical Instruments of North African, Middle
Eastern, and Asian, Origin," *Musica Asiatica* 4 (1984): 170–71. This construction,
where the neck actually enters the gourd, seems to be characteristic of lutes around
Lake Chad.

15 Schlomo Pestcoe, "'Strum Strumps' and 'Sheepskin' Guitars: The Early Gourd
Banjo and Clues to its West African Roots in the Seventeenth-Century Circum-
Caribbean," in *Banjo Roots and Branches*, ed. Robert Winans (Champaign: Univer-
sity of Illinois Press, 2018), 115.

16 Kay Dian Kriz, "Curiosities, Commodities, and Transplanted Bodies in Hans
Sloane's 'Natural History of Jamaica,'" *William and Mary Quarterly* 57, no. 1 (2000),
62; Sloane, *Voyage*, vol. 1, xlvi–xlvii. What Sloane meant by "Indian" is an ongoing
debate. Some scholars believe he means Native Americans, while others believe
he meant people from the Indian Ocean region. In relation to banjo history, the
focus has often been on West African antecedents, but the possibility that Sloane
might have meant people from around the Indian Ocean should make us look more
closely at those instruments.

17 Mary Caton Lingold, "Peculiar Animations: Listening to Afro-Atlantic Music in
Caribbean Travel Narratives," *Early American Literature* 52, no. 3 (2017): 623–50;

Sloane, *Voyage*, vol. 1, 1. I use the male pronoun here because it is very likely that the player was a man. In West African communities, instrumental musicians who play for ritual or ceremonial purposes are usually male, while women sing.

18 Mary Caton Lingold, "In Search of Mr Baptiste: on early Caribbean music, race, and a colonial composer," *Early Music*, 49, 1 (2021): 49–66.

19 Jacqueline Cogdell Djedje, "Song Type and Performance Style in Hausa and Dagomba Possession (Bori) Music," *The Black Perspective in Music* 12, no. 2 (1984): 166.

20 To listen to the pieces Mr. Baptiste transcribed, visit http://www.musicalpassage.org/.

21 Sloane, *Voyage*, vol. 1, lvi.

22 Kriz, "Curiosities," 43.

23 Delbourgo, *Collecting the World*, 84.

24 "Sir Hans Sloane," British Museum website, https://www.britishmuseum.org/about-us/british-museum-story/sir-hans-sloane; Delbourgo, *Collecting the World*, 187–90; James Delbourgo, "Slavery in the Cabinet of Curiosities: Hans Sloane's Atlantic World," 2007, http://www.britishmuseum.org/PDF/Delbourgo%20essay.pdf, 5–6.

25 David Bushnell, "The Sloane Collection in the British Museum," *American Anthropologist* 8, no. 4 (1906): 672, 676; Delbourgo, *Collecting the World*, 230.

III—Martinique, 1694

1 Richard Sheridan, *Sugar and Slavery: An Economic History of the British West Indies 1623–1775* (Baltimore: Johns Hopkins University Press, 1973), 496.

2 Quoted in Jeroen Dewulf, *The Pinkster King and the King of the Kongo: The Forgotten History of America's Dutch-Owned Slaves* (Jackson: University Press of Mississippi, 2017), 47; Brent Tarter, "Elizabeth Key (fl. 1655–1660)," *Dictionary of Virginia Biography* (Library of Virginia, 2019), http://www.lva.virginia.gov/public/dvb/bio.asp?b=Key_Elizabeth_fl_1655-1660; Sue Peabody, " 'A Nation Born to Slavery': Missionaries and Racial Discourse in Seventeenth-Century French Antilles," *Journal of Social History* 38, no. 1 (2004): 117, 121.

3 Jean-Baptiste Labat, *Nouveau voyage aux isles de l'Amerique*, vol. 1 (Paris: Guillaume Cavalier, 1722), trans. John Garrigus, http://web.sonoma.edu/users/t/toczyski/labat2.pdf; Everild Young and Kjeld Helweg-Larsen, *The Pirates' Priest: The Life of Pere Labat in the West Indies 1693–1705* (London: Jarrolds, 1965), 43.

4 Suzanne Toczyski, "Navigating the Sea of Alterity: Jean-Baptiste Labat's *Nouveau voyage aux îles*," *Papers on French Seventeenth-Century Literature* 34, no.67 (2007): 490; quoted in Suzanne Toczyski, "Jean-Baptiste Labat and the Buccaneer Barbecue in Seventeenth-Century Martinique," *Gastronomica* 10, no. 1 (2010): 62; Sheridan, *Sugar and Slavery*, 22.

5 David Eltis, Frank D. Lewis, and David Richardson, "Slave Prices, the African Slave

Trade, and Productivity in the Caribbean, 1674–1807," *Economic History Review* 58 (New Series), no. 4 (2005): 677.

6   Labat, *Nouveau voyage*, trans. Garrigus.

7   Jason Kerr Dobney, "Military Music in American and European Traditions," Metropolitan Museum of Art, 2004, https://www.metmuseum.org/toah/hd/ammu/ hd_ammu.htm; Labat, *Nouveau voyage*, 463; S. Zenkovsky, "Zar and Tambura as Practised by the Women of Omdurman," *Sudan Notes and Records* 31, no. 1 (1950): 69; Steven F. Pond, "A Negotiated Tradition: Learning 'Traditional' Ewe Drumming," *Black Music Research Journal* 34, no. 2 (2014): 179. Francesco Turrisi, who plays frame drum and tambourine among many other instruments, helped me understand how drummers use their hands and the placement of their fingers to create tonalities as well as rhythms.

8   Labat, *Nouveau voyage*, trans. Garrigus. Calabashes and gourds are often confused in vernacular speech. Gourds (*Lagenaria siceraria*) are part of the Cucurbitaceae family, related to zucchini and squash, and grow on vines. According to the Missouri Botanical Garden, they can grow in US hardiness zone 2, which extends as far north as Canada and Alaska. Bottle gourds are sometimes referred to as calabash gourds. True calabashes, however, are the fruit of the *Crescentia cujete* tree, which only grows in warmer climates such as the Caribbean and the southern tip of Florida.

9   Gioia, *Music*, 17, 138; S. Koelsch, T. Bashevkin, J. Kristensen, et al., "Heroic Music Stimulates Empowering Thoughts during Mind-Wandering," *Scientific Reports* 9, no. 10317 (2019), https://doi.org/10.1038/s41598-019-46266-w. Gioia notes a study where voices rising together in song causes the pituitary gland to release the hormone oxytocin. The brainwaves of those hearing the music adjust and synchronize to the beat of the drum, which may be one of the reasons that drums are used in ceremonies and religious practices across the world to induce ecstatic trances.

10 M. Adrien Dessalles, *Histoire générale des Antilles*, vol. 3 (Paris: Libraire-Éditeur, 1847), 296–97; Julian Gerstin, "Tangled Roots: Kalenda and other Neo-African Dances in the Circum-Caribbean," *New West Indian Guide* 78, no. 1/2 (2004): 29; Labat, *Nouveau voyage*, trans. Garrigus. The calenda was banned first in Martinique, in 1678, and in 1685 the Code Noir banned it in all French colonies. The Code Noir did not specify that alcohol could not be given to slaves, only that "it was forbidden to give alcohol in lieu of food"; see Sylviane A. Diouf, *Servants of Allah: African Muslims Enslaved in the Americas* (New York: New York University Press, 1998), 120.

11 Gioia notes that oxytocin (the hormone the brain releases when we sing together) "mobilizes people to fight against other groups . . . and can send people into riots or battles" (*Music*, 398). He also writes that music can induce ecstasy and conflict, and that "research shows striking correlations in nervous system activity (heart rate, respiration, body temperature, pulse, etc.) between listening to pleasurable

music and fight-or-flight responses to danger." He argues that "songs are also the strongest team-building and coalition-building forces in human culture" (238).

12 Gerstin, "Tangled Roots," 7.

13 Jereon Dewulf, "From the Calendas to the Calenda: On the Afro-Iberian Substratum in Black Performance Culture in the Americas," *Journal of American Folklore* 131, no. 519 (2018): 16; Dessalles, *Histoire générale des Antilles*, 296–97.

14 Gerstin, "Tangled Roots," 8.

15 John Oldmixon, *The British Empire in America*, vol. 2 (London: John Nicholson, 1708), 123. While he names instruments, Oldmixon doesn't name any dances.

16 I. M. Lewis, *Ecstatic Religion: An Anthropological Study of Spirit Possession and Shamanism* (New York: Penguin, 1975), 47, 58, 132, 205; Gioia, *Music*, 31; Djedje, "Song Type," 169.

17 Sheridan, *Sugar and Slavery*.

IV—New York, 1736

1 Vincent Buranelli, "Peter Zenger's Editor," *American Quarterly* 7, no. 2 (Summer 1955): 174–81.

2 *New-York Weekly Journal*, March 7, 1736.

3 Buranelli, "Peter Zenger's Editor," 176. Greg Adams and Schlomo Pestcoe argue that it must have been Alexander who wrote the letter signed "The SPY," and Buranelli's article on Alexander supports this, given that Alexander wrote much of the copy for the paper. For purposes of clarity, I am using "Alexander" instead of the anonymous "SPY."

4 Arthur H. Bankoff and Frederick A. Winter, "The Archaeology of Slavery at the Van Cortlandt Plantation in the Bronx, New York," *International Journal of Historical Archaeology* 9, no. 4 (2005): 296; Edna Greene Medford et al., "Eighteenth-Century Procurement of African Laborers for New York," in NYABG, vol. 3, 43; Edna Greene Medford et al., "The Ubiquity of Work," in NYABG, vol. 3, 59.

5 While Sloane gives the name as "Strum Strumps," that seems to be a function of the way it is played and a name he gives it rather than what it was called by enslaved Blacks.

6 For more on African American archeology in New York, see Bankoff and Winter, "The Archeology of Slavery"; Marcus Alan Watson, "Kongo to Kings County: African Cultural Continuities at the Lott Farmstead, Brooklyn, New York," PhD diss., City University of New York, 2016.

7 Warren Perrt, Jean Howson, and Barbara Bianco, eds., "Appendix B–2," NYABG, vol. 4, 2.

8 Jean Cerasale et al., "Description of Burials 1 through 200," NYABG, vol. 2; Edna Greene Medford et al., "'By the Visitations of God': Death, Burial, and the Affirma-

tion of Humanity," NYABG, vol. 3, 88; Albert J. Raboteau, *Slave Religion: The "Invisible Institution" in the Antebellum South* (New York: Oxford University Press, 2004), 12.

9 John Sharpe, "Proposals for Erecting a School, Library and Chapel at New York," in Publication Fund Series 13, pt. 5, *Collections of the New-York Historical Society* (New York: New-York Historical Society, 1881), 355.

10 Quoted in Edna Greene Medford, Emilyn L. Brown, and Selwyn H. H. Carrington, "Change and Adjustment," in NYABG, vol. 3, 26.

11 George Julius Miller, "James Alexander and the Jews, Especially Isaac Emanuel," *Publications of the American Jewish Historical Society* 35 (1939): 171–88.

12 TASTD; Paul E. Lovejoy, "Transatlantic Transformations: The Origins and Identities of Africans in the Americas," in *Africa, Brazil, and the Construction of Trans-Atlantic Black Identities*, ed. Boubacar Barry, Livio Sansone, and Elisée Soumonni (Trenton, NJ: Africa World Press, 2008), 87–89.

13 Jeroen Dewulf, *From the Kingdom of Kongo to Congo Square: Kongo Dances and the Origins of the Mardi Gras Indians* (Lafayette: University of Louisiana at Lafayette Press, 2017), 21.

14 *New-York Weekly Journal*, March 7, 1736.

15 *New-York Weekly Journal*, March 7, 1736.

V—Maryland, 1758

1 James Bordley, *The Hollyday and Related Families of the Eastern Shore of Maryland* (Baltimore: Maryland Historical Society, 1962), 289–90; Sarah Anderson to James Hollyday, December 11, 1758, Hollyday Family Papers, Maryland Center for History and Culture. Bordley writes that the exact date of Sally's birth is not known, but based on letters from Sally's mother, Rebecca, Sally was probably born in 1742, making her about sixteen when she wrote to her uncle.

2 Alan Karras, *Sojourners in the Sun: Scottish Migrants in Jamaica and the Chesapeake, 1740–1800* (New York: Cornell University Press, 1992), 85; Galenson, *Traders, Planters, and Slaves*, 68; Bordley, *The Hollyday and Related Families*, 55; "Voyage ID 103914" and "Voyage ID 103916," TASTD.

3 Sarah Anderson to James Hollyday, March 20, 1759, HFP/MCHC.

4 James Hollyday to Dr. (Sir) William Brown, October 1, 1759, HFP/MCHC.

5 For more on enslaved musicians and the advertisements to get them back, see Robert Winans, "Black Musicians in Eighteenth-Century America," in *Banjo Roots and Branches*, ed. Robert Winans (Champaign: University of Illinois Press, 2018): 194–213.

6 *Maryland Gazette*, June 8, 1748.

7 "Matthew Harris," *A Biographical Dictionary of the Maryland Legislature 1635–1789*, ed. Edward C. Papenfuse, et al., vol. 1 (Baltimore: Johns Hopkins University Press, 1985), 414.

8 *Maryland Gazette*, August 30, 1749.

9 Bordley, *The Hollyday and Related Families*, 103.

10 Bordley, *The Hollyday and Related Families*, 103.

VI—Jamaica, 1750

1 Carol Stiles, "Vineyard: A Jamaican Cattle Pen, 1750–1751," master's thesis, William and Mary College, 1985, 15; Trevor Burnard, *Mastery, Tyranny, and Desire: Thomas Thistlewood and His Slaves in the Anglo-Jamaican World* (Chapel Hill: University of North Carolina Press, 2004), ch. 1; Stiles, "Vineyard," 45.

2 Burnard, *Mastery, Tyranny, and Desire*, ch. 1.

3 Thomas Thistlewood, diary entry, December 25, 1750, Thomas Thistlewood Papers, James Marshall and Marie-Louise Osborn Collection, Beinecke Rare Book and Manuscript Library, Yale University; Edward Long, *History of Jamaica*, vol. 2 (London: T. Lownes, 1774), 426. Thistlewood doesn't describe the dancing, so I augmented his account with that of Long.

4 Stiles, "Vineyard," 12; TASTD; Burnard, *Mastery, Tyranny, and Desire*, ch. 1, ch. 5; Thistlewood, diary entry, December 26, 1750, quoted in Burnard, *Mastery, Tyranny, and Desire*, ch. 1.

5 Thistlewood, diary entry, February 2, 1751.

6 Long, *History of Jamaica*, 423–25.

7 Long, *History of Jamaica*, 423–25; Frederic G. Cassidy, "'Hipsaw' and 'John Canoe,'" *American Speech* 41, no. 1 (1966): 49.

8 Burnard, *Mastery, Tyranny, and Desire*, ch. 1. I am choosing not to describe these crimes because I believe that would serve only to retraumatize or titillate readers, a concept that Christina Sharpe explores in her writing about the legacy of slavery and American culture. Thistlewood's disturbing behavior is described in detail by Burnard in *Mastery, Tyranny, and Desire*.

9 Thistlewood, diary entries, November 20, 1773, and December 3, 1771.

10 Burnard, *Mastery, Tyranny, and Desire*, ch. 6, ch. 7; J. S. Handler and K. M. Bilby, "On the Early Use and Origin of the Term 'Obeah' in Barbados and the Anglophone Caribbean," *Slavery and Abolition* 22, no. 2 (2001): 87; Alan Richardson, "Romantic Voodoo," in *Sacred Possessions: Vodou, Santeria, Obeah, and the Caribbean*, ed. Margarite Fernández Olmos and Lizabeth Paravisini-Gerbert (New Brunswick, NJ: Rutgers University Press: 1997), 174; Richard Cullen Rath, "African Music in Seventeenth-Century Jamaica: Cultural Transit and Transition," *William and Mary Quarterly* 50, no. 4 (1993): 723; Mary Turner, *Slaves and Missionaries: The Disintegration of Jamaican Slave Society 1787–1834* (Kingston: University of the West Indies Press, 1998), 53; Handler and Bilby, "On the Early Use," 87; Turner, *Slaves and Missionaries*, 6. According to Richardson, obeah has Ashanti–Fanti origins (communities that live

in present-day Ghana), and is "more purely concerned with magic or sorcery than Voodoo [Vodou]."

11 Quoted in Burnard, *Mastery, Tyranny, and Desire*, ch. 1.

12 Handler and Bilby, "On the Early Use," 32; Burnard, *Mastery, Tyranny, and Desire*, ch. 6.

13 Burnard, *Mastery, Tyranny, and Desire*, ch. 6; Thomas Thistlewood, diary entry, February 3, 1764.

14 Thistlewood, diary entry, November 20, 1773.

VII—Suriname, 1773

1 John Gabriel Stedman, 1790 manuscript, 15–17, 270, 274, John Gabriel Stedman Archive and Book Manuscript, James Ford Bell Library, University of Minnesota Libraries.

2 John Gabriel Stedman, *Stedman's Suriname: Life in an Eighteenth-Century Slave Society. An Abridged, Modernized Edition of Narrative of a Five Years Expedition Against the Revolted Negroes of Surinam*, ed. Richard and Sally Price (Baltimore: Johns Hopkins University Press, 1992), xi, xii, xix.

3 Stedman, *Stedman's Suriname*, 96, 40.

4 John Gabriel Stedman, diary entry, February 9, 1773. This is his redaction of the word.

5 Stedman, diary entries, February–April 1773.

6 Stedman, *Stedman's Suriname*, 42. Stedman gives Mrs. Demelley's full explanation of Joanna's situation and spells his name with a capital D; Nicky Post, "The Free Non-White Ladies of Suriname," master's thesis, Utrecht University, June 26, 2017.

7 Stedman, diary entry, April 23, 1773; Stedman, *Stedman's Suriname*, xxxiii; Hilde Neus, "The Yellow Lady: Mulatto Women in the Suriname Plantocracy," in *Color Struck: Essays on Race and Ethnicity in Global Perspective*, ed. Julius Adekunle and Hettie V. Williams (Lanham, PA: University Press of America, 2010), 115; Stedman, *Stedman's Suriname*, xxxiii. These relationships would be punishable with a fine of two pounds of sugar.

8 Stedman, 1790 manuscript, 24.

9 Stedman, 1790 manuscript, 91.

10 Stedman, diary entry, June 9, 1773; Stedman, *Stedman's Suriname*, 79; Stedman, 1790 manuscript, 250. Stedman spells the name Passalege, but Amsterdam records have the name as Passalaigue.

11 Stedman, 1790 manuscript, 291. The plantation's name is alternatively spelled Fauquenbergh and Fauquembergh.

12 Stedman, 1790 manuscript, 322–23.

13 Stedman, 1790 manuscript, 322–24.

14 Stedman, *Stedman's Suriname*, 158.

15 Stedman spells Gideon's name de Graav and the plantation Knoppemonbo, but the owner's name was also spelled de Graaf and de Graaff, and the plantation Knopem-onbo and Cnobpobmbo. Johannes Petrus van de Voort, *De Westindische Plantagen van 1720 tot 1795, Financier en Handel* (Eindhoven: Drukkerij de Witte, 1973).

16 Stedman, *Stedman's Suriname*, 17; Stedman 1790 manuscript, 84; Stedman, diary entry, January 18, 1776; Stedman, 1790 manuscript, 279.

17 Stedman, *Stedman's Suriname*, 159, 277. Stedman writes "Loango" without further defining what he understood that to mean.

18 Stedman, *Stedman's Suriname*, 159–60.

19 Stedman, *Stedman's Suriname*, 261.

20 Stedman, 1790 manuscript, 346. Stedman spelled the new owner's name Lude, but official records have it as Luden.

21 Vere Langford Oliver, *The history of the island of Antigua, one of the Leeward Caribbees in the West Indies, from the first settlement in 1635 to the present time* (London: Mitchell and Hughes, 1894); Stedman, *Stedman's Suriname*, 193. See Edward Baptist, *The Half Has Never Been Told* (New York: Basic Books, 2014), for more on the use of credit and the economics of slavery.

22 Stedman, *Stedman's Suriname*, 196. This is Stedman's recounting of her words.

23 Stedman, *Stedman's Suriname*, 197. The surviving diaries do not cover the period from May 1774 until October 1775, so all we have to go by is the manuscript written at least a decade later.

24 Stedman, 1790 manuscript, 475.

25 Stedman, 1790 manuscript, 659; Stedman, *Stedman's Suriname*, 74, 273; Stedman, diary entry, August 27, 1773.

26 Stedman, *Stedman's Suriname*, 262–63; Stedman, 1790 manuscript, 669. These are the examples that Stedman gives of what she might command. The mermaid, the creature that straddles the worlds of water and land, appears throughout Caribbean folklore.

27 Stedman, 1790 manuscript, 667, 692.

28 Stedman, *Stedman's Suriname*, 278–80; Stedman, 1790 manuscript, 697.

29 Stedman, 1790 manuscript, 698.

30 Stedman, 1790 manuscript, 698.

31 Interview, Pete Ross, 2019. This is the style of playing associated with the akonting.

32 Stedman, 1790 manuscript, 277.

33 Stedman, diary entries, August 1, 6, and 8, 1776.

34 Stedman, 1790 manuscript, 779.

35 Stedman, *Stedman's Suriname*, 313.

36 Stedman, *Stedman's Suriname*, 313.

VIII—South Carolina, 1780s

1 Shames, *The Old Plantation*, 35, 43. Although records show that the land was along the Coosaw River (which makes it likely that the location was on Ladys Island), the exact location of Rose's property is unknown.

2 Timothy Ford, "Diary of Timothy Ford 1785–1786," *South Carolina Historical and Genealogical Magazine* 13, no. 3 (1912): 143; Johann David Schöpf, *Travels in the Confederation, 1783–1784*, trans. Alfred James Morrison (New York: Bergman, 1968), 158. Susan Shames writes that planters "spent their days in the rice or indigo fields" (35), but this contrasts with the descriptions provided by the two contemporaneous accounts and others, that the landowners were more likely to spend time in town rather than in the fields.

3 Shames, *The Old Plantation*, appendix. On another watercolor sketch of a woman he made, Rose wrote "Miss Breme Jones."

4 Marjoleine Kars, *Blood on the River: A Chronicle of Mutiny and Freedom on the Wild Coast* (New York: New Press, 2020), 77; Hughes, *Apocalypse 1692*, 66; Margaret Washington Creel, *"A Peculiar People": Slave Religion and Community-Culture Among the Gullahs* (New York: New York University Press, 1988), 30.

5 Richard Ligon, *A true & exact history of the island of Barbados illustrated with a mapp of the island . . . other places that are used in the whole processe of sugar-making* (London: Humphrey Moseley, 1657), 46.

6 Ligon, *A true & exact history*, 49; Stedman, *Stedman's Suriname*, 277. Central African (Congo and Angola) marimbas can be struck (like a xylophone) or plucked (like lamellaphones, where smaller pieces of wood serve as keys, not unlike a thumb piano).

7 Hughes, *Apocalypse 1692*, 15; Kars, *Blood on the River*, 40.

8 Ethan Kytle and Blain Roberts, *Denmark Vesey's Garden: Slavery and Memory in the Cradle of the Confederacy, A 150-Year Reckoning with America's Original Sin* (New York: New Press, 2018), 12. For more on Slave Codes in Jamaica, Barbados, and Carolina, see Edward B. Rugemer, "The Development of Mastery and Race in the Comprehensive Slave Codes of the Greater Caribbean during the Seventeenth Century," *William and Mary Quarterly* 70, no. 3 (2013): 429–58.

9 *South-Carolina Gazette*, July 28, 1733, 4; *South-Carolina Gazette*, April 19, 1735, 2; *South-Carolina Gazette*, June 23, 1733, 4; *South-Carolina Gazette*, June 9, 1733, 4; Peter M. Rutkoff and William B. Scott, *Fly Away: The Great African American Cultural Migrations* (Baltimore: Johns Hopkins University Press, 2010), 15.

10 Rutkoff and Scott, *Fly Away*, 17; the idea is also expressed by Dena Epstein in *Sinful Tunes and Spirituals: Black Folk Music to the Civil War* (Urbana: University of Illinois Press, 1977). Estimates are around 75,000 Blacks as opposed to 49,000 whites in 1770. Darold D. Wax, "'The Great Risque We Run': The Aftermath of Slave Rebellion at Stono, South Carolina, 1739–1745," *Journal of Negro History* 67, no. 2

(1982): 144; John K. Thornton, "African Dimensions of the Stono Rebellion," *American Historical Review* 96, no. 4 (1991): 1101–13; John Fleming, "The Stono River Rebellion and Its Impact on the South Carolina Slave Code," *Negro History Bulletin* 42, no. 3 (1979): 67; Wax, "'The Great Risque We Run,'" 139; Annie Campbell, ed., "Excerpts from South Carolina Slave Code of 1740 No. 670 (1740)," U.S. History Scene, https://ushistoryscene.com/article/excerpts-south-carolina-slave-code -1740-no-670-1740/.

11 Creel, *"A Peculiar People,"* 31.

12 Campbell, ed., "Excerpts from South Carolina Slave Code."

13 Quoted in Wax, "'The Great Risque We Run,'" 144.

14 *South-Carolina Gazette*, September 17, 1772.

15 *South-Carolina Gazette*, September 17, 1772.

16 Stedman, *Stedman's Suriname*, 277; J. F. D. Smyth, *A Tour in the United States of America: containing an account of the present situation of that country . . .*, vol. 1 (London: G. Robinson, J. Robson, and J. Sewell, 1784), 46; Schöpf, *Travels in the Confederation*, 260–62; Johann David Schöpf, *Reise durch einige der mittlern und südlichen vereinigten nordamerikanischen Staaten nach Ost-Florida und den Bahama-Inseln: unternommen in den Jahren 1783 und 1784*, vol. 2 (Erlangen: Johann Jacob Palm, 1788). I compared the 1968 English translation with my own for improvements based on my knowledge of banjos and German (gourd vs. calabash, tuned like a chord vs. made accordant).

17 Although the engraving of the Strum Strumps has two long strings, there seem to be short-string pegs on the necks as well.

IX—Cap François, Saint-Domingue, 1782

1 Joseph G. Rosengarten, "Moreau de Saint Mery and His French Friends in the American Philosophical Society," *Proceedings of the American Philosophical Society* 50, no. 199 (1911): 168–78.

2 Laurent Dubois, *Avengers of the New World: The Story of the Haitian Revolution* (Cambridge: Harvard University Press, 2004), 22, 11.

3 Doris Garraway, "Race, Reproduction and Family Romance in Moreau de Saint-Méry's Description . . . de la partie française de l'isle Saint-Domingue," *Eighteenth-Century Studies* 38, no. 2 (2005): 228; 1779 regulation quoted in Dubois, *Avengers*, 62.

4 See Garraway, "Race, Reproduction and Family Romance," and Julia Prest, "Performing the Racial Scale: From Colonial Saint-Domingue to Contemporary Hollywood," *Insights* 10, no. 7 (2017), for more on Moreau de Saint-Méry's views on race and white superiority in the French Caribbean.

5 Médéric Louis Élie Moreau de Saint-Méry, *Description topographique, physique, civile, politique et historique de la partie francaise de l'isle Saint-Domingue . . .*, vol. 1 (Philadelphia: Moreau de Saint-Méry, 1797), 44. "Bamboula" appears many times in this

book in reference to the instrument and music. My French-American banjo-playing friend Cory Seznec pointed out to me that this has become a derogatory term for a Black person in French and is therefore often avoided even when talking about music in French.

6   Jean B. de La Borde and Pierre J. Roussier, *Essai sur la Musique ancienne et moderne*, vol. 1 (Paris: Impr. de P.-D. Pierres, 1780), 291.

7   "Nicolas Ponce," British Museum website, https://www.britishmuseum.org/collection/term/BIOG42342.

8   Moreau de Saint-Méry, *Description topographique*, 51.

9   Quoted in Crystal Nicole Eddins, "African Diaspora Collective Action: Rituals, Runaways, and the Hatian Revolution," PhD diss., Michigan State University, 2017, 93. Original from *Les Affiches americaines*, December 1784, translated in Julia Prest, "Pale Imitations: White performances of slave dance in the public theatres of pre-revolutionary Saint-Domingue," *Atlantic Studies* 16, no. 4 (2019); from *Les Affiches américaines*, January 15, 1783.

10   The original was an intermede, "a theatrical interlude including music and usually ballet performed between the acts of a French play or opera in the sixteeenth and seventeenth centuries."

11   Prest, "Pale Imitations."

12   Prest, "Pale Imitations."

13   Dubois, *Avengers*, 51. Makandal was executed in Le Cap in 1758 for his alleged crimes. "Merry-wang," the name given to the banjo on Jamaica, may be related to the word wanga.

14   Quoted in Prest, "Pale Imitations."

15   Prest, "Pale Imitations," 45; David Geggus, "Haitian Voodoo in the Eighteenth Century: Language, Culture, Resistance," *Jahrbuch für Geschichte Lateinamerikas* 28, no. 1 (1991): 23. Geggus adds that in Fon, *vodu* "refers to a supernatural being, and modern scholars have long identified the Aja–For culture . . . as a dominant influence in twentieth century voodoo" (23).

16   Moreau de Saint-Méry, *Description topographique*, 48; Louis Mars, *The Crisis of Possession in Voodoo* (New York: Reed, Cannon & Johnson, 1977), 19.

17   Moreau de Saint-Méry, *Description topographique*, 48.

18   Alasdair Pettinger, " 'Eh! Eh! Bomba, hen! Hen!': Making Sense of a Vodou Chant," in *Obeah and Other Powers*, ed. Diana Paton and Maarit Forde (Durham, NC: Duke University Press, 2012), 93; Geggus, "Haitian Voodoo," 27. In *Blood on the River*, Marjoleine Kars notes that "Bombas were prominent men on plantations" (16), and though enslaved held a position of power. A 1762 rebellion in Berbice (now in Guyana) was started by a bomba who was also a healer and practitioner of obeah.

19   Geggus believes that Moreau de Saint-Méry didn't witness the "Vaudoux" ceremony himself ("Haitian Voodoo," 23), adding that "whites and free colored police

were known to have spied on the ceremonies" but an oath "bound all participants to secrecy on pain of death" (24). Moreau himself writes that a real meeting "never takes place except secretly" (*Description topographique*, 46) and "whites found spying on the mysteries of this sect and touched by one of the initiates who discovered them then began to dance and agreed to pay the queen to stop the punishment" (50), suggesting that he would never have been able to see a real ceremony since he is not an initiate.

20 Dubois, *Avengers*, 94–101. Sylviane Diouf argues that Boukman could have been a Muslim priest rather than a Vodou priest and suggests that his name means he was a reader of the Koran.

21 Kenneth Roberts and Anna M. Roberts, *Moreau de St. Méry's American Journey, 1793–1798* (New York: Doubleday, 1947), xv; Garraway, "Race, Reproduction, and Family Romance," 229.

X—England, 1787

1 John Gabriel Stedman to John Stedman, January 14, 1787.

2 Stedman, diary entry, July 24, 1778.

3 Stedman, diary entry, May 1796; Stedman, diary entry, July 21, 1776; Stedman, 1790 manuscript, 408. In September 1777, Stedman gives Quacoo to "the countess of Rosendaal" (1790 manuscript, 817) to be her butler. Stedman lists objects that he gave to the Leverian Museum in London, but he must have had more in his collection, including drums and the Creole-bania.

4 Stedman, diary entry, February 21, 1778.

5 Richard de Tussac, *Cri des colons contre un ouvrage de M. l'évêque et sénateur Grégoire, ayant pour titre 'De la Littérature des nègres'* (Paris: Les Marchands des Nouveautés, 1810), 292. Tussac resided in Martinique and Saint-Domingue between 1786 and 1802.

6 De Mey van Streefkerk papers, James Ford Bell Library, University of Minnesota Libraries. A few researchers and scholars have suggested that what is today known as the Creole-bania is in fact a later instrument collected by F. A. Kühn whose route to the Tropenmuseum collections is more easily traceable; that instrument is likely lost. Richard and Sally Price, who found the banjo in the collections of the Rijksmuseum for Volkenkunde (before it was transferred to the Tropenmuseum) told me that they believe this instrument to be the Creole-bania collected by Stedman (email correspondence with author, December 8, 2019). Considering the evidence the Prices present (and the lack of any evidence other than a provenance tracing a banjo's route from Kühn to the Rijksmuseum for Volkenkunde), I agree with them

In a conversation with the Gambian kora player Sona Jobarteh, we talked about gender roles in Manding music. She explained that while women sing and men play instruments in ritual contexts, her family of griot (the word she uses, rather than jeli) performers don't have a problem with her, as a woman, playing kora for secular purposes. For more on gender roles in West African music, see for example Kirsten Marshall, "Changing Gender Roles in Sabar Performances: A Reflection of Changing Roles for Women in Senegal," https://www.ecu.edu/african/sersas/ Papers/MarshallFall2001.htm; Eric Charry, *Mande Music* (Chicago: University of Chicago Press, 2000); and Jacqueline Djedje, *Fiddling in West Africa* (Bloomington: University of Indiana Press, 2007).

7   Stedman, *Stedman's Suriname*, 316; Stedman, 1790 manuscript, 823.

8   Stedman, diary entries, November 5, 1785, and 1787.

9   Stedman, 1790 manuscript, 824–25.

10 Quoted in Robert Smith, "Liberty Displaying the Arts and Sciences: A Philadelphia Allegory by Samuel Jennings," *Winterthur Portfolio* 2 (1965): 88; Guy McElroy, *Facing History: The Black Image in American Art 1710–1940* (Washington, DC: Corcoran Gallery of Art, 1990), 9.

11 Quoted in Robert Smith, "Liberty," 89. Franklin began serving as president in 1787 and died in 1790, while Jennings was working on the painting.

12 McElroy, *Facing History*, 9; Hans Nathan, *Dan Emmett and the Rise of Early Negro Minstrelsy* (Norman: University of Oklahoma Press, 1962), 23–24. A drawing by Sarah Stone for an inventory of the Leverian Museum very likely shows a banjo.

13 William Fox, "An address to the people of Great Britain, on the propriety of abstaining from West India sugar and rum" (London: M. Gurney, 1792), 6.

14 For more on Johnson, see Gerald P. Tyson, "Joseph Johnson, an Eighteenth-Century Bookseller," *Studies in Bibliography* vol. 28 (1975): 1–16.

15 Stedman, 1790 manuscript, 24. For extensive analysis of this, see the introduction to Stedman, *Stedman's Suriname*.

16 Ed Simon, "William Blake, Radical Abolitionist," JSTOR Daily, June 5, 2019, https:// daily.jstor.org/william-blake-radical-abolitionist/; Stedman, diary entry, December 1, 1791.

17 See Richard Price and Sally Price, "John Gabriel Stedman's Collection of 18th-Century Artifacts from Suriname," *Nieuwe West-Indische Gids* (New West Indian Guide) 53, no. 3/4 (1979): 121–40.

18 Quoted in Stedman, *Stedman's Suriname*, lxi.

XI—Albany, New York, 1803

1   Absalom Aimwell, "Pinkster Ode" (Albany: Printed for the Subscribers, 1803). A transcription is available online from the New York State Museum, https:// exhibitions.nysm.nysed.gov/.

2 Aimwell is generally considered to be a pseudonym, and there is no record of an Absalom Aimwell in Albany or the United States generally.

3 *Spooner's Vermont Journal*, September 8, 1794; *Independent Gazetteer*, January 6, 1789. Like the "Pinkster Ode," the "Mechanics' Lecture" uses Greek allegory, biblical references, commentary on contemporary politics, and even similar rhymes and phrases. Harmon Dean Cummings notes that the common knowledge was that Adgate published his secular songster and "Mechanics' Lecture" under a pseudonym because it was not religious music. (The conjecture that Adgate is Aimwell was first published without evidence in Charles Evans's 1912 *American Bibliography* and repeated as fact thereafter.) In his research, Cummings found "no evidence . . . to substantiate or refute that Absalom Aimwell and Andrew Adgate were the same person" (fn 92). The fact that the "Pinkster Ode" was also "by" Absalom Aimwell and the fact that it bears similarities to other poems by the earlier Aimwell suggest that the attribution of this earlier Aimwell's work to Adgate needs to be reevaluated. Harmon Dean Cummings, "Andrew Adgate: Philadelphia Psalmodist and Music Educator," PhD diss., University of Rochester, 1975, http://hdl.handle.net/1802/5998.

4 Quoted in Shane White, "Pinkster in Albany, 1803: A Contemporary Description," *New York History* 70, no. 2 (1989): 195. He is called Charley or Charlie in some accounts, but the two from 1803 both refer to him as Charles.

5 Jeroen Dewulf, "Rediscovering a Hudson Valley Folkloric Tradition: Traces of the 'Pinkster' Feast in Forgotten Books," *Hudson River Valley Review* 34, no. 2 (2018): 4; A. J. Williams-Myers, *Long Hammering: Essays on the Forging of an African American Presence in the Hudson River Valley to the Early Twentieth Century* (Trenton, NJ: Africa World Press, 1994), 87.

6 Quoted in Claire Sponsler, *Ritual Imports: Performing Medieval Drama in America* (Ithaca, NY: Cornell University Press, 2004), 49; quoted in Jeroen Dewulf, *The Pinkster King and the King of Kongo: The Forgotten History of America's Dutch-Owned Slaves* (Jackson: University Press of Mississippi, 2016), 58; White, "Pinkster in Albany," 73; quoted in Sterling Stuckey, *Going Through the Storm: The Influence of African American Art in History* (Oxford: Oxford University Press, 1994), 68.

7 The last people taken directly from Central Africa to New York probably arrived in 1750, making it unlikely they were still alive in 1803. However, Linda Heywood and John Thornton, by looking at the names of enslaved people in New York, believe that a high proportion of the earliest generation—the charter generation—were taken from the KongoAngola region of Central Africa and likely would have practiced a form of Catholicism that was influenced by African spiritual beliefs. Jeroen Dewulf, "Pinkster: An Atlantic Creole Festival in a Dutch-American Context," *Journal of American Folklore* 126, no. 501 (2013): 259; Dewulf, *The Pinkster King*, 141; Leviticus 23:10, 15–21 (King James Bible). Before the fourth century, the Jewish holiday of Passover and the Christian holiday of Easter did coincide, but while Passover follows

the Hebrew lunar calendar today, Easter is the first full moon after March 21, and Pentecost (from which Pinkster is derived) is observed fifty days after Easter.

8   Dewulf, *The Pinkster King*, 27, 56; Bankoff and Winter, "The Archaeology of Slavery," 299–300.

9   Quoted in White, "Pinkster in Albany," 195.

10 David Levine, "History of the 1793 Fire in Albany," *Hudson Valley Magazine*, January 21, 2014. Whether or not they were guilty is another question.

11 "Pinkster festivities," *New York Times*, June 11, 1878, 8; quoted in White, "Pinkster in Albany," 195. The most common sources on Pinkster are whites who saw the events as children. How well they remember what happened, and what was clouded by later memories and exposure to Blackface Minstrelsy, is hard to discern. James Eights specifically mentions the emergence of Minstrelsy when writing his reminiscences of Pinkster.

12 Quoted in White, "Pinkster in Albany," 195; James Eights, "Pinkster Festivals in Albany Sixty Years ago," in *Collections on the History of Albany*, compiled by Joel Munsell, vol. 2 (Albany: J. Munsell, 1867), 323; Pettinger, "Eh! Eh! Bomba, hen!," 83; John F. Watson, *Annals and occurrences of New York city and state, in the olden time: being a collection of memoirs, anecdotes, and incidents concerning the city, county, and inhabitants, from the days of the founders* (Philadelphia: H. F. Anners, 1846), 209–10; "Ran Away from Kensington, Philadelphia," *New Jersey Journal*, June 25, 1794.

13 Quoted in Percy Van Epps, *Contributions to the History of Glenville* (Glenville: 1926), 100–03. Made available online by The New York Public Library: https://catalog .hathitrust.org/Record/102778035. Van Epps published the contract in its entirety, plus information on Yat's (also spelled Yate and Yates) family.

14 Quoted in White, "Pinkster in Albany," 195. In *Going Through the Storm*, Sterling Stuckey writes, "very few, if any, dance formations would have been frozen in time, the impulse to improvisation alone opening the way to ethnic intermingling of dance movement" (67).

15 Edna Greene Medford and Emilyn L. Brown, "New York Africans in the Age of Revolution," NYABG, vol. 3, 100.

16 Quoted in White, "Pinkster in Albany," 195; Geneviève Fabre, "Pinkster Festival, 1775–1811: An African American Celebration," in *Feasts and Celebrations in North American Ethnic Communities*, ed. Ramón A. Gutiérrez and Geneviève Fabre (Albuquerque: University of New Mexico Press, 1995), 17.

17 Quoted in Dewulf, *The Pinkster King*, 166.

18 Quoted in White, "Pinkster in Albany," 192.

19 "Theater," *New York Evening Post*, May 21, 1803.

20 K. Meira Goldberg, *Sonidos Negros: On the Blackness of Flamenco* (Oxford: Oxford University Press, 2019), 118; Watson, *Annals and occurrences of New York*, 178.

21 Quoted in White, "Pinkster in Albany," 195.

Interlude

1 Mbanza would make sense, given that the French-speaking colonies called the instrument a banza, and Turner further explains that in Brazil the words banza and banju are used to describe "an instrument resembling the guitar," with the latter pronounced ban-shu. In Haitian Krèyol, the letter *j* is pronounced like the *s* in measure or treasure, meaning that banja would have been pronounced ban-zha, perhaps explaining alternate spellings. Banja would have a similar pronunciation to banshaw, a word used to describe the banjo on St. Kitts in 1763; Laurent Dubois, *The Banjo: America's African Instrument* (Cambridge, MA: Belknap Press, 2016), 77; M. M. Mathews, *Some Sources of Southernisms* (Birmingham: University of Alabama, 1948), 102.

2 Michael Theodore Coolen, "The Fodet: A Senegambian Origin for the Blues?," *The Black Perspective in Music* 10, no. 1 (1982): 69–84; Schlomo Pestcoe, "The Stedman 'Creole Bania': A Look at the World's Oldest Banjo," *Banjo Roots*, May 5, 2011, http://banjoroots.blogspot.com/; Dubois, *The Banjo*, 77. Pestcoe also notes the use of the word bania, after Stedman used it, to describe banjo.

3 Clazien Medendorp, *Kijkkasten uit Suriname: De Diorama's van Gerrit Schouten* (Amsterdam: KIT Publishers en Rijksmuseum, 2008), 17.

XII—Paramaribo, Suriname, 1816

1 Stedman, *Stedman's Suriname*, 277.

2 Quoted in Trudi Buda, "Banya: A Surviving Surinamese Slave Play," in *A History of Literature in the Caribbean*, vol. 2, *English- and Dutch-Speaking Regions*, ed. A. James Arnold (Philadelphia: John Benjamins, 2001), 617.

3 Quoted in Neus, "The Yellow Lady," 126.

4 Quoted in Neus, "The Yellow Lady," 126.

5 Ursy M. Lichtveld and Jan Voorhoeve, eds., *Creole Drum: An Anthology of Creole Literature in Suriname* (New Haven: Yale University Press, 1975), 23. This is a typical invocation of Mama Aysa for a banya dance.

6 P. J. Benoit, *Voyage à Suriname: Beschrijving van de Nederlandse bezittingen in Guyana*, trans. Michael Ietswaart (Zutphen: Walburg Pers, 2016); Albert von Sack, *Narrative of a Voyage to Surinam of a Residence there during 1805, 1806, and 1807 and of the Author's Return to Europe by the way of North America* (London: G. and W. Nicol, 1810).

7 Lichtveld and Voorhoeve, *Creole Drum*, 18; Stedman, *Stedman's Suriname*, 277.

8 Melville J. Herskovits and Frances S. Herskovits, *Suriname Folk-Lore* (New York: AMS Press, 1936), 72.

9 Von Sack, *Narrative of a Voyage*, 62; J. D. Kunitz, *Surinam und seine bewohner* (Erfurt: Beyer und Maring, 1804), 351.

10 Benoit, *Voyage à Suriname*, 60–61.

11 Medendorp, *Kijkkasten*, 10.

12 Stedman, diary entries, March 23, August 6, and August 8, 1776.

13 Lichtveld and Voorhoeve, *Creole Drum*, 7; Ellen Neslo, "The Formation of a Free Non-White Elite in Paramaribo 1800–1863," *Caribbean Studies* 43, no. 2 (2015): 177–210.

14 Clazien Medendorp, "History in a Diorama," *Bulletin van het Rijksmuseum* 54, no. 3 (2006): 328.

15 "Nut en Schadelijk," *Suriname Plantage*, https://www.surinameplantages.com/archief/n/nutenschadelijk, accessed August 25, 2021.

16 It's unclear whether Schouten knew the name of the dance. Next to his signature on one diorama he wrote the word *feest*, or party.

XIII—New Orleans, Louisiana, 1819

1 Jeroen Dewulf, "From Moors to Indians: The Mardi Gras Indians and the Three Transformations of St. James," *Louisiana History* 56, no. 1 (2015): 7; Benjamin Henry Latrobe, *The Journal of Latrobe; being the notes and sketches of an architect, naturalist and traveler in the United States from 1796 to 1820* (New York: Appleton, 1905), 250; Jean Baker, *Building America: The Life of Benjamin Henry Latrobe* (New York: Oxford University Press, 2020), 22–23. Latrobe thought he was related to Count de Bonneval and would even sign his name with an extra B, for Bonneval.

2 Baker, *Building America*, 135. Yellow fever is caused by a viral infection carried by mosquitoes, but viruses had not yet been discovered.

3 Christian Schultz, *Travels on an Inland Voyage through the states of New-York, Pennsylvania, Virginia, Ohio, Kentucky and Tennessee: and through the territories of Indiana, Louisiana, Mississippi and New-Orleans; performed in the years 1807 and 1808; including a tour of nearly six thousand miles* (New York: Isaac Riley, 1810), 190–91.

4 Latrobe, *Journal*, 175.

5 Baker, *Building America*, 16.

6 Latrobe's observation of a female drummer is unusual, since men usually played drums, although women played rattles.

7 Latrobe, *Journal*, 179–82.

8 Johann Ulrich Buechler, *Land-und seereisen eines st. gallischen kantonsbürgers nach Nordamerika und Westindien . . .* (St. Gallen: Huber und compagnie, 1820), 129–30.

9 Latrobe, *Journal*, 179–82.

10 Thomas Jefferson, *Notes on the State of Virginia* (Philadelphia: Price and Hall, 1788), 150; Latrobe, *Journal*, 179–82.

11 Schlomo Pestcoe, "Banjo Ancestors," in *Banjo Roots and Branches*, ed. Robert Winans (Champaign: University of Illinois Press, 2018), 33. During the periods when France controlled New Orleans, the majority of newly arrived Africans came from Upper

Guinea and Senegambia, but some also came from Lower Guinea and Ouidah. Ned Sublette, *The World That Made New Orleans: From Spanish Silver to Congo Square* (Chicago: Lawrence Hill Books, 2008), 58; Pestcoe, "Banjo Ancestors," 33. Two of the last ships to arrive in Louisiana before the slave trade ban in 1808 were from Mozambique; TASTD.

12 Robert Farris Thompson, *African Art in Motion* (Los Angeles: University of California Press, 1974), 68–69. While far fewer people taken from the Gold Coast were sold into slavery in Louisiana, their art may have impacted the culture developing in the city, through decorative elements like the ones found on the banjo and the presence of the gome drum.

13 Winans, "Black Musicians in Eighteenth-Century America."

14 Gerstin, "Tangled Roots," 29; Le Page du Pratz, *The history of Louisiana, or of the western parts of Virginia and Carolina: containing a description of the countries that lye on both sides of the river Mississippi: with an account of the settlements, inhabitants, soil, climate and products* (London: Printed for T. Becket and P.A. De Hondt, 1763), ch. 4, section 1, https://www.gutenberg.org/files/9153/9153-h/9153-h.htm.

15 Le Page du Pratz, *History of Louisiana*, ch. 4, section 1; Edna Greene Medford et al., "Social Characteristics and Cultural Practices of Africans in Eighteenth-Century New York," NYABG, vol. 3, 67.

16 Quoted in Freddi Williams Evans, *Congo Square: African Roots in New Orleans* (Lafayette: University of Louisiana at Lafayette Press, 2011), 7; Carondelet, "A Decree for Louisiana issued by the Baron of Carondelet, June 1, 1795," ed. and trans. James Padgett, *Louisiana Historical Quarterly* 20, no. 3 (1937): 602. In *The World That Made New Orleans*, Ned Sublette disputes that this was Congo Square as we know it today, since they wouldn't have disrupted the vespers. Instead, he believes that it was "at the market right by the Cathedral," which would imply that "it's being used as a term applied to a place where Africans gathered" (121). However, maps of New Orleans under the Spanish show no "green expanse" near the cathedral, just the plaza and the levee, which were very much in the central part of town.

17 Jason Berry, *City of a Million Dreams: A History of New Orleans at Year 300* (Chapel Hill: University of North Carolina Press, 2018), 37. During Spanish rule, 1,330 people of African descent bought their freedom, when the total population was 4,897.

18 Sublette, *The World That Made New Orleans*, 106; TASTD.

19 TASTD. Some ships did not have a record of how many people were on board. This database only counts ships that had known human cargo and doesn't include people who may have been smuggled aboard.

20 Schultz, *Travels*, 197; Fortescue Cuming, *Sketches of a tour to the western country: through the states of Ohio and Kentucky, a voyage down the Ohio and Mississippi rivers, and a trip through the Mississippi territory, and part of West Florida, commenced at*

Philadelphia in the winter of 1807, and concluded in 1809 (Pittsburgh: Cramer, Spear and Eichbaum, 1810), 333. There are other accounts of African descendants dancing in New Orleans before and around the time of Latrobe's visit (see Epstein, *Sinful Tunes*, 90–99), but none of them mention the banjo.

21 Thomas Fiehrer, "Saint-Domingue/Haiti: Louisiana's Caribbean Connection," *Louisiana History* 30, no. 4 (Autumn 1989): 431; Berry, *City of a Million Dreams*, 91.

22 Pierre Forest, *Voyage aux Etats-Unis de l'Amerique en 1831* (Paris: J. Perret, 1834), 69.

23 Doris Garraway, *The Libertine Colony: Creolization in the Early French Caribbean* (Durham, NC: Duke University Press, 2005), 259.

24 Theodore Pavie, *Souvenirs atlantiques: voyage aux Etats-Unis et au Canada*, vol. 2 (Paris: Roret, 1833), 318–21.

XIV—Haiti, 1841

1 Victor Schœlcher, "Des Noirs," *Revue de Paris* 20 (November 1830): 72. The woman likely wouldn't have arrived from Africa or the Caribbean, since the international slave trade was supposed to have ended in 1808. No registered ships arrived from outside the US with enslaved people to sell in 1829.

2 Schœlcher, "Des Noirs," 72; quoted in Max Welborn, "Victor Schœlcher's Views on Race and Slavery," PhD diss., Ohio State University, 1965, 8.

3 For more on who and what Schœlcher read to support his views, see Welborn, "Victor Schœlcher's Views." In British colonies, abolition began on August 1, 1834; people enslaved in agricultural labor were supposed to serve a six-year apprentice-ship, while those in non-agricultural labor (domestic and skilled trades) were sup-posed to serve from one to four years. Total abolition happened in 1838 after the apprenticeship model failed. In Antigua and Bermuda, the slaveowners voted for immediate emancipation rather than the apprenticeship model (34). Schœlcher also visited Saint-Thomas, Sainte-Croix, Saint-Martin, and Puerto Rico on his trip.

4 Victor Schœlcher, *Colonies étrangeres et Haïti* (Paris: Pagnerre, 1843), 171; Jeremy D. Popkin, "Facing Racial Revolution: Captivity Narratives and Identity in the Saint-Domingue Insurrection," *Eighteenth-Century Studies* 36, no. 4 (2003): 525, 524.

5 Harold Courlander, *Haiti Singing* (New York: Cooper Square, 1973), 49; Dubois, *Avengers*, 94. Schœlcher would point out how religion helped keep slavery in place, believing it "possessed a fatalism which bred indifference and powerlessness in its followers towards injustice" (Welborn, "Victor Schœlcher's Views," 96). Alexan-dre Girard-Muscagorry believes that "Schœlcher was a good enough writer to . . . demonstrate convincingly how music was crucial to survive" and that he could have avoided racist tropes, but also can't explain why Schœlcher didn't include more on Haitian music in his published writing (correspondence with the author, December 11, 2021).

6 Descourtilz, *Voyages d'un naturaliste, et ses observations*, vol. 3 (Paris: Dufart, Père, 1809), 275; quoted in Dubois, *The Banjo*, 128; Descourtilz, *Voyages*, 191. While four strings seems to be the typical description for a banjo, it can vary between two and six.

7 Descourtilz, *Voyages*, 197.

8 Descourtilz, *Voyages*, 192.

9 This watercolor was put up for auction in 1999 but remained unsold.

10 Eddins, "African Diaspora Collective Action," 67.

11 Mungo Park, *Travels in the Interior Districts of Africa* (London: W. Bulmer and Co., 1800), 278.

12 If the banza had a tailpiece to which the strings were attached, it is now missing. However, the banjo in Rose's watercolor seems to have a leather tailpiece, and a recently uncovered banjo now at the Musée des Confluences in Lyon does have a leather tailpiece.

13 For more on the banza's construction and comparison to West African instruments, see Pete Ross, "The Haitian Banza and the American Banjo Lineage," in *Banjo Roots and Branches*, ed. Robert Winans (Champaign: University of Illinois, 2018). The wedge on the banza has been lost, but upon examining the instrument, Pete could tell that it had been there because the neck was loose and there is a lighter, rectangular portion on the back of the neck where the wood is less oxidized and was very likely in contact with the wedge.

14 Ross, "Haitian Banza," 141. For more on these differences, see Schlomo Pestcoe and Greg Adams, "Banjo Roots Research," and Schlomo Pestcoe, "Banjo Ancestors: West African Plucked Spike Lutes," both in *Banjo Roots and Branches*, ed. Robert Winans (Champaign: University of Illinois, 2018); Charry, *Mande Music*.

15 Robert Farris Thompson, *Flash of the Spirit: African and Afro-American Art and Philosophy* (New York: Random House, 1983), 181; Milo Rigaud, *Secrets of Voodoo*, trans. Robert B. Cross (San Francisco: City Lights Books, 1985), 35–36. Rigaud points out that "The asson or calebassier courant makes a perfect geometric symbol in that by itself it is a metaphysical symbol being the abyss and chasm—it represents a sphere or perfect circle . . . In reality, by the sphere or the circle, plus the handle which symbolizes the poteau-mitan or the vertical, the asson becomes a geometrical synergy combining the two activating principals of all magic: the magic wand, which is the handle, and the magic circle" (35–36).

16 Alfred Metraux, *Voodoo in Haiti*, trans. Hugo Charteris (New York: Schocken, 1972), 182; Anthony B. Pinn, *Varieties of African American Religious Experience* (Minneapolis: Fortress Press, 1997), 13; Rigaud, *Secrets of Voodoo*, 46; Courlander, *Haiti Singing*, 51; William S. Pollitzer, *The Gullah People and their African Heritage* (Athens, GA: University of Georgia Press, 2005), 178; John Michael Vlach, *The Afro-American Tradition in Decorative Arts* (Athens, GA: University of Georgia Press, 1990), 143.

17 Thompson, *Flash of the Spirit*, 258.

18 Mary Nooter Roberts, "The Inner Eye Vision and Transcendence in African Arts,"
    African Arts 50, no. 1 (2017): 73; Thompson, *Flash of the Spirit*, 259; Dubois, *The Banjo*,
    130; Gage Averill, *A Day for the Hunter, a Day for the Prey* (Chicago: University of Chi-
    cago Press, 1997), 67. "Twa Fey" has become a Haitian folk song, and Dubois fully
    explores "Twa Fey" and the banza Schœlcher collected in *The Banjo*. In an email to
    Sule Greg Wilson in 2004, Farris Thompson writes, "With the Haitian Banza we
    have another mask of the spirit, eyes and nose clearly rendered, and head coming
    to a decisive point. If the artist knew Yoruba culture we would automatically rec-
    ognize a reference to Ashe and Nego influence that was and is very strong in Haiti"
    (cited in Ross, "Haitian Banza," n. 9).

19 Translation in Saskia Willeart, " 'Finding' the Haitian Banza," in *Banjo Roots and
    Branches*, ed. Robert Winans (Champaign: University of Illinois Press, 2018), 136;
    interview with Alexandre Girard-Muscagorry, January 28, 2022. Girard-Muscag-
    orry adds that he believes the inscription was written on the banza before Schœl-
    cher's trip to Africa (correspondence with the author, December 11, 2021).

XV—Suriname, 1850

1   "Survey of the Missionary Labours of the Brethren's Church during the Period
    between the Synods of 1836 and 1848 including a review of the Occurrences of the
    last-mentioned Year," United Brethren, vol. 19, 113.

2   "Survey," United Brethren, vol. 19, 113.

3   Baker, *Building America*, 10.

4   "Survey United Brethren, vol. 19, 113. These rowers may have been enslaved
    but could also have been free men, with the Moravians having purchased their
    freedom.

5   "Br. Jansa writes," *Moravian Church Miscellany* 1, no. 4 (April 1850): 123–25. The
    editor writes that Brother Jansa had visited "recently" but does not give an exact
    date.

6   David Nassy, *Historical Essay on the Colony of Suriname 1788*, trans. Simon Cohen
    (New York: Publications of the American Jewish Archives, 1974), 159–60.

7   Burnard, *Mastery, Tyranny, and Desire*, ch. 1; Stedman, 1790 manuscript, 761.

8   "Surinam," United Brethren, vol. 20, 534–35.

9   "From Br. Stanke to the Mission-Board, Liliendal, Nov. 14, 1848," United Brethren,
    vol. 19, 204–05; "Br. Jansa of Annazorg," United Brethren, vol. 22, 197.

10 This later became part of the Ethnological Museum in Berlin.

11 I have not found anything in Jansa's notes or reports that discusses specifically
    when he took the panja. It is possible that someone else took it, but the collection
    notes say "collected by Jansa."

XVI—Paramaribo, Suriname, 1855

1 C. J. Hering, *Korte Beschrijving van Mr. H. C. Focke* (Paramaribo: H. B. Heyde, 1903); Neslo, "The Formation of a Free Non-White Elite in Paramaribo," 186. "Free man/ woman of color" and "free non-white" were both contemporary terms used to describe Surinamers with both African and European ancestry.

2 Neslo, "The Formation of a Free Non-White Elite in Paramaribo," 188, 187.

3 George Lang, "Deep Speech," *Entwisted Tongues: Comparative Creole Literatures* (Amsterdam: Rodopi, 2000), 124.

4 H. C. Focke, "De Surinamische Negermuzijk," in *West-Indië: bijdragen tot de bevordering van de kennis der Nederlandsch West-Indische koloniën*, ed. A. C. Kruseman, vol. 2 (Haarlem: A. C. Kruseman, 1858), 93–107.

5 Focke doesn't call this a quaqua, but the quaqua is also played with hard sticks.

6 Drumming is usually the task of men, although around the same time Focke wrote his article, the Moravian Brethren wrote that the woman Hendrina de Parra was a talented drummer who played for dances in Paramaribo.

7 Guda, "Banya," 618, 615.

8 George Yule, *The Study of Language*, 3rd ed. (Cambridge: Cambridge University Press, 2006), 201–03. No African language survived whole-cloth, not even among the Maroons of Suriname, who began escaping into the jungle in the 1600s.

9 H. C. Focke, *Neger–Engelsche Woordenboek* (Leiden: P. H. van den Heuvell, 1855), 8; C. L. Schumann, *Neger–Englisches Wörterbuch*, 3rd ed. (1783), http://suriname-languages.sil.org/Schumann/National/SchumannGerDict.html.

10 Medendorp, *Kijkkasten*, 25; Lichtveld and Voorhoeve, *Creole Drum*, 17, 51; Pinn, *Varieties of African American Religious Experience*, 27. Even when visiting Suriname in 2018, Christine van Rusel-Henar, the director of Het Koto Museum and a preserver of traditional Koto clothing, told me that parents are wary of letting their children learn to dance banya at NAKS (a cultural organization in Paramaribo) because it wasn't Christian.

11 August Kappler, *Sechs Jahre in Surinam oder Bilder aus dem militärischen Leben dieser Kolonie* (Stuttgart: E. Schweizerbart'sche, 1854), 46.

12 "Br. Van Calker," United Brethren, vol. 23, 399.

13 "Br. Jansa writes as follows," United Brethren, vol. 24, 92–93, 98.

14 Focke, "De Surinamische Negermuzijk," 107.

Interlude

1 Much of this is taken from an unpublished paper that I presented in 2018 at the Legacy of Slavery and Indentured Servitude conference in Paramaribo, Suriname.

2 Robert Farris Thompson, "Face of the Gods: The Artists and Their Altars," *African Arts* 28, no. 1 (1995): 50–61; G. M. Martinus-Guda, "Banya: A Surinamese Slave Play

that Survived," in *African Re-Genesis: Confronting Social Issues in the Diaspora*, ed. Jay
B. Haviser and Kevin C. MacDonald (Walnut Creek, CA: Left Coast Press, 2010);
Christine van Rusel-Henar, *Angisa Tori* (Paramaribo: Stichting Fu Memre Wi Afo,
2008); Herskovits and Herskovits, *Suriname Folk-Lore*, 7.

3 *New-York Weekly Journal*, March 6, 1736; Maria Franklin, "Rethinking the Carter's
Grove Slave Quarter Reconstruction: A Proposal," in *The Written and the Wrought:
Complementary Sources in Historical Anthropology* (Berkeley: Kroeber Anthropologi-
cal Society, 1995), 155; Pollitzer, *The Gullah People*, 176.

4 Farris Thompson, *Flash of the Spirit*, 87; Franklin, "Rethinking," 154; Maria Frank-
lin, "Early Black Spirituality and the Cultural Strategy of Protective Symbolism:
Evidence from Art and Archeology" (Williamsburg, VA: Colonial Williamsburg
Foundation Department of Archeological Research, 1997), 8.

5 Creel, *"A Peculiar People,"* 43–44, 290; Franklin, "Early Black Spirituality," 8; Farris
Thompson, *Flash of the Spirit*, 87; Lang, "Deep Speech," n.p.

6 Diouf, *Servants of Allah*, 195; Moreau de Saint-Méry, *Description topographique*, 44;
Eights, "Pinkster Festivals," 323–27; Laurent Dubois, Mary Caton Lingold, and
David Garner, "Musical Passage," www.musicalpassage.org.

7 Smallwood, "African Guardians," 690; Medendorp, *Kijkkasten*, 83 (Medendorp
spells it "kwakwa"); Raboteau, *Slave Religion*, 15; Turner, *Slaves and Missionaries*,
52; Margarite Fernández Olmos and Lizabeth Paravisini-Gebert, *Creole Religions of
the Caribbean: An Introduction from Vodou and Santeria to Obeah and Espiritismo* (New
York: New York University Press, 2003), 9–11.

8 Raboteau, *Slave Religion*, 15; Phyllis Galembo, *Vodou: Visions and Voices of Haiti*
(Berkeley: Ten Speed Press, 1998), 64; Jane Landers, "The Central African Presence
in Spanish Maroon Communities," in *Central Africans and Cultural Transformations
in the American Diaspora*, ed. Linda Heywood (Cambridge: Cambridge University
Press, 2002), 237; Franklin, "Early Black Spirituality," 6; Farris Thompson, *Flash of the
Spirit*, 117; Leland Ferguson, "Early African-American Pottery in South Carolina: A
Complicated Plainware," *African Diaspora Archaeology Newsletter* 10, no. 2 (2007): 4.

9 Medford et al., "'By the Visitations of God,'" 88.

10 Elias Jones, *History of Dorchester County, Maryland* (Baltimore: Williams and Wilkins,
1902),194; Zora Neale Hurston, *Tell My Horse: Voodoo Life in Haiti and Jamaica* (New
York: Harper Perennial, 2008), 220–21.

11 The *Baltimore Sun* reports 1,994 homicides from 2015 to 2020; 1,437 victims were
identified as Black. The number could be higher since the race of some victims is
unknown. Vlach, *The Afro-American Tradition in Decorative Arts*, 143.

XVII—New York City, 1840

1 *New York Daily Herald*, January 16, 1840, 3.

2 *New York Daily Herald*, January 18, 1840, 3. For more about the politics of early Min-

strelsy, see Douglas A. Jones, Jr., "Black Politics But Not Black People: Rethinking the Social and 'Racial' History of Early Minstrelsy," *Drama Review* 57, no. 2 (2013): 21–37.

3 "The Bonja Song" (New York: A. Geib & Co., n.d.), Lester Levy collection, Johns Hopkins University, https://levysheetmusic.mse.jhu.edu/collection/017/064; S. Foster Damon, "The Negro in Early American Songsters," *Papers of the Bibliographical Society of America* 28 (1934): 138. Damon writes that as early as 1767 in New York, a Mr. Tea performed a "Negro Dance in Character," which was sporadically followed by similar performances throughout the late 1700s and early 1800s.

4 Noah Smithwick, *The Evolution of a State, Or, Recollections of Old Texas Days* (Austin: Gammel, 1900). Williamson has been cited by many as the first white man to play banjo, based on this statement. However, since the recollection is from more than seventy years later and refers to Minstrel Shows, the song "Coal Black Rose," and the banjo, the veracity of the account can be questioned. Furthermore, he was clearly influenced by Blackface Minstrelsy in playing this song, rather than playing the banjo as part of vernacular white culture.

5 Sheet music available from the Lester Levy collection, https://levysheetmusic.mse .jhu.edu/collection/017/078. Eric Lott, "'The Seemingly Counterfeit': Racial Politics and Early Blackface Minstrelsy," *American Quarterly* 43, no. 2 (1991), 230–31. Lott writes briefly about the sexualization of Black men on the Minstrel stage and homoerotic undertones of the performances, but the subject needs to be further explored.

6 Jones, "Black Politics But Not Black People," 35; quoted ibid., 33.

7 Nathan, *Dan Emmett*, 50–52.

8 William J. Mahar, "Black English in Early Blackface Minstrelsy: A New Interpretation of the Sources of Minstrel Show Dialect," *American Quarterly* 37, no. 2 (1985): 260–85. Mahar compares this use of language to Black Vernacular English, Pidgin-Creole, and West African Pidgins to explain the change of consonants and vowels that would have made the speech seem authentic in Minstrel Shows.

9 For more on Sweeney, see Bob Carlin, *The Birth of the Banjo: Joel Walker Sweeney and Early Minstrelsy* (Jefferson, NC: McFarland, 2007).

10 Alvin Harlow, *Old Bowery Days: The Chronicles of a Famous Street* (New York: Appleton, 1931), 219.

11 Quoted in Nathan, *Dan Emmett*, 113–19.

12 Quoted in Nathan, *Dan Emmett*, 120; Christopher J. Smith, *The Creolization of American Culture: William Sidney Mount and the Roots of Blackface Minstrelsy* (Chicago: University of Illinois Press, 2013), 76.

13 Charles Dickens, *American Notes for General Circulation* (London: Chapman and Hall, 1842), 61–63.

14 Dickens, *American Notes*, 62–63; James W. Cook, "Dancing Across the Color Line," *Common Place: the Journal of Early American Life* 4, no. 1 (2003).

15 Reprinted in Patricia Cline Cohen, Timothy J. Gilfoyle, and Helen Lefkowitz

Horowitz, eds., *The Flash Press: Sporting Male Weeklies in 1840s New York* (Chicago: University of Chicago Press, 2008), 186–89.

16 In "'Shuffle Along' and the Lost History of Black Performance in America" (*New York Times*, March 24, 2016), John Jeremiah Sullivan doesn't believe that Juba's real name is William Henry Lane or that he was born in 1825, which is cited in sources as varied as Eileen Southern's *The Music of Black Americans* and Edward LeRoy Rice's *Monarchs of Minstrelsy*. He cites an interview in the *Manchester Times* where Juba gives his date of birth as 1830, which accords with British press reports that he was 18 in 1848.

17 Quoted in April F. Masten, "Sporting Men, Vulgar Women, and Blacked-Up Boys," *Journal of Social History* 48, no. 3 (2015): 621; quoted in Masten, "Sporting Men," 606.

18 *Era*, July 30, 1848; *Guardian*, January 24, 1849; *Freeman's Journal*, July 9, 1849.

19 Frederick Douglass, "Gavitt's Original Ethiopian Serenaders," *North Star*, June 29, 1849, 2.

XVIII—New Orleans, Louisiana, 1850

1 Jerah Johnson, *Congo Square in New Orleans* (New Orleans: Louisiana Landmarks Society, 1995), 46.

2 Galembo, *Vodou*, xviii; Raboteau, *Slave Religion*, 25; Carolyn Morrow Long, *A New Orleans Voudou Priestess: The Legend and Reality of Marie Laveau* (Gainesville: University of Florida Press, 2006), 119.

3 Denis Alvarado, *The Magic of Marie Laveau* (Newburyport, MA: Weiser Books, 2020), 83.

4 "A Motley Gathering," *Planters' Banner*, July 11, 1850.

5 "More Voudouism," *New Orleans Weekly Delta*, July 8, 1850.

6 "Voudouism Unveiled," *New Orleans Weekly Delta*, August 5, 1850; 1850 Census Record. Toledano was likely born free; there are no manumission papers for a Betsey Toledano. The 1850 census doesn't give her profession and the Historic New Orleans Collection's survey of French Quarter properties has no records of a Toledano owning a house.

7 "Voudouism Unveiled"; Michelle Gordon, "'Midnight Scenes and Orgies': Public Narratives of Voodoo in New Orleans and Nineteenth-Century Discourses of White Supremacy," *American Quarterly* 64, no. 4 (December 2012): 772.

8 "The Congo Dance," *Daily Picayune*, October 18, 1843.

9 Evans, *Congo Square*, 94–96.

10 Frederick Starr, *Bamboula! The Life and Times of Louis Moreau Gottschalk* (Oxford: Oxford University Press, 1995), 73. Although the exact date isn't known, Starr believes Gottschalk composed "Bamboula" in 1848.

11 Pierre-Clément de Laussat, *Mémoires sur ma vie à mon fils: pendant les années 1803 et suivantes . . .* , vol. 2 (Pau: Vignacour, 1831), 173–74.

12 Starr, *Bamboula!*, 74; Epstein, *Sinful Tunes*, 94. Starr cites the name of this song as "Lolotte pov'piti Lolotte," but I am using the name as given in the most contemporaneous source I can find: William Francis Allen, Charles Pickard Ware, and Lucy McKim Garrison, *Slave Songs of the United States: The Classic 1867 Anthology* (New York: Dover, 1995).

13 Sybil Kein, ed., *Creole: The History and Legacy of Louisiana's Free People of Color* (Baton Rouge: Louisiana State University Press, 2000), 120.

14 Starr, *Bamboula!*, 75–76.

15 Starr, *Bamboula!*, 134; Louis Moreau Gottschalk, *Notes of a Pianist* (Philadelphia: Lippincott, 1881), 46; Starr, *Bamboula!*, 137; Gottschalk, *Notes*, 66.

16 *Zainesville Daily Courier*, March 11, 1853; *Louisville Daily Journal*, March 2, 1853; [Louisville] *Courier–Journal*, March 22, 1853; Starr, *Bamboula!*, 140. "Old Folks at Home" was published in Boston in 1851 and would also become known as "Swanee River."

17 Benjamin Drake, *Tales and Sketches from the Queen City* (Cincinnati: E. Morgan, 1838), 89, 93–94; quoted in Smith, *Creolization*, 50.

18 Quoted in Starr, *Bamboula!*, 140.

19 *Times–Picayune*, April 7, 1853; Willie Prophit, "The Crescent City's Charismatic Celebrity: Louis Moreau Gottschalk's New Orleans Concerts, Spring 1853," *Louisiana History* 12, no. 3 (1971), 247.

20 Starr, *Bamboula!*, 147–48; *Times–Picayune*, January 28, 1853. I don't hear any banjo imitation in "Bamboula."

21 Starr, *Bamboula!*, 147; Gottschalk, *Notes*, 288. Hans Nathan, in *Dan Emmett*, points out that "Clar de Kitchen" has melodies similar to the popular "High Road to Edinburgh." See Smith, *Creolization*, 52, for more of this analysis. In "Gottschalk's 'The Banjo,' op. 15, and the Banjo in the Nineteenth Century" (*Current Musicology* 50, January 1992), Paul Ely Smith writes that "Le Banjo" is the "most detailed and complete surviving contemporaneous record of mid-nineteenth-century African-American banjo music" (47) and that Gottschalk's sources for the piece were African American (53), but he focuses too much on the technique he believes a banjo player would use if playing the music as Gottschalk notated it for piano rather than on the melodic content of the piece, which is clearly derived from Minstrel sources. This doesn't discount the fact that Sweeney and Foster may have used African American sources for "Johnny Boker," "Oh Susanna," or "Ring, Ring, de Banjo." However, unless "Le Banjo" can be directly tied to an African American source beyond these, it seems much more likely that Gottschalk heard Minstrel music, realized how popular it was, and was inspired to use similar melodies in his composition.

22 W. T. Lhamon, *Raising Cain* (Cambridge, MA: Harvard University Press, 2000), 138–39.

23 Pete Ross helped me immensely with identifying "Johnny Boker" and discussing

how "Le Banjo" sounds like a Minstrel tune. I also corresponded with Seth Swingle, who has studied both Minstrel-era banjo and Mande music in Mali. He couldn't discern a specific Mande melody, which he believes would be the only way to say for certain that the tune came from a Mande source.

XIX—Washington, DC, 1857

1 Quoted in [Washington, DC] *Evening Star*, March 5, 1857.

2 *Dred Scott v. Sandford*, 60 US 393 (1857); "Dred Scott v. Sandford," Oyez, https://www .oyez.org/cases/1850-1900/60us393.

3 Quoted in Patricia Hills, *Eastman Johnson* (New York: Whitney Museum of Art, 1972), 14, 22. Elsewhere, Hills writes, "We do not know the specific catalyst for Johnson turning to the subject of slave life in 1857 . . . but certainly the subject was timely in that turning-point year." Patricia Hills, "Painting Race: Eastman Johnson's Pictures of Slaves, Ex-Slaves, and Freedman," in *Eastman Johnson: Painting America*, ed. Teresa Carbone (New York: Brooklyn Museum of Art, 1999), 122.

4 John Davis, "Eastman Johnson's Negro Life at the South and Urban Slavery in Washington, D.C.," *Art Bulletin* 80, no. 1 (1998): 73.

5 John Michael Vlach, *The Planter's Prospect: Privilege and Slavery in Plantation Paintings* (Chapel Hill: University of North Carolina Press, 2002), 17–18.

6 Davis, "Eastman Johnson's," 78.

7 Hills, "Painting Race," 122; Patricia Hills, Eastman Johnson Catalogue Raisonné, https://www.eastmanjohnson.org/catalogue/index.php, accessed September 8, 2021.

8 Hills, "Painting Race," 128.

9 The white woman in the painting may suggest the reality that the enslaved were always being surveilled, even when they had precious free time for themselves.

10 Davis, "Eastman Johnson's," 78; Hills, "Painting Race," 126. Johnson could have found models in Washington or New York. Free Blacks lived in his father's home, as did the woman whom Johnson's mother-in-law owned. He could also have hired free Blacks in New York to pose for him.

11 Mary Ellen Hayward, *Baltimore's Alley Houses: Homes for Working People Since the 1780s* (Baltimore: Johns Hopkins University, 2008), 23–33.

12 The information on William Boucher, Jr., comes from Greg Adams, Pete Ross, and Robert Winans's text and exhibit outline, "Making Music: The Banjo, Baltimore and Beyond," Baltimore Museum of Industry. Conversations with Pete Ross also helped with this section.

13 Interview, Pete Ross, September 8, 2021. They vary in size, but are frequently twelve inches. A triangular piece of wood is added to the back of the neck so that it swells slightly where it reaches the body.

14 Ross, "Haitian Banza," 147.

15 Thomas F. Briggs, *Briggs' Banjo Instructor* (Boston: Oliver Ditson, 1855), https://archive.org/details/briggsbanjoinstroobrig/.

16 "Editor's Easy Chair," *Harper's New Monthly Magazine* 19 (1859): 126 (they noted that the piece "immediately sold for $1200," which would be $40,000 in 2021); *New-York Tribune*, May 21, 1859, 6.

17 Quoted in Hills, *Eastman Johnson*, 34; Davis, "Eastman Johnson's," 86.

18 Hills, "Painting Race," 24, 131.

19 Hills, "Painting Race," 133. For a critical discussion of Beecher's auctions, see Jason Stupp, "Slavery and the Theatre of History: Ritual Performance on the Auction Block," *Theatre Journal* 63, no. 1 (March 2011).

20 Quoted in Samuel Charters, *Songs of Sorrow: Lucy McKim Garrison and Slave Songs of the United States* (Jackson: University Press of Mississippi, 2015), 103.

21 Creel, *"A Peculiar People,"* 298.

22 Charters, *Songs of Sorrow*, 199; Allen et al., *Slave Songs*, xviii–xvi; Raboteau, *Slave Religion*, 245.

23 According to Laura Town, quoted in Charters, *Songs of Sorrow*, 109; Creel, *"A Peculiar People,"* 299; Charters, *Songs of Sorrow*, 198; Creel, *"A Peculiar People,"* 208. Lorenzo Turner posited that the Arabic word *saut* was used among Muslims in West Africa in the motion of walking and running around the Kaaba (Diouf, *Servants of Allah*, 68). However, William Pollitzer believes, "It is virtually impossible to identify religious belief or practices of the sea islands with any particular African ethnic group, as so many were involved, and changes have taken place on both sides of the Atlantic" (*The Gullah People*, 142).

24 Quoted in Raboteau, *Slave Religion*, 66; Creel, *"A Peculiar People,"* 101, 73, 225, 277; Rutkoff and Scott, *Fly Away*, 28; Pollitzer, *The Gullah People*, 138. Pollitzer writes, "Spirit possession was reinterpreted in Christian terms."

25 Quoted in Charters, *Songs of Sorrow*, 207, 282; Creel, *"A Peculiar People,"* 202–03.

26 Frederika Bremer, *The Homes of the New World: Impressions of America*, vol. 1 (London: A. Hall, Virtue, 1853), 369; Creel, *"A Peculiar People,"* 297; quoted in Stephen Nissenbaum, *The Battle for Christmas: A Cultural History of America's Most Cherished Holiday* (New York: Vintage, 1996), 269. Bremer writes that he (she never gives his name) sang "songs universally known and sung in the South by the negro people, whose product they are, and in the Northern States by persons of all classes, because they are extremely popular." She doesn't name the tunes. Her description makes it sound as if she is referring to something as popular as Blackface Minstrel music. She also flat-out dismisses Minstrelsy: "I have seen their imitators, the so-called 'Sable Singers,' who travel about the country painted up as negroes," and trying to imitate Black people which "for the most essential part of the resemblance fails—namely, the life."

27 Elizabeth Fenn, "'A Perfect Equality Seemed to Reign': Slave Society and Jonkonnu,"
    North Carolina Historical Review 65 (1988): 129; Dougald MacMillan, "John Kuners,"
    Journal of American Folklore 39, no. 151 (1926): 55, 57. The drum was also called a goom-
    bay or gombay and played in the Florida Keys, Belize, and the Bahamas.
28 Quoted in Charters, *Songs of Sorrow*, 130.
29 Charters, *Songs of Sorrow*, 117–18, 130.
30 Allen et al., *Slave Songs*, vi–vii.

Coda

1 "The Thang: The Affrolachian On-Time Music Gathering" brochure, 2020.
2 *The Librarian and the Banjo*, documentary film, directed by Jim Carrier, 2013.
3 Ulf Jägfors, "Scott Didlake and the origin of the banjo TBI 1992," YouTube, October
   6, 2006, 10:11, https://youtu.be/L4a4FxaRjQk; *The Librarian and the Banjo*; Pete Ross,
   postcard to Dena Epstein, October 17, 1997.
4 Epstein, *Sinful Tunes*, 348.
5 Valerie Díaz Leroy to the author, July 17, 2021.
6 Dena Ross Jennings in discussion with the author, March 2021.
7 It was at the Thang in 2018 when I first read a section from this book, very close to
   the opening you read.
8 Lillian Werbin in discussion with the author, November 2021.
9 "The Arnold Shultz Fund," https://bluegrassfoundation.org/arnold-shultz-fund/,
   accessed November 28, 2021.
10 Valerie Díaz Leroy in discussion with the author, March 2021 and November 2021.
11 These lessons are available for free on the NMAAM website and from Quaver Ed.
12 Jake Blount in discussion with the author, November 2021.
13 Hannah Mayree in discussion with the author, November 2021.
14 I want to add that I realize that by condensing and transmitting our conversations
    to you, I am using their stories for my book. You might think that is wrong, or you
    may not have thought about it at all.
15 Alexandre Girard-Muscagorry, email to Pete Ross, November 4, 2021.

$Index$

Page numbers in *italic* represent illustrations. Note: In the index, Haiti is "Haiti" after the Revolution and "Saint-Domingue" before.